AFRICAN PRESENCE

in

EARLY AMERICA

Edited by

Ivan Van Sertima

Transaction Publishers
New Brunswick (U.S.A.) and London (U.K.)

ISSN 0270-2495
ISBN 0-88738-715-2 (paper)
Printed in the United States of America

Cover design by Jacqueline L. Patten-Van Sertima

African Presence in Early America

Incorporating *JOURNAL OF AFRICAN CIVILIZATIONS,*
December 1986 (Vol. 8, No. 2)

Contents

FIFTEEN YEARS LATER
[An Introduction and Overview]

Ivan Van Sertima

It is now fifteen years since *They Came Before Columbus: The African Presence in Ancient America* was first published. It appeared from Random House in January of 1977 and is now in its seventeenth printing. Like most controversial works, it has attracted the most extreme and vicious criticism as well as the most enthusiastic praise. Like most controversial works also, its most voluble commentators have either read it superficially or have misread it, for it is often praised and attacked for the wrong reasons, for saying things I did not say, for advancing positions I would neither entertain nor defend. The time has come to present some of the new evidence that has emerged since then in this steadily expanding field. It has also become necessary to clarify the stands I took nearly a decade ago and to reexamine the case for pre-Columbian contacts between Africans and native Americans with a greater scholarly precision and lucidity.

Narrative Style in *They Came Before Columbus*

Not only the matter but the manner in which the case was presented has been the subject of criticism. Some critics have confused method with substance and have referred to the dramatized openings of chapters in *They Came Before Columbus* as "fictionalizations." One critic has placed the strange hybrid label "faction" (fiction plus fact) upon these dramatized sections. It is a word coined, I believe, by Alex Haley or one of his critics, who, in a discussion of *Roots*, use it to depict that special blend of historical fact and symbolic fiction. With all due respect to Haley, whose work I admire, the term may be apt for his kind of historical saga but not mine. What Haley has done is significant in that he has used the frailest threads from the web of ancestral memory to spin a story of the African's brutal crawl through the gloom of the Middle Passage and the slave plantation. Other have attempted this before but never with such dramatic power and skill and inspired by what seems to be an actual personalized linkage to the African continent.

In such a narrative it is possible to use history as a painted backdrop to the stage upon which the drama of families and individuals is played out, but the detail of happenings may often be created freely by the author so that both the manner and the matter is novelistic, that is, invented, fictionalized. This need not detract, as Haley has persuasively shown, from the broad symbolic truth of the past.

What I set out to do, however, was quite different. First of all, my concern was with the reconstruction of those aspects of African ancestral history which transcend and redeem that later colonial chapter of debasement and humiliation. More importantly, it was through the meticulous examination of historical narratives that I was galvanized by a desire to draw the reader into the living skin of lost times and thus adopted a dramatic mode of presentation. The facts were well researched, notes indicating the archival sources were always given, the skeletal data buried in musty volumes were fleshed and animated with startling but authentic moments of history. This is a method used by the best of historians to bring a vanished world and ghostly figures to life. It is neither fiction nor "faction." Used sparingly and cautiously, and with a respect for the authenticity of detail, it can make a difference between opening a door to the past or closing it to all but a few.

This method brought life stirring afresh from the tombs of the archives. The curtain lifted on Columbus sitting at dinner in the court of King John II in the valley of Paraiso. Concentrated in that single selected incident, we can see the personal ambitions and duplicities of the man, the intrigues and rivalries of the powers that were about to alter the destiny of Africa and America. When I entered the world of medieval Mali in the early fourteenth century it was with the telescopic lens of the historian and the microscopic focus of the novelist. I found it was the only way to see, in the broadest and yet the most intimate terms, the life of the Mandingo prince, Abu Bakari II, and the life of his court at Niani on the banks of the Sankarini river. Every detail of this court was drawn from first-hand travellers' accounts. They were not created for the purpose of drama but dramatized for the purpose of recreation.

In like manner one should look at the evocation of medieval Tlatelulco with the mist of morning over the lake, the hollow scream of the sacred conches, the crack of the fisherman's paddle on the glass of the water, the ash and bloom of the volcanoes sleeping in the clouds. I was amazed to receive a letter from someone who had lived there, had awakened at morning like my Aztec featherworker on the edge of the lake, had watched the volcano fusing its distant wisp of smoke with a passing cloud (an eminent authority, moreover, on Mexican colonial art, Judy de Sandoval) I was amazed to receive a letter from her in which she said she was so moved by the authenticity of the description of her childhood village that she wept. I must confess that I have never seen the island in question and I want to emphasize this in order to show the care with which I have applied this method and technique to dead documents in my attempt to breathe life into ancient peoples and places, times through which we can no longer pass, streets we cannot walk, worlds we can no longer visit.

But let us leave the question of manner and method aside. What of the new facts that have emerged that undermine or consolidate my case? What fresh light is thrown upon the thesis by what I have found since then and what others have unearthed?

The Olmec Stone Heads

First of all, I have restated the Olmec case in the essay "Egypto-Nubian Presences in Ancient Mexico" republished in this volume. The most remarkable of the new finds is that of the Olmec head discovered since 1862 but which had never appeared, it seems, in any work on the subject, outside of Mexico. It is not featured in the works of Michael Coe, Matthew Stirling, Alexander Von Wuthenau, Rafique Jairazbhoy nor in my own book, *They Came Before Columbus*. It is a significant omissio῀ because it is the most persuasive evidence of an African type among ? the stone heads found to date. It was brought to my attention in 1984 ῀ Wayne Chandler and Gaynell Catherine who had rephotographed it from ._ archives. In 1985, while spending a week in Mexico at the house of my friend, Alexander Von Wuthenau, he drew my attention to its description in a Spanish work—*Las Cabezas Colosales Olmecas*, by Beatriz de la Fuente. The head, by the way, was found by Jose Melgar, probably the first nineteenth century Mexican to write seriously about Africans in America before Columbus. The comment by Beatriz de la Fuente is worth quoting:

> If in some moment one happened to ponder on the existence of negroes in [early] Mesoamerica, such a thought would surely occur after you have seen the head at Tres Zapotes (Tres Zapotes 2) the most remote in physiognomy from our indigenous ancestors. The elevated position of this personage is revealed in the headdress, from the back of which dangles seven bands which figure braids that taper off into rings and tassels. *(my translation)*

The Terracotta Evidence

The clay sculptures of African types in ancient America are even more impressive than the heads, since many of them evoke the coloration of the skin and the texture of African hair. They corroborate the evidence of the stone colossi and are found on Olmec pre-Christian sites in growing numbers. My visits to Von Wuthenau's chateau and studio at San Angel—an almost yearly pilgrimage—brought yearly surprises. He is an indefatigable researcher and collector, a man of great vigor and intellectual curiosity at 85, living a more active life than most people I know at 40. For thirty years he had the chair of Pre-Columbian Art History at the University of the Americas. He founded the *Humanitas Americanas* collection in his studio at San Angel. This houses more pre-Columbian African terracottas than any art gallery in

Von Wuthenau's studio at San Angel, Mexico, which houses the Humanitas Americanus collection.

the world. My last visit in 1985 came a few weeks after the publication of *Unexpected Faces in Ancient America* in the Spanish language. I quote from one of our taped conversations during the visit, to highlight the importance of the terracotta evidence to American history.

VON WUTHENAU:

The Spanish title of the book means *America: Melting Pot of the Races of the World.* This, in my opinion, is what really happened . . . and it should be used as a point in our conception of the historical record in ancient America because the writing that survived is negligible. Very little was left after what the Spaniards destroyed. The only thing that can really take us to the source is the pictorial document. We have to know more and more about the portraits

Van Sertima and Von Wuthenau holding a discussion on pre-Columbian terracotta.

of ancient America, which thousands, in fact tens of thousands, of gifted artists made on our continent, and which have been overlooked so far in serious studies.

VAN SERTIMA:

May I interject here, Alex, to consolidate what you are saying because many people are not aware of the fact that it is necessary, far more necessary than in Europe, to concentrate on other areas of evidence than the written document. It is relatively easy for historians to reconstruct early passages of European history from the written document because Europe had the good fortune to maintain an archival continuity. In spite of all its wars, its libraries were not destroyed. Yet here, in America, as you have just pointed out, you have a virtual absence of documents. As in the case of Africa, my friend, it was not the lack of writing as most people want to believe, but a destruction, an almost systematic destruction, of documents. One remembers the exhortation of that bigot, Bishop de Landa, ordering the destruction of native American books in the Yucatan. "Burn them all," he said, "they are works of the devil." So it has become necessary in the reconstruction of American history to concentrate on other areas of evidence and, as you say, these figures, these faces, these human images, are witness to a whole sequence of ages, a whole sequence of cultures . . .

VON WUTHENAU:

More than that. They are portraits of the living by their contemporaries. No professor nowadays has seen a living Olmec. The carver of the Olmec saw these people and they are the ones who transmit the truth of the history. You cannot make up all these things in your imagination. It's impossible that all the differentiation of races which were so meticulously and precisely por-trayed by the artist were never here. We are looking into the faces of actual people who lived here. That is why it is the backbone of our research into the ancient history of the whole American continent. Mexico is just a part of it . . .

The Skeletal Evidence

Frederick Peterson, whom I quoted in my book to establish the African skeletal evidence in the Olmec world, turned on his words in a 1985 letter to Keith Jordan (see Jordan's essay in this book). Peterson disavowed his com-ment on the "Negroid" element among the priest-caste of the Olmec at Tlatilco but then cited as his source for this bold (and, for him, regrettable) comment, scholars far more reputable than himself (Dr. Davalos, future head of the National Institute of Anthropology in Mexico, and Luis Covarrubias, brother of the renowned Mexican scholar, Miguel Covarrubias). As Keith Jordan points out, the revelations made in the disavowal gives more credence to his original statement than if he had left it hanging on his own authority. What it also shows is that major Mexican authorities in the field of physical anthropology had already come to the conclusion that there was a "Negroid" element among the Olmec, even before the Polish craniologist Wiercinski established this on a more substantial basis.

Wiercinski assessed the presence of a "Negroid" pattern of traits on the basis of a detailed analysis of a large set of skull traits which differentiate between Black, Yellow and White racial varieties. The traits analyzed included "degree of prognathism, prominence of nasal bones, height of nasal roof, width of nasal root, shape of nasal aperture, position of nasal spine, promi-nence of nasal spine, shapes of orbits, depth of canine fossa and depth of maxillary incisure." Wiercinski sees the colossal stone heads as representing individuals with "negroid" traits predominating *but with an admixture of other racial traits.* On this matter I am afraid Keith Jordan seems to have misread me, seeing a conflict between my conclusions and that of Wiercinski, a conflict which does not exist. Jordan brings into question "the pure African pedigree claimed by Van Sertima for members of the Olmec ruling class."

I have never claimed anything of the sort. I must draw the reader's attention to page 147 of my book *They Came Before Columbus* in which I make my stand emphatically clear.

"The Olmec were a people of three faces, that is, a people formed from three main sources or influences. One of these faces was Mongoloid. Elements of this Mongoloid strain may have come into America from Asia even after the Bering Strait migrations but they would have blended indistinguishably with the Ice Age Americans. The second face or influence was Negroid. The third suggests a trace of Mediterranean Caucasoids or Semites (probably Phoenician) but this will be shown to be related historically to the second. These faces became one face, to which the broad name "Olmec" was given. I think it is necessary to make this clear—since partisan and ethnocentric scholarship is the order of the day—that the emergence of the Negroid face, which the archeological and cultural data overwhelmingly confirms, in no way presupposes the lack of a native originality, the absence of other influences, or the automatic eclipse of other faces."

Keith Jordan introduces something else to the discussion which is new and important. That is the work of A. Vargas Guadarrama. Guadarrama's independent analysis of Tlatilco crania revealed that those skulls described by Wiercinski as negroid were radically different from the other skulls on the same site. Guadarrama noted similarities in skull traits between these "negroid" finds in the Olmec world and finds in West Africa, Egypt and some parts of Peru.

Evidence from Ancient Maps

Joan Covey brings something fresh and extremely persuasive to the discussion—the study of ancient maps. Four maps are given special attention, three of which show parts of South America before the European "discovery" (the Hamy-King, the Piri-Re'is, the Mercator) and one of North and South America (the Hadji Ahmed map). The years in which these maps were discovered or redrawn actually postdate the so-called "discovery" but they could not possibly have been drawn at that time without recourse to ancient maps. They either involve knowledge of territory then unknown or are too accurate to have been drawn by the Greek mapmakers or the Renaissance explorers.

Greek mapmakers like Eratosthenes and Ptolemy could not have been responsible for sections of these early maps since there is no hint of America,

North and South, on "World Maps" made by the Greeks. As for the later European explorers of America (15th-17th century) "it was not only impossible for them to find longitude," Joan Covey points out, "they also had great difficulty transferring their geographical knowledge to maps." One hundred and fifty years after Columbus, it was still believed that "not only is longitude undiscovered, but . . . undiscoverable."

The Hamy-King map (redrawn from earlier maps and made available between 1502-1504) shows the coast of America. It also shows detailed coastlines of Africa and precisely charted sources of the Nile. This could not simply be an updated composite of ancient and medieval maps. "This mapping of the Nile, of the coast of Africa, and of parts of America was completed in ancient times by people who could measure longitude with great accuracy. The longitude between Africa and South America is off by only 2 degrees."

Only the Piri Re'is map is more accurate. This map is featured in my book (Plate 39). It is the most astonishing document to come out of the ancient world. Eight of the twenty maps of which it is composed are survivals from the sacked library of Alexandria in Egypt. Those are the ones, Ms. Covey informs us, that deal with North and South America. Although there are errors in this map due to use of different grids by different mapmakers over a long period of time, "the original mapmaker found the correct relative longitude across Africa and across the Atlantic, all the way from the meridian of Alexandria (Egypt) to Brazil."

The details of South America in this map must rank among the hardest evidence available in any discipline of the visit of ancient Old World peoples to South America.

"The Andes are shown on this map of 1513. The Andes were not discovered until 1527 by Pizarro. The Atrato River (in present day Colombia) is shown for a distance of 300 miles from the sea. Its eastward bend at 5 degrees North latitude is correct. Someone explored this river to its headwaters in the western Andes before 1513. The Renaissance explorers did not leave a record of any exploration of this river. The Amazon river is shown . . . the actual course of this river . . . while all representations of it in later maps of the 16th century bear no resemblance to its real course."

Pyramids, Measures, and Numbers

As I had pointed out in my book, pyramid-building was revived in the eighth century B.C. by the Nubians. Professor Lumpkin shows that this revival was attended by certain technical innovations. Although the Nubians built much smaller pyramids the superstructures were more solid. Also, instead of five or six steps as in the Third dynasty, they introduced many small steps. It looked more like the many-stepped stairways of the American pyramids. Other correspondences between the pyramids of the Nile Valley and those in early America include (a) the north-south orientation of the structures, which was a sudden development in Olmec Mexico, coinciding with the first appearance of the African-looking colossi on the La Venta ceremonial platform (see my essay in this volume) (b) sacred pools and systems of moats and drains as part of the pyramid complex (c) sides of the pyramids facing the cardinal points of North, East, South, West (d) use of the corbelled arch (e) use of a wall to enclose the pyramid complex (f) use of the pyramid for astronomical alignments (g) roads radiating from the construction, not unlike pyramid causeways. Professor Lumpkin is careful also to point to the differences, since she feels that, if a valid connection exists, it is, as I have suggested, more in the nature of "a stimulus, an influence."

Provocative new comment on the pyramids comes from an unexpected source—a musician, Bart Jordan, whose extraordinary mathematical ability at a very early age led him into an audience with Einstein. I quote from a communication he sent to the *Journal* on March 18 of this year:—

"No edifice in the Old World has drawn more scholarly notice than the Great Pyramid at Giza. None has been more intensively probed yet extensively misread. This is understandable. The casing and capstone are gone from this wonder of wonders, making certain measures difficult, others impossible. While the base of this great stone tent is tolerably measured, all efforts to recover the intended height have failed. Hence, wholly original perspectives and techniques are needed, causing this writer to reconstruct the following schedule of "source numbers" for the probable height. *These source numbers are not merely speculative in that they parallel the tetrachordal cubit measures mandated by Agatharchides (a Greek geographer who examined the pyramid when all was still intact).*

SOURCE NUMBERS FOR
PYRAMIDION OF 33.13 INCHES

1/120 Statute Mile	528 inches
Synodical Mercury	116 inches
Synodical Venus	584 inches
Synodical Mars	780 inches
Synodical Jupiter	399 inches
Synodical Saturn	378 inches
1/120 Statute Mile	528 inches

SOURCE NUMBERS FOR
PYRAMID OF 5806.08 INCHES

Ten Palindromic Miles: 48384 feet or 580608 inches

- The pyramidion, or capstone, begins and ends with the Statute Mile/120 measure, establishing the foot and inch as we know them. Embraced within these inch-per-foot measures are the inch-per-day measures of the synodical planet schedule, resulting in a total of 3313 inches to be

divided by 100. The pyramid itself reflects ten of what may be called the
**Palindromic Mile (note: 48384 reads the same from right or left), resulting
in 580608 inches to be divided ny 100. Dividing evenly into the**
5806.08 inches are 280 Saturn Cubits, 320 Jupiter Cubits, 336 Mars
Cubits, and 448 Mercury Cubits (original nomenclature). The other
cubits, those of Earth/Moon and Venus, divide unevenly and function
uniquely.

- The sum of 33.13 and 5806.08 is 5839.21; this is highly significant in
  that it is precisely ten times the synodical revolution of the planet
  Venus. If the true height of the Great Pyramid be 5839.21 inches and the
  true transit of the Great Star is 583.921 days, then Venus must preside
  over the edifice and its measures. Therein lies a consideration. Whatever
  may be assigned in the future to other aspects of Cheops' Pyramid, one
  would hope for some resonance with the recovered measure.
- For this is the way of ancient thought. Measure is emblematic and
  systematic. Above all, it is sacred. That which appears arbitrary by ancients is mostly misunderstood by moderns. And what is true of the Old
  World is true of the New. *In the Caracol at Chichen Itza, for example,
  there is yet another setting of the 583921 calculation enshrined in the
  height of the Great Pyramid at Giza.* Coincidence? Perhaps, but how
  many coincidences make a fact?*

Bart Jordan is now working on a report of "such coincidental measures
regarding Old World and New World edifices" which we hope to publish in a
later edition of this book.

Dating of the Ancient Voyages

Rafique Jairazbhoy dates the coming of the Egyptians to America in the era
of the Rameses. Alexander von Wuthenau follows that scenario. I am now
persuaded by new evidence to accept this earlier dating as more probable. I had
opted for the later phase of the radio carbon dating of the ceremonial platform
at La Venta where the first sequence of the colossal stone heads were found.
That dating is 814 plus or minus 134 B.C. (that is, between 948 and 680 years
before the Christian era). I had concentrated in *They Came Before Columbus* on
the twilight phase of the Bronze Age. This I saw then as the most likely period
of contact since the blocking of the Asiatic sea routes by the Assyrians and the
quest for tin, copper, purple dye and iron encouraged the drift of fleets west of
the Mediterranean towards the Atlantic. *I have since pointed out, however, that
both the capacity for ocean travel as well as the pressures of war and trade
could have facilitated these movements at either end of the dating equation.*
The matter, however, does not end there. It involves a debate over the
question of motives for such a voyage (which I do not feel was necessarily
deliberate) as well as the very nature and extent of the African influence

---

*(Copyright, Bart Jordan, 1987).

(which I see as stimulating, but not as creating, Olmec civilization). I would like to clarify my position more thoroughly here, although I touch on this in my essay "Egypto-Nubian Presences in Ancient Mexico."

I am aware of the very early sites and settlements of the Olmec. San Lorenzo was occupied, according to Coe, as early as 1500 B.C. and *The Washington Post* reports stone structures found on the Olmec site of Copalillo as early as 1200 B.C. (see *Ancient Olmec Site Unearthed in Mexico*, The Washington Post, April 26, 1986). None of the colossal stone heads are found on any of these first phases of occupation or construction. The first stone head found on the newly discovered site of Copalillo dates from the third phase of the construction 800-600 B.C. Guadalupe Martinez Donjuan, who excavated the site, has made that clear, even though we do not yet know what this head looks like. Native or "negroid," the point is, it is much later in the day.

Datings therefore of sites, as such, are irrelevant to the dating of contact with outsiders. Ignacio Bernal has perceptively noted that the colossal sculptures cannot be dated by site occupation dates but only by the buildings or structures with which they are associated. Michael Coe himself has conceded in a private communication to Bernal, that the colossi at La Venta are older than those at San Lorenzo, even though LaVenta was not occupied until c. 1255 B.C., about quarter of a millenium later than San Lorenzo. San Lorenzo architecture displays a lower level of development and the stone heads found there are introduced much later than the slipshod and irregular San Lorenzo structures. The Egypto-Nubian elements do not seem to have left the same enduring and impressive impact on San Lorenzo as on La Venta. According to Coe, there was a revolution. Some of the colossal heads were thrown into a ravine, many of the sculptures were smashed and defaced. The natives probably grew to resent the intrusion of a powerful foreign element within their ruling caste. Perhaps the same thing happened later at Monte Alban, where some of the rulers were not only murdered but castrated. The dance of the so-called "Danzantes" was the dance of the damned.

At La Venta, the key to the dating of the heads, we find that the pyramids (the first miniature *step-pyramid* in America and the first *true* pyramid which was made of clay, probably eroding through weather into the shape of a fluted cone) the colossi, the altars, the stelae, and that phase of the ceremonial center (three times renovated) associated with these monuments, were all placed on a north-south axis, with a slight deviation west of north. This apparent deviation from true north has now been explained (see Lumpkin in this issue, as well as Aveni, ed. *Archeoastronomy in Pre-Columbian America*). No American structure that observes this alignment goes back before the first appearance of the Africoid stone heads.

By the time any outsiders came in any significant numbers, the Olmec would already have had some kind of home-grown civilization. A priest-caste would have emerged, an elite group that governed the rural villages and started to put a stamp, a distinctive stamp, upon the culture, like the jaguar motif for example. This motif is already in evidence in the 1200 B.C. find at Copalillo. This motif sprang out of the real physical and immediate environment. It was not imported. It was the familiar feline of the Gulf Coast jungle. I have never argued (although there is a cat-cult in Nubia, some of the black kings of the eighth century B.C. having cat names—Shabaka, the male cat, Shabataka, the male-cat's son) that this was brought to America by outsiders. Whatever the arguments of my colleagues, and I say this with the deepest respect, they are too apt to assume a native vacuum in pre-Christian America. On the contrary, a cultural vacuum would have voided the impact of the Nile Valley visitors.

I cannot subscribe to the thesis that civilization suddenly dropped onto the American earth from the Egyptian heaven. According to Jairazbhoy, who believes the Egyptians founded rather than influenced Olmec civilization, there was "no organisation of labor, trade network, gods or religious symbolism" when the contact took place. If this were the case, the expedition walked smack into the steaming Gulf Coast jungle peopled by roving and scattered bands of primitives. The Egyptians then began to organise these natives into an Egyptian-style colony. This would have been an impossible task. It took 18,000 workers nearly one million man-hours to construct the conical pyramid at La Venta. These visitors found, I contend, a native elite, a significant minority whom they could influence. Through that elite who incorporated them (hence their appearance in the royal graves) filtered major aspects of their ritual and technology. The native culture was then transformed and raised to a higher level through a mixture of elements from both civilizations. It was not so fully formed and fixed as to be impervious to foreign elements nor so primitive as to be unable to exploit the sophisticated element of a more advanced civilization.

To assume that one can only significantly influence a civilization at its birth is to underestimate the fluidity and openness of man's social structures. A certain kind of giving calls for a certain state or level of readiness in the receiver. Hunters and gatherers have never been organized and transformed overnight by the technology of urban peoples.

South America

Having said all this, however, I want to make it clear that Jairazbhoy's work is of the utmost importance. No one has amassed such a staggering list of cultural parallels between the Olmec world and that of the Egyptian. Problems of dating, possible errors in some of his basic assumptions, does not invalidate the painstaking and microscopically observant work he has done both in Mexico and South America. Many of the ritual parallels cited in this work between Olmec and first millenium B.C. Egypt are taken from his work.

There is no question that Olmec culture in Mexico and the Chavin level of pre-Inca culture in Peru were intimately related. Trade networks, shared cultural parallels too identical, arbitrary and complex to be dismissed, establish this early connection. Jairazbhoy, who sees the Egyptian voyage as inspired by a religious motive (the search for the Underworld or paradise in the West) follows the trail of ritual correspondences over a vast area. He ties together the apparently scattered pieces by relating them not only to visual counterparts in ancient Egypt but to an overall conceptual framework that meets one of the acid tests in the study of cultural diffusion. Here, single traits which may be dismissed in themselves as coincidence, when shown to be functionally related like strands in a web, make the incidence of coincidence cancel out the statistical probability of a mere coincidence.

Jairazbhoy cites the traditions of the ancient Americans who, according to Sahagun, said that "the bookmen (*amoxaque*) went taking their writings, the books, the paintings, the crafts and the casting of metals." The use of the term amoxaque in Mexico turns up as amoutas in Peru for these travelling bookmen. This word (like *Ra* for sun and *yaru* for paradise) which the Egyptian (*Re, iaro* or *yaro*) share with the pre-Inca people of Peru, has led to a very interesting revelation.

"As per your request," writes Dr. Charles Finch, in a letter to me dated January 20, 1987, "I have investigated the possible Egyptian etymologies of the pre-Columbian Meso-American word "amoxaque" and the pre-Columbian Peruvian word "amoutas." The two words mean in Egyptian "book men," "teachers," "sages," or really any meaning that has the connotation of "learned" or "instructed" men.

The root of "amoxaque" and "amoutas" is the Egyptian "ām" and "ym" both of which mean "to know, to learn, to understand." It is derived from the original meaning of the word "ām" which means "to eat, devour, digest." "Ym(i)" also has the meaning of "within, dweller, 'he who is within,'" and is frequently a title or cognomen of a "priest" or "follower." In "amoxaque" the "x" is pronounced like our "ch" and is interchangeable with "k" or "kh." Thus "xaque" = "khekh" in Egyptian and Khekh is the Egyptian god of learning and letters. Thus "amoxaque" = "ym-khekh" which would mean "priest or follower of Khekh," that is the "follower of the god of learning." In "amoutas," "outas" is equivalent to the Egyptian "ud" which means "writing or written words." Thus, "amoutas" = "ām-ud" (Eg.) which means "to know, to understand written words," highly appropriate for men whose function it was to teach writing to a highly select group of initiates. In any linguistic cross-comparative analysis, the two words being compared have to conform in structure (morphemes), sound (phonemes), and meaning. I think that all three of these are satisfied in the above etymologies."

Jairazbhoy's main preoccupation is with ritual. Readers should complement this study with a closer look at technological parallels. These are very striking. Among those I have noted in my book (pp. 167-171) which may be consulted for further references, are identical horizontal and vertical looms in Egypt and Peru, spindle whorls, *the* cire-perdue *method of bronze-casting (known as the lost-wax technique), Peruvian bronze of the same quality as the Egyptian in spite of missing evolutionary stages (the tin phase, the crude-bronze phase)** the use of an identical mummification formula in both places, a formula not developed in Egypt until about 1090-945 B.C., trepannation (a specific form of skull-surgery) and fitted megalithic masonry. Hereydahl has also investigated the use of identical reed boats and Jairazbhoy has pointed to Egyptian-type sun-doors in a pyramid complex at Tiahuanaco, also the use of Egyptian dove-tails or clamps to keep stone blocks together while the mortar was setting.

There is much left to be done in this field. The most exciting investigation that lies before us now, I feel, is Mochica culture in South America. No one

Mochica Negroid portrait vessel from Peru circa A.D. 900.

has yet probed deeply enough the mystery of the black figures that stand out in this culture from between 900-600 A.D. Who were these people? Did the

* Note: The metallurgical advances (that is, the sophisticated bronze-casting in Peru) belong, according to Dr. Kelley, to another chronological plane, *later* than the Chavin phase, and are therefore to be questioned as one of the evidences of outside influence in this ancient period.

Moors venture out to the Americas? Michael Coe, who is extremely skeptical of pre-Columbian African contact has, nevertheless, in correspondence with Keith Jordan, dropped hints of this.

"On the other hand," he wrote to Jordan, a few years ago, "if you want to pursue this subject, you might look into the report by the 16th century friar, Alonso Ponce, who reported that on the coast of Campeche in pre-Spanish times, a large boatload of "Moors" had landed and terrorised the natives." Ponce would have used the word "Moor" with some knowledge of its implications since Moors were the masters of Spain for half a millenium before Columbus. But this is just a tantalising tidbit. The Mochica chapter has not yet been opened.

Leo Wiener—Reviews and Reassessments

It is now nearly seventy years since Leo Wiener published the first volume in his trilogy *Africa and the Discovery of America*. It is a seminal work and indeed, without Wiener, *They Came Before Columbus* could not have been written. He was the father of the subject in a way. Although a few Mexicans had attempted brief essays on the subject, nothing remotely comparable with this massive work has appeared before or since. Readers, however, should be warned that it was written before Olmec civilization was discovered, before the scientific expeditions to the pre-Christian settlements of America had been launched, and before reliable dating methods (like carbon-14, therminoluminescent dating of pottery) even basic divisions into periods like pre-Classic, Classic, post-Classic etc had been attempted. My assessment of Wiener is that of a grateful but hypercritical student. Many of his primary sources I used but I disagreed with his conclusions on many matters. He was wrong about most of his plant transfers and he was blissfully ignorant about some of the most critical aspects of African civilization which, he assumed, in spite of his liberalism, to be at its best when it was simply the conduit of Arab cultural electricity.

Wiener's first volume was reviewed in the Journal of Negro History (Vol 5, No. 3, July 1920) The reviewer, Phillips Barry, refers to the Mandingo as "Arabicised Negroes" and since he cannot conceive of Africans as having come to America by themselves he writes: "The question arises whether or not there had been a colony of Europeans, with African slaves in America, before the arrival of Columbus." Later on in the review he concludes from reading Wiener, "there had been in Hispaniola, a pre-Columbian colony of European adventurers, with their African slaves, who taught the Indians the Negro words for 'farm, gold, frog, bush, itch' etc. and also African folklore. No other hypothesis is possible." This is so absurd. Why would the slaves teach African words to the Indians for things so basic that they would have arrived at these in their own languages long before outsiders came? Of course this was back in the 1920's and Wiener is not responsible for the follies of his reviewer but some of the hidden racial assumptions are shared. Other aspects of the review—the summary and elucidation of some of Wiener's labyrinthine linguistics—may prove helpful, but readers should be extremely skeptical about the claim of the tobacco plant as an African introduction into America. Innovations in pipe manufacture and certain uses of tobacco may be valid as African loans but *not* the plant, as such. Wiener's dating of objects in the mounds is also highly questionable (see criticism of Wiener and Van Sertima in the appendix to Keith Jordan's article).

Dr Muffett's review is to be taken more seriously. It is particularly valuable as a biographical note on this important pioneer, however outdated some of Wiener's data and naive his assumptions about African civilizations. I tend to agree with the *Dictionary of American Biography* when it says "His broad knowledge, industrious research, and scholarly enthusiasm were, to some extent, counterbalanced by too great a reliance on intuitive decision and too little patience with the formalities of scholarly discipline." The Muffett essay is particularly illuminating when it comes to his comments on the Ra I and Ra II, ancient African boats used to make the trans-Atlantic crossing. A former British administrator in Africa, Dr Muffet is also an expert on early boats (see his letter to me in "The Lost Sciences of Africa"-*Blacks in Science: Ancient and Modern*, 1983).

Mandinga Voyages to the New World

Attention has shifted considerably since Wiener's time from the late pre-Columbian journeys which engaged his attention to those that affected the first major civilization in the New World—that of the Olmec in Mexico and the pre-Inca world of Peru. This has been so not only because the most intensive excavations now being attempted are in the Olmec world but because many investigators believe that while the West African voyages of the fourteenth and fifteenth centuries may have introduced isolated African communities along the Atlantic seacoasts of America, these are too late in the day to have been formative and seminal and therefore are not as important, in a cultural sense, to the study of Old World influence on New World civilization.

While my own interest, even in the process of writing *They Came Before Columbus*, shifted sharply to the early pre-Christian era, I do not agree that the later medieval contacts between Africans and Americans were too late in the day to matter. In a letter I wrote Jairazbhoy on October 2, 1976, I pointed out "Apart from the trade journeys of the late 15th century, which are unusual in that they are among the first proven "return" journeys (American things begin turning up in Africa, like *gossypium hirsutum var punctatum*, a native Caribbean cotton, for example, in the Cape Verde) there are two major migrations in the early fourteenth century, just before the founding of modern

Mexico. This was a fluid period. All sorts of people were gravitating towards the spot that was to be the site of Tenochtitlan and while a great deal was formed in the native American world by then, it was by no means impervious to outside influences. In fact, the first quarter of the fourteenth century was a period of melting and mixing and considerable fusion and change in Middle America."

It is therefore refreshing that we have a scholar who has thoroughly researched the last of the pre-Columbian voyages. This is Harold Lawrence (also known as Kofi Wangara) who was the first African-American scholar to pursue this subject seriously after Wiener (see *The Crisis*, 1962). W.A. Rogers and Carter Woodson had mentioned it in their works but they were merely echoing Wiener. Lawrence went further. He returned to primary sources and even learnt Arabic. He extended on some aspects of Wiener's linguistic base, clarifying, organizing, updating it. His work on the *guanin* complex of words, for example, is eloquent proof of this. He has demonstrated a larger range of usage of the word in West Africa, which could account for other variants of its use in the Americas. He has pointed also to surviving Mandinga words in modern 19th century America and while one may argue that these can just as easily be post-Columbian (the African slaves, after all, left their own linguistic mark) the evidence builds up too compellingly for it to be easily refuted.

"As late as the mid-nineteenth century," writes Lawrence, "a number of Mandinga place names still survived in Panama. The name Mandinga itself

Mandingo head in 14th century Mexico. Made by the Mixtecs, from Oaxaca. Josue Saenz collection, Mexico City.

appeared as a township, a river, a bay and an anchorage on the bay; Mali designated the identical area where Balboa and Colmenares reported that Africans lived in the fifteenth century; Cana was the site of the oldest known gold mine in the country; the mine was in use before the Spaniards arrived . . ."

His case for the Mandinga contact is very well presented. His style at least in this excerpt, is scholarly, precise and cautious. He realizes that a case like this has to be built up like a tower of matchsticks and that the strength of the tower depends on the most fragile stick. He is not dogmatic. He does not stick to the original date (1307) given in *The Crisis* for the Mali expedition but accepts that my suggestion of a later date (1311-1312) might, in the light of further considerations, be equally valid. His contribution to the evidence for contact during this particular period considerably enhances and consolidates the case. One can only hope that he will find a way to complete his work and publish it. This thesis needs not one book or two or three but a whole library in order to change the opinion of the world on these matters.

I would like to draw your attention now to a dot-and-crescent script that I found in the Reef Bay Valley at St John's in the U.S. Virgin Islands (see plates on adjacent page). Comment on this is reserved for the sequel, *African Voyages Before Columbus*.

Africoids Out of Asia

The final section of the book is devoted to the Africoid element in the earliest migrations across the Pacific from Asia to America. Runoko Rashidi reviews Harold Gladwin's thesis on this subject. Gladwin, an American archeologist and historian, is the author of a controversial, and now relatively rare, volume entitled *Men Out of Asia*. It was published in 1947 and is important because it is one of the few studies backed by specialized field research that persuasively argues that some of the earliest American populations were Black people.

Through *Men Out of Asia* Gladwin was, with the admittedly "disconnected and fragmentary evidence of archeology," attempting systematically to build up a new theory to explain how the native American civilizations originated." He sought to determine "the number, variety and location of the different peoples who were on hand when the seeds of American civilizations first began to sprout."

The Gladwin thesis revolves around the first four separate and distinct migratory waves of peoples to enter the New World: Australoid Blacks, Asiatic Blacks, Algonquin (whose phenotype Gladwin is uncertain of) and Eskimo. All four migrations were sporadic, probably unplanned, extremely gradual, and entered North America from Asia by crossing either the Bering Isthmus or (depending upon the geological period involved) the Bering Strait. His research enabled him to identify major elements of the cultural prototypes of each migratory group and subsequently locate, trace, and verify their presence

Dot and crescent formation on rock at bottom of the Reef Bay Valley, St. John's, U.S. Virgin Islands. Verified as Tifinag branch of a Libyan script by Libyan Department of Antiquities.

B-B —K K $\overset{W}{D}$ $\overset{K}{D}$ $\overset{W-S-\overset{\cdot}{A}}{D\cdot A\text{-}D}$ S-K $\overset{K-}{(q)}$ $\overset{\overset{\cdot}{A}}{W}$ ←Start

Reading from right to left, in Libyan Arabic,

W-a-q k-s d-a-d a-s-w k-d w-d K −K-b-b, or, rendered in modern Arabic

و اِقٌ كس صاد اسو لكد ودِ كلٌ دكً سُرُ

"Plunge in to cleanse and dissolve away impurity and trouble; this is water for ritual ablution before devotions."

Barry Fell's Decipherment

in the New World. Although he believed that scattered bands of Diminutive Blacks were in all likelihood the first people to physically stand on American soil, Gladwin qualified these four major groups as actual migrants because they came to the Americas in relatively large numbers.

1. The first actual migration to America, according to Gladwin, was that of black Australoids. It began about 25,000 B.C. and lasted for several millennia. These people are called Australoids because of their close physical and cultural relationships to the people who as early as 38,000 years ago colonized Australia and Eastern Asia.

2. The second migration, Asiatic Black, began about 15,000 years ago. The physical appearance of these migrants closely resembled the Black Islanders of the South Pacific. After having first penetrated their way northward up the coasts of Asia, they began to enter North America gradually where they ultimately developed the historically pivotal Clovis and Folsom fluted-point tool industries.

3. The third migration was that of the Algonquin, of whose physical appearance Gladwin was uncertain.

4. The fourth migration to the New World was that of the Eskimo, whom Gladwin says were the first Mongoloid types to enter the Americas. Mongoloids were soon arriving in the New World in such large numbers that they eventually almost totally absorbed the earlier arrived Blacks, pushing them into the misty realms of fairy tales, myths and legends.

Both the essays of Rashidi and Clegg deal with prehistoric black migrants who would, in all likelihood, have faded into the billion-bodied gene pool of the Mongoloid many millennia before the Olmec era. They are not to be confused therefore, with the later pre-Columbian Blacks from the Nile Valley area and West Africa. The later migrants are the subject of discussion by the other essayists. The very ancient presence of an Africoid element among the original aborigines of America is of historical interest, to be sure, but it is the majority opinion of the contributors to this symposium that they are too early in the day to have made an impact on formative high-cultures of America— the Olmec, the Mayan, the Chavin. Rashidi's outline and evaluation of Gladwin's work, however, is valuable and timely and brings a comprehensiveness to the symposium.

Wayne Chandler, following in the path of R.A. Jairazbhoy (*Ancient Chinese in America*) and Betty Meggers, argues that the Shang dynasty of early China affected the Olmec. His approach to this controversial thesis, however, contrasts sharply with that of Jairazbhoy and Meggers. He is speaking of a "Negroid" Shang, and his photographs, supplementing those of James Brunson (see revised edition of *African Presence in Early Asia*, co-edited by Van Sertima and Rashidi—September, 1987) seems to bolster his case more persuasively than any argument. There is no doubt that there was a Negroid element among the ruling Shang (the Chou, themselves, who succeeded the

Shang, describe them as "black with oily skin") but some may dispute whether the Shang, as such, were a predominantly black Chinese population at that late point in time. (1766 B.C.-1100 B.C.)

Chandler sees the Shang arriving on the Pacific Coast and extending their influence down into central and South America, whereas the Egypto-Nubian influence, according to him, arriving from the Atlantic coast, penetrated the Gulf and spread across the interior of the landmass. He sees these two outside influences fusing eventually with native elements in the Olmec world. While **I have my own reservations about this thesis of a Pacific-Atlantic fusion and** diffusion, his comparative photographs are vivid and compelling and fill a void left by the destruction of early American books.

In closing, I would like to point out that the editor does not necessarily share the opinions of all the essayists in this book. My views have been made very clear on the matter of the Nile Valley presence in Olmec civilization and on the nature of the African presence in the much later fourteenth and fifteenth century journeys by West Africans of the Mali and Songhay empires. This thesis, however, has to open out into other areas and periods and it will attract over time many more investigators and commentators. It cannot be the task of a mere handful of scholars to attempt to revise early American history and the role of the African in that history. Our great hope is that, as the field widens, cautious and meticulous scholarship will not give way to over-enthusiastic speculation. That hope, we would like to believe, is largely fulfilled by this symposium.

Ivan Van Sertima

Postscript

Confusions arising among readers of my chapter "Among the Quetzalcoatls" (Chapter 5 of *They Came Before Columbus*) has prompted me to add a detailed note on this figure in Mexican mythology.

Quetzalcoatl is seldom represented with human features. The origin of Quetzalcoatl as a mythical figure (plumed serpent) is ancient but Quetzalcoatl as a man in Mexico is medieval, dating from the tenth century.

As a man he was a native Mexican, the son of the Toltec king, Mixcoatl. He disappeared from the Toltec capital of Tula in AD 999, heading east into the Atlantic Ocean in a flotilla of boats, promising to return.

Quetzalcoatl as a god, however, has many representations or aspects. As a god he is always represented in the Mexican valley documents, painted black. Neither his coloration nor his features are that of a European outsider. Many have claimed this and so he has been referred to in certain post-Columbian fables as "the white god of civilization." Quetzalcoatl was not modeled on a "white" outsider but neither was he modeled on a black outsider, for black in this context is a symbolic and ceremonial color. That, however, is not the end of the story. It is just the beginning. For, as so often happens, the symbolic can sometimes be transposed upon, and become inextricably linked to, the literal. We shall show how this confusion occurs in the legend of both a post-Columbian white and a pre-Columbian black Quetzalcoatl, both based upon erroneous notions but upon real men.

Let us look first of all at the representations of Quetzalcoatl as *Ehecatl* (pronounced A-heck-atul) the wind god. Here we see him painted black and with prominently bulging nose and heavy, protruding lips.

These physiological characteristics—beaked nose/duck-billed lips—spring from the fact that he is wearing a bird mask. The wind-god flies through the heavens like a great bird, sweeping the roads of the sky in preparation for the rain. He and the rain god, another aspect of Quetzalcoatl, has the color black probably because black is the color of rain cloud. Black is also the color of the sacrificial cattle and the ceremonial clothing both West African and Mexican magicians wore in rain ceremonials. This blackness has nothing to do with race.

However, and this is what is most interesting, the symbolic and the literal often become confused. C. Nunez, the Mexical codex scholar, pointed out that a "negroid" figure was mistaken for the Mexican god, *Tezcatlipoca*, and venerated by the Aztecs simply because he had the right color associated with that god. Tezcatlipoca is black because he is god of the dark forces. Still we see the image of a pre-Columbian African being worshipped by the Aztecs simply because the symbolic black has become indistinguishable from the literal black, "black force" becoming "man of black race."

This same kind of confusion occurred among the first Spaniards to come to America. They did not realize "white" was being used as a symbolic color for an aspect of Quetzalcoatl, that Quetzalcoatl was referred to as "white" when he stood in opposition to Tezcatlipoca, the dark force, "white" in this context meaning the force of light, the polar opposite to darkness. "The god with yellow beard," in an oft-quoted mistranslation of an oral tradition, was really the god with beard of gold, once again a symbolic statement. For gold was seen as the flesh of the sun and the sun was a god and the rays of the rising sun (golden) were the hairs of god. Neither "white" nor "gold" were being used in a racial or literal sense. These terms, as conventions for human colorations, were exclusively European and post-Columbian, not native American. When the Mexicans, therefore, told the Spanish that Quetzalcoatl was a "white god" and that "like them" he came from the east, the Spanish assumed erroneously that the natives were talking about a man with "white" skin like theirs. The sun rises in the east and the gods were supposed to come like the sun across the water from the east. Also, Quetzalcoatl, the man, had disappeared in boats going east.

That is why Cortez was mistaken for a Quetzalcoatl. He came from the east in boats and he arrived on the shores of Mexico at the end of a cycle, a year of expectation among the Mexicans. In like manner presumably was Abu Bakari, the black king, similarly mistaken for a Quetzalcoatl for he arrived (1311) precisely six cycles after the true Quetzalcoatl disappeared on the sea (999) and precisely four cycles before Cortez (1519). His "white" robes would have fitted in with the image of the symbolic "white, bearded figure" while his black skin would have been the right ceremonial color of the rain-god and wind-god aspects of Quetzalcoatl. His appearance in boats from lands of the sun and the time of his appearance would have all combined to place him among the many legends and representations of Quetzalcoatl.

Ivan Van Sertima

Notice to Readers

Ivan Van Sertima appeared on November 1, 1991, before the Smithsonian Institution to deliver an address: *Evidence for an African Presence in Pre-Columbian America.* He spoke for 1½ hrs.to an audience of more than one thousand in the main auditorium of the American Museum of Natural History. His lecture was accompanied by 68 slides.

Because of problems of securing permission for reproduction of these slides in time for this publication, the lecture is reproduced in its entirety without them. Van Sertima, however, describes the visuals so as to evoke them in the minds of readers.

It is hoped that the full reproduction of the lecture with *all* the visual data will be released in the spring of 1993 when the sequel *"African Voyages Before Columbus"* is published. This will be a major chapter in the sequel (see advertisement in this volume).

A tape of the address to the Smithsonian is available for $10, from "Legacies, Inc.".

EVIDENCE FOR AN AFRICAN PRESENCE IN PRE-COLUMBIAN AMERICA

— AN ADDRESS TO THE SMITHSONIAN* —

Ivan Van Sertima

I would like to thank the Smithsonian Institution, in particular Dr. Vera Hyatt, the main mover behind this symposium, for allowing me this opportunity to present the main outlines of this highly controversial thesis, the thesis that Africans made contact with the Americas in more than one historical period before the discovery of "India" in the west by Columbus. My contention is, and I shall here set out the case in outline, that at least two of these contacts or contact periods were significant. I'm only allowed one hour and it should be appreciated that this is not the total case but only the main outlines thereof. I shall divide my presentation into two parts. The first part will deal with evidence for contact in the early fourteenth century extending up to the time of the Columbus voyages and, in one or two instances, even beyond. The second part will deal with evidence for contact in a much earlier period — the pre-Christian era, in fact, and the possible influence of that contact on an early American civilization. I would like to request at the beginning that I not be judged today on all the positions I held fifteen years ago, but on what I say now. In such a broad ranging exploration where one is walking on ground that is partly lit and partly hidden in the grayness of antiquity, one is bound to make a few stumbles. As an honest scholar, whenever one discovers that one has erred, one should admit it. I wish that were true of many scholars. A foolish consistency is the hobgoblin of little minds. But having said all that, let me also say that the elements of contestable data that I shed are minor and are replaced today, fifteen years later, by new and more formidable bodies of evidence. The fundamental thesis, therefore, is in no way weakened, but reinforced. One proceeds with far greater caution but with far lesser doubt.

I'm not the first person to suggest that there were Africans in America before Columbus. Nor was José Melgar, Leo Wiener, Alexander Von Wuthenau, Harold Lawrence, or Rafique Jairazbhoy.[1] Columbus, himself, was the first person to suggest it. He says in his *Journal of the Second Voyage,* and this is quoted in many places, not just in his journal, that when he

---

* This lecture was delivered to the Smithsonian Institution on Nov. 1, 1991. It was part of the symposium *"Race," Discourse and the Origin of the Americas: A New World View of 1492.* The fully illustrated address is to be published in 1993.

was in Haiti, which was then called Española, the native Americans came to him and told him that Black-skinned people had come from the south and southeast in boats, trading in gold-tipped metal spears. Here it is recorded in Raccolta, Parte I, Volume I: "Columbus wanted to find out what the Indians of Española had told him, that there had come from the south and southeast, *negro* people who brought those spear points made of a metal which they call *guanin*, of which he had sent samples to the king and queen for assay and which was found to have 32 parts—18 of gold, 6 of silver, and 8 of copper."[2] Now, he may or may not have believed the story, but Columbus was meticulous enough to send samples of these spears back on a mail boat to Spain to be assayed and the ratio or proportion of gold, silver and copper alloys were found to be identical. Not just similar. *Identical* with spears then being forged in African Guinea.

There are at least a dozen European explorers of the Columbus contact period who, within the first 50 years or so of the European encounter, saw black Africans among the native Americans. Ferdinand Columbus, one of the sons of Columbus, reported in a book on the life of Columbus, that his father told him that he had seen Blacks north of the place we now call Honduras.[3] Vasco Nuñez de Balboa in September 1513, coming down the slopes of Quarequa which is near Darien, which we now call Panama, saw two Black men who were captured by the native Americans, and he asked them, where did these Black men come from. They were not Black "Indians" or he wouldn't have asked that. In fact, he used the word "Negro," in case you have any doubt about what Black means, because that seems to be in question, too. And the native Americans said, "We do not know. All that we know is that they are in a large settlement nearby and they are waging war with us."[4] Peter Martyr, the first important historian of the European contact period, reports on this meeting. Martyr says that Blacks had been shipwrecked in that area and that they had taken refuge in the mountains. Martyr refers to them as pirates, Ethiopian pirates.[5] He uses the word Ethiopian which was then a general word for African. Lopez de Gomara describes some of the Blacks they found in that area. He said they were identical with Africans. I quote him. "These people are identical with the Negroes we have seen in Guinea."[6] L'Abbé Brasseur de Bourbourg, reporting on Blacks in Panama speaks of two indigenous peoples, the *Mandinga* (Black skin) and the *Tule* (red skin).[7] Fray Gregoria Garcia, though in a slightly later period, reports on Blacks seen off Cartagena, Columbia. He says, "these are the first Negroes we have seen in the Indies."[8] Michael Coe, who is no friend of this thesis, nevertheless noted, in a letter to one of my students, that Alonzo Ponce had reported on Blacks landing on the American coast in pre-Spanish times. Ponce uses the term "Moors" here as a deliberate racial reference. He speaks of a boatload of "Moors" who landed off Campeche in pre-Columbian Mexico and terrorized the natives.[9]

Alphonse de Quatrefages, author of *The Human Species*, speaks of distinct Black tribes among the native Americans – Black communities like the Jamassi of Florida, the Charruas of Brazil, and a people in St. Vincent.[10] He cites the work of Captain Kerhallet. He actually presents a map drawn by the sea-captain, Kerhallet, a map of independent black settlements along the South American coasts, where there were landfalls by Black Africans.[11]

The question arises: How could Africans cross the Atlantic? That is really a major question in most minds. Such a voyage seems incredible because early Africans have been studied primarily in one particular context. That is something most of us do not seem to understand. When I left my homeland – Guyana – and I went to study in London I was so keen to learn about Africa. I studied at the School of Oriental and African Studies, London University. Never in all my years there did I learn of any significant African civilization. I began with an enormous respect for my professors. I was told that they were world authorities. I soon discovered that it was quite easy to become a world authority because all you had to do was to look for some insignificant, peripheral African tribe, study it to death, come back with kinship charts mapping out who was one's mother's brother's sister's father's son and all the little rituals and customs and sayings, and you were well on the way to becoming a world authority on some quaint, simple, exotic folk. Now, I'm not dismissing primitives. I lived for more than a decade in the jungles of Guyana. Guyana, mind you, is no jungle. It has sophisticated towns and villages on the coastland. However, when I was a baby my mother and father were divorced and I was taken into the jungled interior. The British put my father in charge of all road and river transport in that jungle. I stayed there until I was nearly 14. My boyhood imagination was shaped by that jungle. It was the kind of jungle you see in *Raiders of the Lost Ark*. So I have no disrespect for people who grow up in the jungle. Early anthropology focused on these jungle tribes and wanted to capture them before they vanished because they were under the assumption (which all of us shared to a greater or lesser degree) that these were the lowest levels of people and that, like monkeys, you had to study them in order to acquire insights into the groundings of advanced societies. We wrote thousands of books about primitives assuming that we had captured the essence of Africa.

We do not indulge in these fantasies in Europe. Now, I have lived everywhere in the world, except Asia, *lived*, not passed through. I not only came out of South America where I spent 24 years. I spent $10^1/_2$ years in Europe. Not just Western Europe. I lived in Eastern Europe as well. I spoke Hungarian. I lived on the Hungarian/Czechoslovakian border. Not just in the big cities. I savored life in villages far from Budapest and I saw people living like people in what we now call "The Third World." Very few of you know that Europe. When we study Europe, we study the best, the shining cities of

Western Europe. I was startled by the incredible poverty in many of these places. You shall soon have a taste of what I speak when we try to rebuild them. I went into villages where they had never seen a Black man in all history, except on television. I found villages where people did not even have a flush toilet. They were using crude latrine pits infested by hundreds of flies. They did not even have showers. They bathed, as we did in parts of the Third World, with water collected from the standpipe in buckets. As I say, you do not know that Europe. We do not study that Europe because if we want to get the essence of Europe, the grandeur of Europe, the technological ingenuity of Europe, we go to the sophisticated centers. But we ignored the centers of Africa. It was not only because of prejudice. We could not study it easily. It was a shattered world and that is one of the things I want to make clear from the beginning. You cannot study America and you cannot study Africa the way you study Europe. Europe has, in spite of its many wars, what I would like to call "an archival continuity." Africa does not. America does not. There were three systematic and deliberate destructions of documents in this country. Bishop de Landa in the Yucatan said, "Burn them all. They are works of the Devil." That is why it has become necessary to adopt what some people like to call an "ahistorical" method. It is, in fact, the only possible historical method for dealing with such shattered worlds. You can't just go into the little books that we think are complete and study what happened in early America. You have to go to botany and linguistics and oceanography and into studies of crania and pottery and cartography in order to find the missing pieces of these shattered worlds.

This time, this place, is no longer the America we are examining, the America we are debating. Look around this room. There is probably no native American in this room. You could go to parts of Africa, too, like Cairo, and you stand in a room lecturing and there are almost no indigenous Egyptians. An awesome catastrophe has happened in these broken worlds. And one is not saying this out of protest. One is just making clear a historical reality that we have to come to terms with. To do so we have to change our methodologies, our approaches. It doesn't mean that we have to surrender to the fantasies of wild diffusionists, of which I, by the way, do not consider myself a part. Some of them are making absolute fools of themselves, claiming everything to be African. I'm not here to do that. One wants to put this subject on a respectable basis so that it can be studied by experts in various fields. The evidence does exist in various fields.

There were other reports and sightings. There is Father Ramon Pane, who speaks of the Black "Guanini," the gold merchants.[12] There is Riva Palacio who speaks of the Jarras and the Guabas, corresponding to the Diara and the Kabba, two Mandinga clans.[13] We have evidence from the Smithsonian itself, the discovery of African skeletons in the U.S. Virgin Islands. I think it was in 1974 or 1975. And I'm going to say what they said. They said these skeletons were morphologically African. They said that they were the bones of two Black males in their thirties and they were found in a pre-Columbian grave at Hull Bay in the Virgin Islands. They said they were probably pre-Columbian because the layer or strata in which they were found was dated about 1250 A.D. They also found something that was typologically pre-Columbian. A pre-Columbian native American ornament around the forearm of one of these skeletons.[14] But when they went into the lab to carbon date them, they couldn't. Now, I do not want to embarrass anyone. I have been told privately why there could be no proper carbon dating. It has nothing to do with this thesis and we share (the Smithsonian and I) a common concern that nobody should know about it. But it is necessary for me to say that it was in bad grace for them to suggest, as one of them did in a newspaper, that Van Sertima is a man who sees a horse and calls it a cow and that the reason why they could not carbon date the skeletons is because of the interference of sea water. That explanation is not valid. Even more extraordinary was one report that the skeletons had to be post-Columbian because they found a nail associated with the skeletons. What is the conclusion? *Africans cannot make nails.* You see what happens when your main focus is on primitives.

Peter Schmidt and Donald Avery of Brown University in Rhode Island found Africans smelting steel 1500 years ago along the lakes of Tanzania and Uganda, in machines that achieved temperatures 200 degrees higher than any machine in Europe until the late nineteenth century. These African blast furnaces produced steel in a single-stage process. Even when in the mid-nineteenth century, the German scientist, George Wilhelm Siemens, developed a machine for manufacturing steel, the nineteenth-century Europeans did it in two crude processes. First, the sintering of solid particles and then the final stage. Africans in an industrial site in Tanzania were doing this in a single stage. They were doing it because they were making steel from iron crystals which calls for a semiconductor technology, unknown in the world until the late nineteenth or early twentieth century. *They were doing this in the fifth century.* And then the investigators found, to their astonishment, that they were doing it using less fuel than the Europeans.[15] And these are the primitives who we are led to believe cannot make nails. And so if you find a nail in the layer where the skeletons are found, they are automatically post-Columbian. Prejudices seriously affect science. They are bound to make a difference.

Columbus sent back spears which natives in the Caribbean claimed to have come in with black traders. The metallurgists in Spain were able to identify them as something identical with spears being forged in African Guinea. We have found no evidence of a metal alloy industry in the pre-Columbian Caribbean and it would be unthinkable that both Atlantic communities could automatically arrive at the same proportion of alloys, even if we had found such evidence. And it doesn't just stand on the metallurgical assays. If it did, we might be inclined to dismiss it. There is the linguistic connection. Whatever Leo Wiener's faults, for he blundered in many matters, and in a few, in spite of my reservations, I may have followed him a bit too trustingly, but in this matter—the matter of the *guanin* complex of words—there is no question whatever of a connection. Both the late Harold Lawrence and I have checked this out in the West African languages. The word for the spears and several variants of this word, appear in both language areas. Among the Mandinga, we have *ghana, kane, kani, kanine, Ghanin.* In the Caribbean, we have *goana, caona, guani, guanin, guanini,* etc. There are even variants far removed from the *guanin* complex, which are almost identical. Another word used to refer to gold, and metal with gold alloys, was, as Las Casas reports, *nucay* or *nozay.* This is close to the Mande *negé* (pronounced nuh-GHAY) and *nexe* (pronounced nuh-KHUH) which stands for any kind of metal ornament or jewelry.[16]

The botanists have provided further corroborative evidence. The Portuguese were in West Africa, since about 1450, in fact before. The Portuguese found a cotton growing plentifully in West Africa and they took this cotton and planted it into the Cape Verde islands in 1462. Thirty years before Columbus. They assumed it to be indigenously African. When it was studied in the twentieth century, they found it was not African at all. It was *gossypium hirsutum var punctatum,* which was grown in the pre-Columbian Caribbean and in parts of South America. It is not African, yet it was transplanted to Africa and was growing plentifully there before Columbus.[17] Not only that. We've also found *zea mays* in pre-Columbian Africa. American *zea mays!* Professor M.D.W. Jeffreys of Witwaterstrand University, a brilliant South African linguist, showed how American maize had travelled to Africa. It is distinct from African sorghum. It had moved across the African continent and he traced it down meticulously through linguistic footprints.[18] And the Russians picked it up as it moved from Africa into Asia. Botanists Kuleshov and Vavilov identified it. They showed that American *zea mays* had entered Asia before the time of the Columbus voyages.[19] All this we ignore.

On the Third Voyage also, when Columbus' ships landed on the northeastern coast of South America, his crewmen describe a certain dress of the identical material and design as the *almayzar* which the Portuguese found Africans wearing in Guinea.[20] In South America the European visitors found plants brought in through earlier contacts. Take the banana! The banana is not African. It is an Asian cultigen. However, we do not find the banana on the Pacific coast, the "Asiatic side" of South America. It is found in east Peru and along the Amazon—the "Atlantic" side. We found the medieval Peruvians digging up bodies and reburying them, feeding them symbolically with certain fruit. In the graves of the reburied dead, in late pre-Columbian strata in South America, we find the banana. The Arabs introduced the Asian banana in their trade with Africa since the twelfth century. They took it out of Asia and introduced it to Africa. All the African, as well as the Arab-African, words for the banana run through the South American languages in recognizable form. Let us, for the sake of illustration, look at the indigenous African word for the banana, unrelated to the more popular Arab-African word *platano* and *platena*, which had been introduced a century earlier into Spain through Moorish trade. The African word for the banana is *bakoko*. In the South American language Galibi we find the African banana word *baccuccu*; in the Oyapock language, the banana word *baco*; in Oyampi, the word *bacome*; in Tupi, the word *pacoba*; in Apiacas, the word *pacowa*, in Puri, the word *bahoh*; in Coroada, the word *bacoeng*.[21] There is also the plantain variety, the sister of the banana. The early sixteenth century explorer Orellana tells us that he saw the plantain in ubiquitous cultivation along the Amazon.[22] One thing is clear. There was no native South American banana. That has been very clearly established. Its appearance in pre-Spanish Peruvian graves and the ubiquity of its sister, the plantain, along the Amazon, in 1513, cannot be explained by an introduction after Columbus.

Now the ocean always seemed to be an impassable barrier to travel and that is why conventional anthropologists have assumed that Africans could not make it. First of all, because we were studying primitives we assumed Africans only had dugout canoes and could not cross oceans. That is one of the things I believed until I was 30. I was brought up on Tarzan. I did not know that Africa had two of the longest rivers in the world (the Nile dwarfs the Amazon) and that a lot of their trade was along those rivers and that the French and others had noted huge boats, not just the canoe, of 70 tons burthen, trading daily along the Niger.[23] And the Africans didn't just sail on lakes and rivers. They had ocean-going craft. Heyerdahl tested one of these — an ancient pre-Christian craft. Heyerdahl felt that the sweep and curve of the ship, the sail, the great steering oar, suggested that these ships were designed for ocean travel, not just confined to lakes and rivers. Scientists mocked at Heyerdahl. A papyrus reed boat? Nonsense! If you take a craft made of papyrus reed and put it on the ocean, it would soon get waterlogged and sink! And they actually tested this hypothesis. They built a tank and they put papyrus reed in the tank and it sank. But Heyerdahl reasoned thus: If one were to take a piece of the Queen Mary, which is made of iron, and put it in a tank, it would also sink. So he rebuilt the ancient African reed-boat, which he call *RA*. He got the Buduma people on Lake Chad, under Abdullah Djibrine, to build the boat and it was built. And in 1969 the Africans set out from Safi in North Africa on that pre-Christian boat, venturing upon the vast Atlantic.[24] They had studied paintings of this boat on the walls of ancient temples. They used these paintings as models for the reconstruction. The Africans made one or two mistakes. They made a mistake with the great steering oar which functions as a rudder. Eventually the rudder broke. But that was not the end of the journey. That made it even more remarkable. The boat in the final stages drifted to America by itself. It got as far as Barbados. *How*? The answer is simple to those who know the sea. So few anthropologists had bothered to learn even the basic lessons of oceanography. They had just assumed that the Atlantic Ocean was a vast wilderness of wind and wave and the peoples along the Atlantic coasts could not make contact with each other because it was a dead sea, a forbidden zone, until the caravels of Columbus came along. We have found, in fact, three powerful currents in the Atlantic which take you automatically, irresistibly, into the Americas unless you have engines to break the almost magnetic pull of the water.

There is one off the Cape Verde islands, there's one off the Senegambia coast, there's one off the southern coast of Africa.[25] Anything sailing or drifting about a hundred miles off Africa, caught in a squall or a storm, is blown automatically towards America. You have to come in this direction unless you have an engine or unless the fish get you first. It is right there at the landfalls, the termini or end-points of these currents, that we have found the African presence. In parts of South America, in parts of the Gulf of Mexico, in parts of the Caribbean. I have not claimed, and this is something that I really resent, the accusation that I claimed that Africans founded the first significant American civilization.

There are one or two people who have stated that. Not me. I have not. I have never said so. Aboriginal or native Americans were here for thousands of years. How could migrants crossing the oceans, save those who came later in a massive movement of millions, *totally* alter the face of their civilization. I pointed to specific influences which the evidence seemed to suggest. Alien groups, however small, migrants from outside, can impact significantly on a native civilization. This is true of all the world's civilizations. Whether they be African, or Asian, or European, they are affected by other civilizations. That is the very nature of civilization. The only people who are not easily affected are primitives. They live in an impervious glass bubble, most of them. That's why they remain fairly static and unchanged for thousands of years. In civilization, though, there is a greater richness and variety and complexity due to the fact that civilizations reach out and draw things into their systems. They take the other, the alien, the new. They transform it. They make it their own. They have their own thing but they draw incessantly from others. This is natural. It has nothing to do with cultural inferiority or superiority. Let me make it utterly clear. I'm not trying to build some new Afrocentric model of superiority.

So far we have been talking about African voyages in the fourteenth and fifteenth centuries. But there was a visit or visits which occurred much earlier, in the pre-Christian era, in fact . . . I shall shift now to the slides. I would like you to follow in images what I am saying.

First, examine the map of the Gulf of Mexico. This is the terminus or end-point of the currents that sweep from Africa towards the Americas. Those diamond-points on the map are the points where we find sculptural and skeletal evidence of an African presence in early America. (Plate 1 – Map of the Olmec World)

This Gulf Coast area was occupied and dominated by the Olmec, the first major high-culture or civilization that we know of in North America. It is considered the mother-culture of America. It was, in my opinion, as in the opinion of most Americanists, a home-grown civilization. But I think only a very closed mind would assume that it developed in total isolation. As the International Congress of Americanists declared in 1964, "There cannot now be any doubt but that there were visitors from the Old World to the New before 1492." America is no laboratory for the study of virginal culture. It shows not only traces of an alien presence but of an alien penetration.

In 1858, peasants at Tres Zapotes found an enormous stone head which was described as having pronounced Africoid features. But in 1862 came an even more significant discovery [Plate 2/3 Tres Zapotes head. *Front* (Plate 2) *Side* (Plate 3)]

Look at the front and side of this head. A very broad nose, pronounced prognathism, very full-fleshed lips. But you cannot be sure of its African-ness just by examining the front because some anthropologists will argue to the death that it is just a plain clear case of an Asiatic. As Bernard Ortiz de Montellano would say, this ancient stone head in America is a "spitting image" of the people living there.[26] Aguirre Beltran will tell us that these are human-jaguar combinations. That accounts, he claims, for the "snarling lips." Some have even claimed that these are "baby faces" and that is why they are so pug-nosed and heavy-jowled. Michael Coe, author of ancient Mexico, claims that the reason they have such broad noses and thick lips is because the tools the carvers used were blunt and they could not make the features any thinner.[27] Ignacio Bernal argues that they could not be African because Africans do not have epicanthic folds (I shall come back to the problem of the epicanthic fold a little later). But now look at the back of the head. (Plate 4 – Head with seven braids)

Look at it very closely. You are seeing something hidden from public view for fifty years. Probably the most well-kept secret in Mesoamerican archeology. This head, although covered by a helmet (as most of them) shows the hair. The carver or carvers went to the trouble of representing the hair against the helmeted dome. Note the unique, extraordinary braids. There is no evidence before this, or since, of any native American with a seven-braided hairstyle. Beatrice de la Fuente, in *Las Cabezas Colosales Olmecas*, comments on this head.

> If in some moment one appeared to ponder on the existence of negroes in [early] Mesoamerica, such a thought would surely occur after you have seen the head at Tres Zapotes (Tres Zapotes 2) the most remote in physiognomy from our indigenous ancestors. The elevated position of this personage is revealed in the headdress, from the back of which dangles seven bands which figure braids that taper off into rings and tassels (translated from the Spanish).

No one who was on that site when the discovery was made doubted that they were seeing something very different from the native. Even the natives themselves felt they were in the presence of something foreign. José Melgar, who excavated this head, wrote the first essay on an African presence in pre-Columbian Mexico.[28] Yet the head disappeared from photographic collections. It reappeared in my anthology *Nile Valley Civilizations* in 1984 because of the photo-research done by Wayne Chandler and Gaynell Catherine.[29] I had not seen it when I wrote *They Came Before Columbus*. Alexander Von Wuthenau, who had done the most exhaustive work of excavation and classification of terracotta in ancient America, had never seen it. Rafique Jairazbhoy, one of the most meticulous scholars on cross-cultural diffusion, who has done a microscopic examination of ritual correspondences between the world's civilizations, had never seen it. National Geographic never published it. This photograph was kept in the dark (and I think the blackout was deliberate) for about fifty years.

Let us move on. Look at this color plate. (Plate 5) It shows us, in one of the rare realistic portraits of the races of man in ancient times, how the Egyptian saw himself, how he saw the Indo-Aryan, how he saw the Blacks to the South, how he saw the Semite. This is 1200 B.C. in Egypt. This is the time of the reign of Ramses III, which Rafique Jairazbhoy chooses as the most likely date of pre-Christian contact between Africa and America. Let me explain the great importance of this plate. Drucker, Heizer and Squier had carbon-dated the wooden platform at La Venta (capital of the Olmec) at 814, plus or minus 134 B.C. (that is, between 948 and 680 years before Christ.[30] This is the platform on which the first sequence of stone heads appear. Michael Coe and Ignacio Bernal are agreed on that.[32] Jairazbhoy selected the earliest dating as the most likely. Van Sertima, in his 1977 model, opted for the latter end of the dating equation. He pointed out, however, that the cultural complex that obtained in the later world of Nubian supremacy (the 25th dynasty) duplicated to a great extent that which was classically Egyptian (that is, it was not that much different in its major particulars from the Ramessid dynasty traits).[32]

There was the conventional assumption, however, that the Black figure did not come to the fullness of his power until the evening of the Egyptian dynasties. This was a Eurocentric myth, to which many students of Egypt, including myself, had once subscribed. The discovery of a pharaonic dynasty, a Nubian dawn dynasty at Ta-Seti, by an American archeological team has exploded that myth.[33] But, even beyond the dawn dynasties, we have this plate before us, a window on one of the noonday dynasties of the Egyptians. This color plate shows that the Black African actually played a dominant role in the Old World at either end of the dating equation, be it 1200 B.C. or 700 B.C.

Look at the Black Egyptian nobleman on the far left. He sees himself as first power in the world at that time. The Indo-Aryan (pink to yellow skin, long straight hair, robe flowing to his ankles) ranks second in ascendancy. The Black to the south of Egypt comes after, and the Semite, a mixture of all, stands at the end of the line of power. Note that this painting faithfully and minutely portrays skin-color, hair-texture, facial form, ethnic costume, yet the Egyptian makes no racial distinction between himself and the Nubian in any particular. Same hair, same skin-tone, same facial type, same cut and color of clothing. The Indo-Aryan is represented as strikingly different in all these respects. The distinction between Egyptian and Nubian is made in terms of power and status. It is subtle but it is very clear. There are three banners floating from the robe of the Egyptian but only two from the robe of the Nubian, his black brother in the South.

Here is another head, not far from where José Melgar found the one with braids. It is known as Tres Zapotes F. (Plate 6) It is even more "amazingly Negroid" in its physiognomy (to use Matthew Stirling's phrase for a La Venta head). Most unusual of all, the stone from which it is carved is of a jet black color. Unlike most of the heads, too, it has no helmet, so that the tuft of close-cropped hair is exposed. Look at the next plate (Plate 7) where the art historian Alexander von Wuthenau compares this head with that of a Nuba chief. You feel you are looking at members of the same family, in fact at twin brothers. Now study the helmet in the next slide. (Plate 8) Note the main features of this helmet (probably made of leather). Note the parallel incised lines, the straps falling along the side of the face, the circular ear plug. Rafique Jairazbhoy has shown the same features on helmets which cap colossal heads at Tanis, the sea-going port in the Egyptian delta. Compare it with this slide (Plate 9) showing obvious similarities to the headgear of the Egyptian military in the same period. Look also at this other helmeted Africoid head in Egypt, probably a Nubian. (Plate 10)

Here is a spectacular new stone head found only a few years ago (Plate 11). It is staring up at us from the belly of a swamp. Nobody would move it. The federal government of Mexico, I have been made to understand, feels it is the responsibility of the state in which it was found to take care of it. The locals feel it is not their responsibility but that of the federal government. I have sometimes had a secret overwhelming urge to hire a helicopter and lift it out of the swamps under the shadow of night. But this phenomenal thing weighs, as the other stone heads do, between ten to forty tons. Brood on that fact! For the nearest quarry, rich in this basalt stone, is 60–80 miles downriver and the stone can only be transported by water to the ceremonial platform where they were found. There is a twenty-two foot wide gorge that makes the overland route from the quarry to La Venta an impassable nightmare.[34]

Now we are not in the least suggesting that the Egyptians taught native Americans their portrait art. But we are faced with some facts here that do not fit neatly within the conventional isolationist model. For early Olmec art shows no transition from the beautiful little pieces of fully-formed humans or jungle cats, demonic masks or fierce were-jaguars, to this monumental concentration, this fascination, this obsession with bodiless heads, heads so colossal that, were bodies attached to them, they would rise fifty feet or more above the earth. Second, the heavy transport techniques used by the Egyptians and Nubians to move colossi across the waters on barges and rafts are unique in the ancient world. The Japanese found in the 1970's that they could not replicate this technology.[35] Barges carrying much lighter balls of stone sank or capsized. Yet Robert Heizer, who was no diffusionist, tells us that there were startling identities between the unique heavy transport techniques of the ancient Americans and Egyptians. We search in vain for antecedents for this development in the American archeological record. Although San Lorenzo has occupation datings centuries before La Venta (where the experts agree that the first in the sequence of stone heads appear) we have absolutely nothing like it. The stone heads found on the San Lorenzo site appear there much later than at La Venta. Coe and Bernal and all the dating experts, I repeat, are agreed on this.

The Africans are still making these colossal heads. Look at this modern one (Plate 12), now on display at the Boston Museum. It is almost as high as the first floor of the museum.

Now we come to the question of the epicanthic fold raised by Ignacio Bernal, who claims that Africans do not have the epicanthic fold. Those who have never studied Africa do not know of its many types. Meek and Seligman and Evans-Pritchard have all shown us examples of unmixed Africans from Nigeria and Ethiopia who have the epicanthic fold.[36] These three slides demonstrate that clearly. (Plates 13, 14 and 15) But that is not the only answer to this objection since the migrants could not all have come in with epicanthic folds. We must consider too the habitual and standardized representation of the eye in ancient American art. The Buddha looks half-Indian, half-Greek, in Hellenistic art.[37] But most importantly, we are not dealing just with pure Africans but with migrants who are intermarrying with the native population. Let me use an illustration from my own family.

My uncle, Alick Van Sertima, married a Chinese woman and my first cousins, Sheila and Anita, have the epicanthic fold. You can acquire this feature in nine months.

To conclude the panorama of stone heads, let us look at two more of these. They were found within the same area where the head with seven braids was found. (Plate 16 — Tres Zapotes 1 and Plate 17 — Tres Zapotes 2).

But the sculptural evidence does not merely lie in the stone heads, some of which, as I have indicated, are racial mixtures, as indeed they should be. There are many terracotta figurines which represent Africoid types. Some are rather stylized and we can dismiss them with a contemptuous wave of the hand but some are so startlingly realistic that we ignore them at the peril of an objective vision of history. My good friend, Alexander von Wuthenau, who has excavated and classified more of these terracotta than any other investigator, presents at least a hundred of these in *The Art of Terracotta Pottery in Pre-Columbian America* and *Unexpected Faces in Ancient America*.[38]

Comas said there were no such terracotta, that no image in American sculpture looked like anything other than the typical Mongoloid type that came across the Bering Straits from Asia.[39] His latter-day disciple, de Montellano, sings the same tune. They are all "spitting images of the native."[40] Michael Coe told the *Science Digest* in 1981 that he had never seen any terracotta in Mexico that looked African.[41] This is not necessarily dishonesty on the part of Comas and Coe. They may have never, in their earlier studies, had a chance to be exposed to the range and variety of ancient American terracotta. The Museum of Anthropology in Mexico City, for example, puts on display less than half a dozen of these among their thousands of exhibits, and the references to them are designed to give the public the impression that they are post-Columbian. For those who would like to follow this official line, let me warn them. A few of these have been subjected, at Von Wuthenau's expense, to thermino-luminescence dating. His organization of these into specific time-frames or historical periods, therefore, is not mere guesswork. It is related not only to stratigraphy and typology but, in some cases, to the most advanced methods of dating. You can visit the finest collection of these Africoid heads at his chateau and studio at San Angel. (Plate 18)

Here are a few from that collection.

This head from the central plateau of Mexico shows not only the African features but the unmistakable kink and coil of African hair. (Plates 19 & 20)

Another pre-Christian African head from Tabasco, La Venta. (Plate 21) Note particularly the representation of the hair. Even in some of the early art of Europe, of Asia, of Africa itself, these tiny circular patterns have been used to represent kinky hair.

Here is a striking one with a nose-ring, from Morelos. (Plate 22)

A nose decoration first appears on the La Venta ceremonial platform next to the first sequence of stone heads. Here is this strange figure carved on a stele with an enormous nose. (Plate 23) It actually looked as though it had a plug in its nose. This is not from the Von Wuthenau collection but an unusual recent photographic discovery by Chandler and Catherine.

Note now the dramatic alteration. (Plate 24) *The large bulbous nose has been recut. It has actually been made to look aquiline.* Once again, in the face of an apparent deception, we are called upon to be gracious. The nose, we must assume, appeared too big, too broad, too bulbous to be real. How could the discoverers not but conclude that vandals or the blows of time had damaged it? So what were they expected to do to restore this ancient personage to its original dignity? Why, history had already suggested the perfect solution. The huge African nose on ancient royal sculpture had led Napoleon's army to shoot off its cannon. Later invaders were to fracture and flatten this nose, shatter and splinter it. But these good gentlemen went one step further. They filed it down to fit in with their fancy or fantasy of what it should be. They resculptured the objectionable protuberance. They "refined" it.

Here now is an Olmec mask. (Plate 25) But in this instance we must be wary. The face is unusually stylized. Unnaturally slanted slits for eye-sockets, tiny pinholes for eyes, abnormally large ears and nose and lips. We might well be looking at the ritualized representation of something monstrous than at the exaggerated caricature of an African.

Here is a naked Olmec woman from Xochipala in pre-Christian Mexico. (Plate 26) Observe her again. (Plate 27) Unlike the mask, you are dealing now with the faithful portrayal of a human, skillfully carved. I have held this doll-like marvel in my hands in Von Wuthenau's studio at San Angel. It is about 3000 years old, yet it looks today as it did before Christ. Perfect in its proportions. The mouth, the teeth, the eyes, the African coiffure, the ear-pendants. Everything is detailed — all of her front teeth, every one of her ten fingers and toes, the fluid curve of her arms, the delicate bulb of her nipples, and when she turns, the voluptuously sculptured cheeks of her buttocks. It is rare in ancient American art.

Here is another woman from Xochipala. Very Africoid features and hair-style, in a sitting position. (Plate 28) And here is an acrobat from the Diego Rivera museum (Plate 29) with superbly detailed Africoid hair, mixed Afro-Asiatic features, sculpted in charcoal black clay. Finally, two Africoid heads with beards, one from Tabasco (Plate 30) the other from Guerrero (Plate 31), all from the Olmec world and time.

But the iconographic evidence cannot and does not stand alone. Even the most stunning visual witnesses will elicit the cry: These are just "spitting images of the native." They merely look African, our detractors will say, because of stylization. Hence, it is necessary to show a corroboration of the sculptural evidence by an equally meticulous examination of the skeletal remains in the graveyards of the Olmec.

This seemed at first a problematic proposition since the corrosive humidity of the soil destroyed the bones in the humid capitals of the Olmec. But in the drier centers — Tlatilco, Cerro de las Mesas and Monte Alban — the Polish craniologist Andrez Wiercinscki found ample and indisputable evidence of an Africoid presence. Wiercinski, in 1972, assessed the presence of a negroid pattern of traits on the basis of a detailed multivariate analysis of a large set of skull traits which differentiate between Africoid, Mongoloid and Caucasoid racial varieties. The traits analyzed included "degree of prognathism, prominence of nasal bones, height of nasal roof, width of nasal root, shape of nasal aperture, position of nasal spine, prominence of nasal spine, shapes of orbits, depth of canine fossa and depth of maxillary incisure."[42] Wiercinski sees the colossal heads as representing individuals with "negroid" traits predominating but with an admixture of other racial traits. That is what I have said.

The work of A. Vargas Guadarrama is an important reinforcement of Wiercinski's study. Guadarrama's independent analysis of Tlatilco crania revealed that those skulls described by Andrez Wiercinski as "negroid" were radically different from the other skulls on the same site. He also noted similarities in skull traits between these "negroid" finds in the Olmec world and finds in West Africa and Egypt.[43]

But evidence of a physical presence is only one half of the story. What influence did these outsiders have, if any, on the native? Before I answer that question I want to make it clear once again that any contact between two peoples and cultures can lead to a cross-fertilization. And that to find a dozen or even a score amidst a hundred and one elements in a civilization that strongly suggest borrowing, does not negate a native originality nor an indigenous base for the civilization. Nor does it necessarily constitute a claim that the outsider is superior to the native. In fact, there are instances in history where the invader is more affected by the civilization of the invaded than vice versa. [A classic example of this, though still unacknowledged, is the impact on the culture of the conquering Greeks by the conquered Egyptian.]

There are ritual parallels between the Olmec and the Egyptian that are so startling that they bear serious examination, especially in the light of a highly probable physical presence. All sorts of claims have been made by diffusionists but the few I shall present here meet a very rigorous criteria. (1) Traits that appear in an interrelated cluster rather than single-trait correspondences. (2) Traits that are unique to the two culture areas, in that they appear nowhere else in the world save where they can be shown to have diffused from what we claim to be the outsider or donor culture. (3) Traits that are so complex or arbitrary that it is remotely unlikely that they should occur in the same form and with the same function in cultures far apart. (4) Traits for which there is abundant evidence of antecedence in the donor culture and no such known evidence at the moment in the supposed recipient.

Let us look, first of all, at monarchic traits—traits associated with the priest-caste or ruling elite of both civilizations. I shall cite half a dozen of these, two of which were noted in my earlier work. Let us begin by looking closely at just one, which would seem at first glance to be so simple that it could crop up in any place at any time. Use of purple as an index of royal or noble rank, for example. The religious value of purple and its use to distinguish priests and people of high rank is well known among the dynastic Egyptians. What is little known, however, is that it grew out of very unique circumstances and is found nowhere in the Old World save where it can be shown to have diffused from its original center. Sanctity was attached to shell purple because the murex shell, from which it was extracted, revealed by the sequence of colors through which it moved, before acquiring its final fixed purple, a parallel to color changes of the Nile in flood.[44] The Egyptians therefore considered purple a noble and sacred color, and, through the Phoenicians, who adopted the purple industry, the association of purple with royalty, the priesthood and the high-born, spread throughout the Mediterranean.

We find purple having the same value in the Olmec world. Both Matthew Stirling and Professor Zenil Medellin noted that a patch of purple appears on one of the monumental stone heads at San Lorenzo. Medellin in fact claims that some of the heads were originally painted but that the paint faded over time.[45] In the Nuttall Codez, Zelia Nuttall, the discoverer of the codex, notes "pictures of no fewer than thirteen Mexican women of rank wearing purple skirts and five with capes and jackets of the same color. In addition, 45 chieftains are figured with short, fringed, round purple waistcloths, and there are also three examples of the use of a close fitting purple cap."[46]

Mention has also been made of the artificial beard as an index of royal rank in both cultures but although a case has been made for this,[47] it is probably too simple for us to contend that it was an influence. The Indian scholar, Rafique Jairazbhoy, presents far more persuasive evidence of shared monarchic traits.

Observe this Olmec dignitary at Cierro de la Piedra. (Plate 32) This is clearly a native American. He is probably a king and has one of his subjects bound and seated at his feet. Look at the royal head. Upon this head stands something so unique that only the priest-kings in two culture-areas in the world have been known to wear it. This is the double-crown. The double-crown in the Egypto-Nubian world grew out of very special historical circumstances. It signified the joining of the two lands, the north and south, Egypt and Nubia. But there is more to it than that. Far more unique is the bird and serpent motif on royal diadems and crowns. Yet here, in this extraordinary glimpse of an Olmec king, we see the duplication of not one, but two, indisputable unique traits. Not just the double-crown, but the lower crown with the head of a serpent and the upper crown with the head of a bird (the plumed serpent motif).

I do not exaggerate when I say that it would be impossible to find a mirrored duplication of such a complex and arbitrarily fused twin-trait, in any other cultural context, in any other historical period, in any other part of the world, without some demonstrable evidence of contact between the mother of the original trait and her daughter or duplicate.

Observe the bird and serpent on the crown of the boy-king Tutankhamun, son of the Nubian queen, Tiye. (Plate 33)

Observe it again on the head of yet another Olmec dignitary. (Plate 34)

Lastly, on the head of a Mayan Chief, to whom it diffused from the Olmec high-culture. (Plate 35)

There is the royal crook and the royal flail, part of the ceremonial regalia of priest-kings in both areas. Jairazbhoy cites an Olmec painting at Oxtotitlan where the Olmec king seated on the throne has the same type of flail as the Egyptian and it is in the same position behind his head.[48] But there is also, in this interconnected cluster of monarchic traits, the sacred boat or ceremonial bark of the priest-kings. What is so remarkable about this is that it not only has the same function but the same name (*sibak* in Egyptian, *cipac* in Mexican. The *b* and *p*, of course, are interchangeable plosives).

I had noted the parasol or ceremonial umbrella in my earlier work, as something reserved for royalty in both civilizations. It is actually recorded in Mexican tradition as having come across the water from the east by way of foreigners. Here again Jairazbhoy cites this little known oral tradition recorded in the Titulo Coyoi, one of the surviving texts of the Quiche Maya, influenced by the ancient Olmec. The tradition harks back to early visitors. "These things came from the east," it says, "from the other side of the water and the sea: they came here, they had their throne, their little benches and stools, they had their parasols and their bone flutes."[49]

Jairazbhoy also draws our attention to another unusual monarchic trait duplicated in the Olmec world — feathered fans used by Egyptian royalty that are almost identical in shape, style and color as royal fans found in ancient Mexican paintings in the pyramid of Las Higueras. These fans were painted in an area once dominated by the Olmec and in a culture clearly influenced by them, even though the culture itself (Totonac) belongs to a slightly later period. The fans are made of feathers arranged in concentric circles of blue, red and green. In Mexico they are blue, red and light blue but the Mexican light-blue is the nearest thing on the color spectrum to the Egyptian green.[50]

It does not stop at shared royal paraphernalia and indices of rank. The parallels and identities between some of their ritual ceremonies and ceremonial objects are not to be found anywhere else in the world. Singly, some of these traits can be dismissed as coincidence. The density of the cluster, however, the range and extent of the duplication, with very minor local variations, especially in the light of what we have seen of the iconographic and skeletal evidence, cancels out such a simplistic explanation. As I have said in my earlier work, "the overwhelming incidence of coincidence argues overwhelmingly against a mere coincidence."

Let us look closely now at about a dozen of these which strongly suggest a cultural influence.

First, this plate (Plate 36) shows us ceremonial balls of incense served up in hand-shaped incense spoons. The Egyptian king is throwing pellets of incense into a hand-shaped incense spoon. The Mexican priest below (as portrayed in the Codex Selden) is dropping balls of incense in a hand-shaped incense spoon. The incense also is identified by roughly the same sounding name, *kuphi* (pronounced ku-pi or ko-pi) in Egypt, while we have *copal* (pronounced ko-pul) in Mexico.[51]

Here is another ceremony (Plate 37) where another combination of near-identities occur. The Egyptian papyrus painting above is taken from the Book of the Dead. It depicts the Opening of the Mouth Ceremony. Compare it with the wall painting below from a cave at Juxtlahuaca. The priests in Mexico and Egypt are wearing the skins of beasts, whose heads cover theirs, like masks, and whose tails hang in the identical manner between their legs. They both proffer a snake-headed wand or stick, as well as another object (unidentifiable but similar) to a bearded, seated figure before them.[52]

Observe another. (Plate 38) In Egypt the Pharaoh is purified by the gods Thoth and Horus, pouring crossed streams of libation over him. In the Mexican Codex we see the same ceremony. Here are two underworld gods pouring crossed streams of libation over a third god.[53] The blackness of the third god has been noted but here the color is ritual, not racial.

Another ritual ceremony is the phallic cult. Here is the god Min in Egypt holding his phallus in the same manner as the Mexican as seen in the Codex Borbonicus (Plate 39) and again (39 A) a phallic procession of ancient Mexicans, holding artificial phalli.

Among the most startling of identities between the two cultures because they are found nowhere else in that phase of time is the human-headed bird, the Ba and Ka[54] (Plate 40A). Observe the comparison in ancient Egypt. (Plate 40B) These human-headed birds are found on sarcophagi in both Egypt and Mexico and holes are cut in the tombs in both places so that the soul of the deceased, which it represents, can come and go. There is also the human-headed dog, Anubis. I have seen this in the museum of Villahermosa which houses many of the treasures of ancient La Venta. At least 48 people can bear witness that I brought it to their notice in this museum in the summer of 1984.[55] In spite of the restrictions of the museum (we were not allowed to use flash) some of us persisted and got a blurred impression of the object under the glare and mist of glass. The latest information reaching me from recent visitors to the museum is that this object has now been removed. (I say this as a simple fact. I am not suggesting any ulterior motive.)

But note another remarkable pair of human-headed objects. (Plate 41) These appear in my earlier work. The one above from early America, Costa Rica, with a very realistic African head at one end and a penis with two stylized footrests at the other. The one below — a human-headed coffin from Argin in ancient Nubia — has the African features like the American one above, spectacularly sculpted into the funerary wood.

Jairazbhoy demonstrates the remarkable similarity between several gods in the Egyptian underworld and early Mexico. I would like to point to just two of these, which are particularly convincing. The god Sokar. (Plate 42A) This god is a winged god who stands (as you can see) on the back of a double-headed serpent. Compare this ancient Egyptian papyrus painting of the Underworld with this god at Izapa in Mexico. (Plate 42B) In Egypt the god stretches out his hand to hold up his wings. The Mexican god does the same. Both Egyptian and Mexican also stand on the back of a serpent with the same unique mythological formation — a head where his head should be *as well as a head where his tail should be.*

Visually striking also is the Mexican duplicate of the double-rope swallowing god, Aken (Plate 43) "a serpent without eyes, nose or ears, a nonarticulated ophidian."

Mummification among the Olmec is another claim that has been made but the evidence is scanty. This may be due to the fact that the corrosive humidity of the soil destroyed much of the skeletal material. But, as we have shown, there are significant centers where crania were found in good enough condition to be analyzed. There are mummified remains in Mexico, to be sure, but no hard evidence, it seems, that the manner of the mummification or the formula for mummification is close enough to suggest an influence. In Peru, however, Professor Ruetta has cited such evidence.[56] In Olmec Mexico Rafique Jairazbhoy presents a very unusual sculpture from Oaxaca (Plate 44) with rib cages outlined as those of a dead man and arms folded in exactly the same way as in some Egyptian mummies — arms crossed over chest, fingers open.

Certainly unusual in the ritual of the ancient world was the plucking out of the human heart. Here is a representation of it in Egypt (Plate 45) where the enemies of the sun-god have their hearts plucked out. This was simply symbolic in Egypt but it became terrifyingly real in Mexico, where human hearts (often from the breasts of subject tribes) were torn out and fed to the sun-god. It can be argued, however, that the idea blossomed independently, by sheer coincidence, among these two peoples and cultures, although one would be hard put to show its parallel elsewhere in the ancient world.

But here is another so-called coincidence that is much harder to explain. Let us look at the ceremonial platform at La Venta where the first sequence of stone heads appear. (Plate 46) Here, in spite of earlier centuries of occupation of Olmec sites like San Lorenzo, (as early as 1500 B.C.) we are witnessing the very first pyramidal construction at La Venta (948–680 B.C.). Not just the conical pyramid but the step-pyramid. And further, the first use in America of a north-south axial orientation for ceremonial structures. This axial orientation for pyramids is not only unique to Egypt and Nubia. It has an indisputable antecedence.

Now, what have the isolationists said about this? They have ducked this one rather awkwardly. The large construction at one end of the platform is not a pyramid at all, they say, but "a fluted cone." This (Plate 47) is meant to represent, they claim, "a volcano." This explanation ignores two very important things.

First, that it was built of clay, not stone, as in the Old World prototype. Also, it was built in a swampy area. The sides would inevitably collapse inwards with time, as do all earthen hills, and the construction would naturally lose the sharpness of its original slopes. All formations of this nature, not set in natural rock or man-made stone, suffer the same fate.

Second, how can we ignore the miniature step-pyramid at the other end of the platform, which is clearly and undeniably related? Is this then a baby volcano? Come on. If our critics are going to be absurd, let them be absurd logically.

Now, I have never claimed that Africans built this pyramid or any other pyramid in America. It would have been most unlikely. This is about 103 feet high. It is three and a half million cubic feet in volume. It is estimated that it took 18,000 men one million man-hours to construct. There could not have been that many foreign migrants to the Olmec world. What we are talking about is a stimulus, an influence. The natives had never built a full-blown pyramid before. They had never placed a miniature step-pyramid on a ceremonial platform before. They had never carved colossal stone heads before. They had never transported 10–40 tons of basalt on rafts or barges before.[57] They had never used a north-south axial orientation before. Earlier sites tell us this. San Lorenzo was occupied half a millennium before La Venta. Yet none of these things are in evidence. It needs repeating once again, for those who find it difficult to separate occupation-phase datings from datings of structures on a site, that the stone heads at San Lorenzo appear much later than those at La Venta. None of the structures at San Lorenzo observe any axial orientation. They are slipshod, poorly planned, irregular and uneven. We are facing something *new* at La Venta, something both native and foreign. How can we insist categorically that this is a virginal culture when we have a corroboration of iconographic and skeletal evidence and such provocative ritual identities and correspondences?

Now we return to the question of boats. Here is a representation of the typical African dugout. (Plate 48) But the dugout is a mere template or building block for extension and expansion techniques. Africans had many other types of boats. Apart from 3000 years of shipping on the Nile, we find a considerable range of watercraft on the Niger, a marine highway that is two thousand, six hundred miles long. On this highway one could find reed boats with sails, like the reed boats of ancient Egypt and Ethiopia; log-rafts lashed together; enormous dugouts as wide-berthed, long and sturdy as Viking ships; double-canoes connected catamaran fashion like the Polynesian; lateen-rigged dhows, as used by the Arabs and African maritime peasants on the Indian Ocean; rope-sewn plank vessels with cooking facilities in the hold; jointed boats fitted out with woven straw cabins.[58]

Here is the famous reed-boat, RA I. (Plate 49) This is the boat the Buduma people rebuilt for Thor Heyerdahl. It is an ancient pre-Christian vessel. In 1969 the Africans set out from Safi in North Africa and crossed the Atlantic, getting as far as Barbados. They had crossed 2,000 miles of ocean using a vessel they had at their disposal even as early as Olmec times. Bear in mind that Africa, at its nearest point, is only 1500 miles away. Europe, by the way, is twice as far from America as is Africa and it does not have the advantage of the currents off the Atlantic coast of Africa. But there are even more important experiments with African boats than those attempted by Heyerdahl. Dr. Alain Bombard took an African raft in 1952 and sailed from Casablanca in North Africa to Barbados. Hannes Lindemann made the journey from Africa to America in an African dugout in 52 days. Vespucci took 64 days to do this, not counting the days travelling from Europe. He actually set out from an advantageous position in Africa in 1502 in a Portuguese caravel and yet Lindemann's African dugout beat him by 12 days. Bombard did it without a crew, without any stored food or water, with only a cloth net for small sea fauna, a fishing line with hook for tunny, and two spears. Lindemann did the same in the African dugout but, in addition to a fishing kit, he took along an instrument to squeeze liquids out of fish in case no rain fell on the ocean. Both men survived in perfect health.[59]

Here is an African ship (Plate 50) also built before Christ — on the opposite side of the continent. This is the *mtepe,* used by the Swahili on the Indian Ocean. There is also the *dua la mtepe,* which has banks of oars as well as a sail. Africans were not a boatless people. The Chinese report Africans transhipped an elephant to the court of China two hundred years before Columbus.[60] You cannot ship elephants to China in a dugout.

Now look at the map of currents which leave Africa for the Americas. (Plate 51) This is a United States oceanographic map. It shows you clearly three powerful currents which, like marine conveyor belts, take everything that remains afloat to the Americas. It is at the termini of these currents that we have found the African presence.

Here now is a map which is the most extraordinary piece of evidence that Africans crossed the Atlantic in early times. (Plate 52) This map is, beyond the shadow of a doubt, pre-Columbian. It was redrawn in 1513 from pre-Christian maps found in the sacked library of Alexandria. It is called the Piri Reis map from the Turkish admiral who found it. It has its meridian in Egypt, in the area later called Alexandria by the Greeks, later called Cairo by the Arabs. It definitely precedes them. Their maps do not show these things. The mid-Atlantic islands are shown with remarkable accuracy. The Cape Verde, Madeira Islands, and the Azores are shown in perfect longitude. The Canary islands are only off by 1 degree longitude. The Andes are shown on this map. This was only seen by Europeans in 1527 when Pizarro claimed to have "discovered" it. The Atrata River in Columbia is shown for a distance of 300 miles from the sea. The Amazon River is shown, the actual course of the river, while the 16th century European maps bear no resemblance to its real course. Even more remarkable is the near-accuracy of the longitudinal and latitudinal coordinates between the African and the American coasts.[61] No European map came even close to this until the eighteenth century. 150 years after the death of Columbus, European encyclopedias declared that longitude had not been discovered and was probably undiscoverable.

So far we have been looking at faces from the pre-Christian world in Mexico. There were obviously descendants of these Africans and, on some occasions, new arrivals, not just in the later Mandingo voyages of the fourteenth and fifteenth centuries. The African image can be seen in various periods—pre-Classic, Classic, post-Classic. I shall present just a dozen of these visible witnesses. Observe this African figure from Vera Cruz with turban and ritual scarification (Plate 53), this African drummer from Colima (Plate 54), this African woman from the Pyramid of Teotihuacan (Plate 55A). Observe the startling realism of this piece, down to the headkerchief, the ear pendants, the blackness of the skin. Compare with the next slide (Plate 55B) where Von Wuthenau shows us a near identical counterpart from the African continent, both in facial form and cultural accoutrements. Look at the bearded African with the topknot hair style from Tabasco (Plate 56) and what is perhaps the finest representation of an African in pre-Columbian art (Plate 57), a Mandingo type found among the Mixtecs at Oaxaca.

Here is another African from the Mandingo period. (Plate 58) This is from the Josue Saenz collection in Mexico City. As realistic in every detail as the previous one, which is now in the Stavenhagen collection in Germany. Here, heavily tattooed, in roughly the same period, is an African from the province of Guanacaste, Costa Rica. (Plate 59) Here is another in a portrait vessel from Oaxaca. (Plate 60) Another, now in the National Museum in Mexico City. (Plate 61) Von Wuthenau says that this figure was worshipped by Aztecs in the province where it was found because it had the right ritual color of one of their gods, Tezcatlipoca. This has nothing to do (please do not misunderstand) with them mistaking it for a god. It was just an appropriate image for that ritual purpose. The next, however, is the black god of jewelers, Na-ua-pilli. (Plate 62) Stylized though he may be, everything is done to emphasize his Negroid or Africoid element. It is hard to dismiss this as purely accidental or arbitrary since the Mandingo traders were associated with the gold trade. According to Ramon Pane, as I mentioned before, they are called the "black guanini," the black gold merchants. The final selection is of a black in the Mexican marketplace. (Plate 63) A red-skinned native is standing by a stall where the trader, his Africoid features heavily emphasized down to the painted exaggeration of his lips, is offering his wares.

We shift now to something that came about as a result of the Smithsonian find of African skeletons in a pre-Columbian grave in the Virgin Islands. The skeletons could not be dated and so the matter remains inconclusive, at least where the bones are concerned. But not far from Hull Bay, where these skeletons were found, at the bottom of the Reef Bay Valley on St. John's, something unusual has emerged.

This script (Plate 64) is found at the bottom of a waterfall in the Reef Bay Valley and it is reflected in the water. The unusual regularity of the dot and crescent formation is what attracted me to it and away from the relatively meaningless carvings of animals further up the rock-face. It has been deciphered by Barry Fell, professor emeritus of Harvard. Fell has got into a lot of trouble over some of his decipherments but this has been carefully checked out. Scholars in the Libyan Department of Antiquities arrived at the same decipherment as he did. It has been identified as the Tifinagh Branch of the Libyan script. This was used not only by Southern Libyans but by people in some parts of medieval Mali and by the Tamahaq Berbers which, in the period of which we speak, were not the heavily mixed Euro-African people they are today. The inscription reads: "Plunge in to cleanse yourself. This is water for purification before prayer."[62]

The African presence is also found in South America. The heads that now follow (Plates 65, 66, 67 and 68) clearly show Africans in Ecuador and Peru. These are far too realistic to be brushed aside. But we cannot deal with that chapter of the African presence in this lecture. There is one, however, which we must comment upon as we close. That is this remarkable portrait of the sons of African governors in South America. (Plate 65 repeated) These Africans are chieftains from Esmeraldas in what is now Ecuador. They visited Quito in 1599. They are shown here in Spanish dress and Indian ornaments but were descendants of a group of 17 shipwrecked Africans who gained political control of an entire province of Ecuador in short order.[63]

Let me close by saying, this is not all diffusionist fantasy and all I ask is that there should be a little more tolerance and openness to discussion and examination of this subject. It will take a lot of time and study by many experts, in many fields, to settle upon the validity of some of the data and to distinguish an apparent influence from a mere coincidence, but we cannot approach the study of shattered worlds like Africa and America the way we approach the study of Europe. We are forced to venture into several disciplines today because of destruction of documents, in order to grasp the true complexity of these vanished worlds. But America was not the tidy, closed world we would like to think it was. The Negroid or Africoid type, depicted in the terracotta and in the bones and stones, was not the result of local micro-evolution but hybridization through migration. The Atlantic was never an impassable sea of darkness. Its currents were living, moving roads, marine conveyor belts. The only cultures in the world that we have found, built up over millennia in almost pure, impervious bubbles of glass, are the cultures of jungle primitives.

No great civilization, be it African, Asian, or European, developed in total isolation. Why should America then? Why should we assume that a world, so vast and various, that the peoples in Mexico alone spoke fourteen languages, rotated away from the rest of humanity for tens of thousands of years, until a little gold-hungry adventurer, Christopher Columbus, suddenly discovered that the people here were really living in India, that Cuba was the continent, South America an island, and the Caribbean Sea the Gulf of the Ganges?

Thank you.

RESPONSE TO DR. KELLEY

Van Sertima: I just want to respond very quickly to one or two things raised by Dr. Kelley. The question, for one, of Wiener's linguistics. I think, in quite a number of cases, Wiener's linguistics were very poor and I have made that very clear. From the very beginning of my first essay into this subject, I spoke of the fragile pillars of philology upon which so much of his thesis was built. Everything he had to say about plants, for example, was wrong. I ventured into botany and took a close look at the plants. Wiener did not know anything about cotton. All of his linguistic arguments about cotton were absurd. Nevertheless, his instincts had taken him down the right road even though he made the wrong turning. For we did find that the two tetraploid cottons of America — Gossypium hirsutum and Gossypium barbadense — are the result of a marriage between an Old World diploid cotton and a wild ancestral American cotton. The Old World cotton could not have come from Europe, for cultivated cotton only entered Europe in the 9th century A.D., more than three millenia after the marriage of Old World, New World cottons. It could not have come in from Asia, since the closest Asian candidate — Gossypium arboreum — is more distantly removed from the American family of cottons than is the African putative father. Not only that, it is actually a stepchild of the African, a mutation of the African diploid cotton, Gossypium herbaceum. Everyone who has studied this problem knows that the herbaceum is the best candidate. But there is a problem. It is African, you see. Africans, as we know them, are too primitive to have domesticated plants that early. Another problem. The cotton had to cross the ocean and Africans, as we know them, are good at crossing jungles, not oceans. Perhaps, say the botanists, after the failure of 'oceanic drift' and 'bird-migration' theories, it may be best to leave this one as a mystery. Then we do not have to deal with the African. But perhaps — and here is a chance for a new departure that may solve other problems — perhaps we have to start dealing more seriously with our vision of the African.

We face the same problem in South America. An African jackbean (canavalia virosa) intermarried with an American jackbean (canavalia plagiosperma) to produce, by repeated backcrossing in the Andean lowlands, the African-American jackbean (canavalia piperi). Like the cotton, it did not happen yesterday. Like the cotton too, it could not survive transoceanic drift or come flying down from the clouds in the bellies of migrating birds. Birds do not eat cotton balls or jackbean seeds for lunch.

Now Dr. Kelley has explained to us that the Vikings left a building and this is what makes Lief Erickson's voyage more believable to the conventional anthropologist. But are the plants less substantial, less permanent?

No, but let us concede the point. *L'Anse aux Meadows* is impressive as a single isolate, yes. But the Vikings brought no new plant, influenced no art, introduced no ritual. Like a wave they broke on alien sands and then receded. . . .

Let me respond to another point in reference to Wiener. I have never accepted his evidence on tobacco. I argued clearly that he was dead wrong to state that tobacco was brought to America from Africa. I pointed out, in my appraisal of the case, that the evidence pointed to both an African and an American tobacco. Even when my good friend, the late Chiekh Anta Diop, reported to me the find of tobacco in the belly of Rameses II, I questioned this find as foreign in origin although it seemed to support my thesis. Diop sent me a letter saying, "Here is apparent evidence on behalf of your thesis." I said "No, no. If you check it out, you will probably find it is *not* American tobacco."

Tobacco is not simply an American indigene. It is also found in Africa. The African type has stronger narcotic qualities. I have never followed Wiener on these matters. There is some evidence of African influence on American medieval pipes and vice versa but it is not true that Africans brought the pipe itself. This was a mistake. I was extremely critical in a later work I edited, attacking Wiener. I even invited one of my students to spend a semester to check out the validity of everything that Wiener had to say about the mounds. When he showed me the misdating of certain objects in the mounds and exposed certain errors in Wiener's conclusions, I published his essay. This thesis will not rise or fall on little things. Give Leo Wiener his due. He was a pioneer. It is true that he made a lot of mistakes but he also opened the field. He probed the unknown with an open mind. That is more than can be said of many of us.

EGYPTO-NUBIAN PRESENCES IN ANCIENT MEXICO

Ivan Van Sertima

> We can trace the progress of man in Mexico without noting
> any definite Old World influence during this period
> (1000-650 B.C.) except a strong Negroid substratum con-
> nected with the Magicians (high priests).[1]
> —Frederick Peterson, Ancient Mexico
>
> The startling fact is that in all parts of Mexico, from Cam-
> peche in the east to the South coast of Guerrero, and from
> Chiapas, next to the Guatemalan border, to the Panuco
> River in the Huasteca region (north of Veracruz), arch-
> eological pieces representing Negro or Negroid people have
> been found, especially in Archaic or pre-Classic sites.
> —Alexander von Wuthenau, Unexpected Faces in[2]
> Ancient America

In my book They Came Before Columbus *(Random House, 1977) I deal with contacts, both planned and accidental, between Africans and Americans in about half a dozen historical periods. In this essay, however, I confine myself to a particular geographical region (the Gulf Coast of Mexico), a particular culture complex or civilization (known as Olmec), and a particular period of history (948-680 B.C.).*

The Olmec are known as the People of the Jaguar or the Jaguar-Mouth People. The jaguar hovered on the fringes of their first major settlements, dominating their consciousness, and so it became a central motif in their art. Yet, contrary to what scholars have claimed, it is often clearly distinguishable from the art of human portraiture. Jaguar mosaics, jaguar masks, even human-jaguar combinations stand side by side and in contrast with some of the most vivid, monumental and realistic human portraits in clay, jade and stone. Therefore, no obsession with the jaguar, no artistic style suggested by this jungle cat with the snarling mouth, can account for the clearly Africoid features of some of the colossal stone heads, clay figurines and masks found in the Olmec world.

Speculations as to a possible African element in the first major American civilization go back more than a century to the year 1858, when the first colossal

This article originally appeared in *Dollars & Sense* magazine, February/March 1983 (vol. 8, no. 6). Copyright © 1983 by National Publications Sales Agency, Inc. Reprinted with permission.

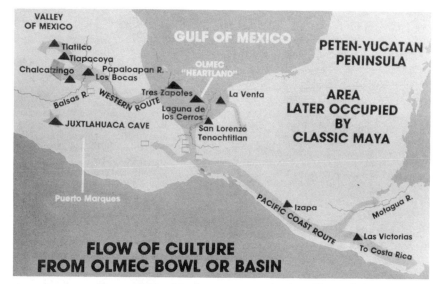

stone head was discovered by Mexican peasants in the village of Tres Zapotes. These very early speculations by scholars like Jose Melgar[3] and Orozco y Berra[4] were easily dismissed because far too little was known at the time. It was not until 1938 that intensive scientific excavations of Olmec sites began. In that year an archeological team directed by Matthew Stirling rediscovered this huge stone head with a helmeted dome.[5] Eight feet in height, 18 feet in circumference, it weighed over 10 tons.[6] Stirling found it, in spite of its great size, to be carved from a single block of basalt and to be a head only. In its realism, its size, its awesome bodilessness, its alien features and headgear, it stood out among American sculptures. Only the colossal bodiless heads of Nubian blacks and other racial types found at Tanis, the harbor for seagoing ships in Egypt, can parallel this head in scale or conception in the ancient world.

"Cleared of the surrounding earth," wrote Stirling, "it presented an awe-inspiring spectacle. Despite its great size, the workmanship is delicate and sure, its proportions perfect. Unique in character among aboriginal American sculptures, it is remarkable for its realistic treatment. The features are bold and *amazingly negroid* in character."[7]

Fourteen years before Sterling's expedition to Tres Zapotes, a team from Tulane University had found a giant stone head pushing out of the ground at La Venta in the Mexican state of Tabasco, about 18 miles inland from the Gulf of Mexico. The Tulane team was only passing through the area and did not have time to dig out but they recorded their find in a photograph.[8] After his return from Tres Zapotes Stirling saw this photograph and was struck by something in it: Although only the top of the head could be seen, the domelike helmet on this buried figure seemed to match the one he had excavated at Tres Zapotes.

Among the first stone heads found, with Africoid features. *Front view*. Tres Zapotes. This was found in 1862. It is now located at Tuxtla.

Side-view of the Tres Zapotes head.

Back of the Tres Zapotes head, showing Ethiopian-type braids. This unusual photo is by anthropo-photo journalists Wayne Chandler and Gaynell Catherine.

Suspecting a link, he headed toward La Venta on his next expedition in 1939. La Venta was later to turn out to be the holy center of the Olmec world, the home of the Olmec priest-kings and of the Olmec elite—the very heartland of their civilization.

After a relentless search by Stirling's team, the head recorded in the photograph was located. It was found to be 8 feet high and, like the one at Tres Zapotes, it also looked African.[9] Three more African-looking heads were uncovered at La Venta. Two of them were so realistic in detail that they even had their teeth carved out, a very unusual thing in American art. Massive and military, like tough warrior dynasts they stood, faces of pure basalt stone, dominating the ceremonial plaza in which they were found. The lines of cheek and jaw, the fullness of the lips, the broad fleshy noses, the acutely observed and faithfully reproduced facial contours and particulars, bore wit-

New head found at San Lorenzo, still lying in the swamp.

The rain god at La Venta

ness to an African presence. One of the African-looking colossi, 8 feet and 6 inches high and 22 feet in circumference, wore earplugs with a cross carved in each.

The cross, which first appears in ancient America on this site, conveys the same idea of fertility as the Egyptian cross. Like the Egyptian cross it is the symbol of life and generation. The Mexican word for the cross, which was later to appear in the Olmec-influenced city of Teotihauacan is *To-naca-qua-hui-tl* "tree of life." It is possible to argue that the duplication of this motif and its meaning is a coincidence, but how can we explain the duplication of the helmets found on most of the African-type sculptures?

If we examine some of these helmets we find they are uncannily similar to leather helmets worn by the Egyptian-Nubian military in the era of the Ramessids (Egyptian pharaohs) and in the first millenium B.C. They completely cover the head and the back of the neck and they have tie-ons attached to the crest and falling in front of the ears. The details on some of them, although almost 3,000 years old, have become a little obscured, but there is one in particular, now in the Jalapa Museum, which can be examined for comparative purposes. It has the circular earplug and incised decorative parallel lines found on other colossal Nubian heads in the Egyptian seaport of Tanis.

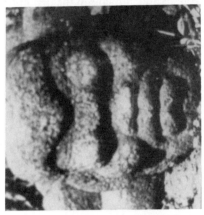

These heads, following the orientation of the ceremonial center on which they were found, were placed on a north-south axis. So was the pyramid at La Venta, the first to be found anywhere in ancient America. This north-south axis corresponds to the axial orientation of the pyramid complex in Egypt and the Sudan. (We shall return to the issue of the pyramid later. Suffice it to say, that although earlier settlements have been found in America—as early as 2,000 B.C. among the Maya—the pyramids are later than the one at La Venta.)

The largest of the African heads at La Venta—9 feet high—had its domed head flattened so that it could function as an altar. A hole may be seen at the left ear, running like a tube through the head itself to form a small opening at the center of the mouth. This head was used as an oracle, a "talking" god. "In grayest antiquity," wrote Constance Irwin in *Fair Gods and Stone Faces*, "a priest of the Olmec whispered into that giant ear, and his sonorous words emerged from the great stone lips."[10] It is strongly reminiscent of the technique used in the talking god of the Etyptians and Nubians in the first millenium B.C.—Amon-Ra. The blacks made Amon-Ra into an animated god. By its oracular pronouncements and the illusion of animation, they could invoke the unchallengeable authority of a god on earth. The statue of Amon-Ra was jointed, a priest being especially appointed to work it, and, in the sanctuaries, hiding places were arranged in the thickness of the wall from which the priest skillfully arranged for the oracular voice of the god to be heard.

The significance of the oracular stone head and of the other objects found on the La Venta site could not be assessed until some very firm dating by scientific methods could be obtained. This was accomplished by means of carbon 14 (a radioactive isotope of carbon) datings during excavations conducted in 1955 and 1956 by members of a joint National Geographic-Smithsonian-University of California expedition. The results were released in 1957 and were astonishing.

At the place where the African-type stone sculptures were found—the La Venta ceremonial court—nine samples of wood charcoal were taken. Five of these samples related to what was believed then to be the original construction of the court. They gave an average reading of 814 B.C., plus or minus 134 years,[11] which is nearly 3,000 years ago.

While most archeologists have accepted the 800 B.C. date as the average of the La Venta ceremonial court, the most recent redatings by archeologists Berger, Graham, and Heizer seem to suggest that the first phase of the ceremonial court is nearer to the 948 or circa 1000 B.C. date.[12] (This redating does not affect my emphasis on the Nubian 25th dynasty, 800-654 B.C., because the earliest dating relates to the first occupation of the La Venta ceremonial site—it was rebuilt twice by the natives—and not necessarily to the later phase of the African colossi and the pyramid. Even if it did, I had made allowance for both extremes of the dating equation.)

Let it be noted that the Nubian military, the most powerful militia in Africa at the time, had become the main force behind power factions in Egypt and had functioned as backroom power brokers in Egyptian politics since 1085 B.C. They held this position of ascendancy for centuries, even though it was not until the beginning of the 9th century B.C. that the establishment of the royal house of Kush in Nubia and the total conquest of Egypt by Nubian kings were finally achieved. Nubia, both as the creator of Egyptian civilization (as the recent archeological discovery of the black kingdom of Ta-Seti has shown)[13] as well as its unifier and conqueror in the 8th century B.C., was the preserve of classical Egyptian culture. It ushered in a renaissance of cultural traits, like mummification and pyramid building that had lapsed in Egypt but had been perpetuated in Nubia all through the period under study (948-680 B.C.). To restore these and other traits to Egypt clearly indicates that the Nubian was in the mainstream of Egyptian culture and quite capable, if thrust by accident or design into an alien environment, of transmitting Egyptian traits.

La Venta was not alone in its sculptural representation of African-type heads in stone. Apart from the four found there, two were excavated at Tres Zapotes and six at San Lorenzo in Veracruz, one of which, the largest known, is 9 feet, 4 inches high. Some of these heads weigh between 30 and 40 tons. The San Lorenzo site was occupied even earlier than La Venta (circa 2000 B.C.) but the Africoid stone heads appear much later.

Even Michael Coe, the leading American historian on Mexico, who has on occasion disputed my findings, agrees that the heads at La Venta are the first in the sequence and that the carbon dating there is the most relevant.[14] Coe, in response to an interview with *Science Digest* in 1981, contended that the reason the stone heads had broad noses and thick lips was because the tools used to cut them were too blunt to make sharper noses and thinner lips. He also contended that the sculptors wanted to avoid "protruding or thin facial features that might break off."[15]

This is the latest explanation by the "establishment." Earlier on, scholars had argued that these were idolized Mongoloid babies or monsters or throwbacks or were influenced by the jaguar motif in Olmec art. These explanations do not take into account that side by side with the stone representations of African types there are also many sculptures in clay with African-type features as well as African-type hair—both head-hair and chin-hair.

When Coe was asked by *Science Digest* whether he knew of these clay sculptures corroborating the stone-head evidence, he confessed that he had never heard of them. Few traditional scholars of Mexico know of these terra cottas (clay pieces). There are only about half a dozen of them among the pieces displayed in the Museum of Anthropology in Mexico City. One must visit the Diego Rivera Museum, the Josue Saenz collection and the Alexander von Wuthenau collection to see these remarkable and unmistakable Africoid men and women—chiefs, dancers, drummers, wrestlers, priests, women of great beauty, men of great authority, Olmec, Mayan, Totonac, Zapotec, Mixtec, Aztec. It is fortunate that in spite of the great official opposition to the idea of Africans in ancient

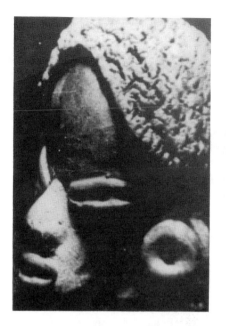

Pre-classic clay sculptures identifiable as African, not only by nose, lips and general facial structure, but also by color of skin and texture of hair. *Top*: Sculpture from the central plateau of Mexico, Olmec period. *Center*: Sculpture from Tlapacoya. (Photos from Homo Americanus Collection: Von Wuthenau) *Bottom*: Sculpture from Chiapas emphasizes moustache and beard. (Photo by Jacqueline Patten)

America, President Portillo of Mexico and the wife of former President Echeverria have given their support to the work of von Wuthenau in establishing this pre-Columbian presence, particularly in the medium of clay.

Clay is the medium *par excellence* for portrait art. It is impossible to list all of the African pieces found thus far in the Olmec world (or in the pre-Classic period when that civilization flowered), but an examination of them reveals the unmistakable combination of kinky hair, broad nose, generous lips, frequency of prognathism (abnormally projecting jaws), occasional goatee beard, and sometimes distinctively African ear pendants, hairstyles, tattoo markings and coloration. With respect to coloration, the clay chosen or the oxide dyes used to evoke the blackness or dark brownness of the skin is particularly striking because they are reserved for the types with the non-native noses, lips, hair textures, etc. These were deliberate choices of artists dealing with living, human models. (I have been to these collections on several occasions and have held many of these pieces in my hands. They are works of incredible skill, some so tiny that only a modern carver of genius could capture the complex delicacy of detail on such a miniature scale. I present with this article some of the terra cottas that were not in my book along with a few that were. I must draw special attention to the drummer from Colima, the three women from Xochipala, Guerrero, and the African acrobat. With the exception of the last named, which is in the Diego Rivera museum, the other four are new acquisitions by von Wuthenau and stand in his San Angel collection, which should become the focus of any pilgrimage to Mexico by African-Americans.)

What clinches evidence of the African presence, however, are skulls and skeletons of Africans found on Olmec sites. The study of crania (skulls) came into disrepute in the early part of this century since it had been used by unscrupulous racists to show that Africans had brains inferior to Europeans. Skull study has matured, however, in spite of early frauds, into a fairly exact science and the Russians can now reconstruct a face with computerlike precision from the skull of the dead. One of the world's leading skull experts, Polish professor Andrzej Wiercinski, announced to the 41st Congress of Americanists in Mexico in September 1974 that African skulls had been found at Olmec sites in Tlatilco, Cerro de las Mesas and Monte Alban.

"These show," said Wiercinski, "a clear prevalence of the total Negroid pattern that has been evidenced by the use of two methods: (a) multivariate distance analysis of average characteristics of individual fractions distinguished cranioscopically and (b) analysis of frequency distributions of mean index of the position between combinations of racial varieties."[16] There is no easy way to break this down into laymans' language but, roughly speaking, the three main races of men show differences in skull shape and in the formation of the bones of the face. It is possible to make distinctions in noses, jaws, brow ridges, etc. and in the way these are put together in terms of very minute variations of distance between the parts.

Pre-classic acrobat. (Photo by Jacqueline Patten)

Woman from Xochipala. (Photo by Jacqueline Patten)

Woman from Teotihaucan. (Photo by Jacqueline Patten)

Since in extreme instances, one race may fade into the other, in the sense of unusual types of one race having average characteristics of the other, a further close check has to be made to ensure that this possibility is not distorting the picture. In very mixed populations this would be a very difficult process, open to much error, but in the dry areas of the Olmec civilization Wiercinski found clear evidence of a racial type different from that of the native population appearing as a significant minority. All the indices used to distinguish races through the study of surviving skulls and close comparison with skulls found in continental African and native American graveyards make it quite clear that a foreign racial element (African) entered the Olmec world at this time.

That does not make the Olmecs *African* as several diffusionists have claimed. It means that the African element became a significant group and influence among the native American Olmecs. Africans not only came here (before the Vikings or any other Old World group) but they left an impact upon America's first major civilization. The Olmec civilization was formative and seminal: it was to touch all others on this continent, directly or indirectly. (But I have never claimed that Africans created or founded the Olmec civilization. Such a claim would be extreme. They left a significant influence upon it, as we shall show, and that is more than can be said of any other Old World group visiting the native Americans or emigrating to this continent before Columbus.)

A number of extremely interesting facts emerged from a study of the skeletal evidence. Wiercinski noted that 13.5 percent of the skeletons examined in the pre-Classic Olmec cemetery of Tlatilco were African, yet only 4.5 percent of those found later at Cerro de las Mesas from the Classic period were African. This indicates that the African element intermingled until it almost fused with the native population. Female skeletons found in the graves from the pre-Classic period, and lying side by side with African males, are racially distinct from them (that is, native American Females, foreign African males), but they appear racially similar to their male companions at a *later* "Classic" site, indicating progressive intermixture and the growing absorption of the foreign African element into the largely Mongoloid (Asiatic) American population.

This makes it very clear that the Olmec-African element was a distinctive, outside injection that came and crossbred in the Olmec time period and that it did not represent "proto-Australoid" or "proto-negroid" aborigines who trickled into America from the Pacific in the very ancient glacial epoch when the very first Americans came. According to Wiercinski's skeletal statistics, they would have disappeared millenia ago into the American gene pool if they could fade from 13.5 percent to 4.5 percent in a few brief centuries. The two major Pacific migrations of the first Americans occurred, after all, about 50,000 and 20,000 years ago, respectively, according to the most recent datings. (Some have put it as early as 70,000 years ago, others as late as 13,000. In terms of the point I am making, the fading of an African element that came in at the very beginning of the Bering Strait migrations, the current dispute over those dates does not matter.)

The Ra I built by Africans in 1969 crossed from Safi, North Africa, to Barbados in the Caribbean, using power and the direction of the currents and trade winds.

In the Olmec world (948-680 B.C.) we are not dealing with African elements that survived the Pacific crossing many thousands of years ago. Wiercinski has pointed out that these skulls in Olmec strata are of a continental African type, such as we find in West Africa today, and not those of Pacific negritos, who could have come in much earlier. The continental African migrated in huge waves to Nubia and Egypt in the pre-dynastic era following the drying up of the green, fertile lands of the Sahara. This physical type, in spite of minor Asiatic and Caucasoid infusion into the north of Egypt, remained predominantly unchanged until wave after wave of conquerors and successive invasions of Assy-

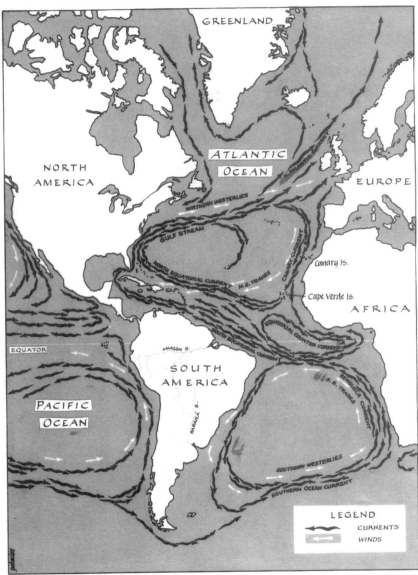

Currents map shows the flow of the ocean from Africa to America.

rians, Persians, Greeks, Romans, Arabs, etc. followed upon the decline of Egypt as a world power at the close of the Bronze Age.

Blacks were particularly dominant in the political and spiritual life in Egypt in the period of contact with the Olmec world and explain the presence of this racial type in colossal African heads in stone, in clay sculptures (terra cottas) and in the skeletal remains found among the Olmec high priests and magicians.

Apart from the African, there is another element that is represented in the native American sculptures of this time. It is not as important as the African in the political and religious hierarchy of the Olmec (no colossal monuments were built to it), but it is associated with the African in the Olmec milieu, with the Egypto-Nubian navies of the first millenium B.C., and even with the indigenous North African on the edge of the Atlantic basin.

That other element is Phoenician. A figure with curved aquiline nose, thin lips, and flowing beard stands on the same plaza as the African figures, although his is a flat representational portrait etched in the slab of stone and does not, therefore, have the same awesome bodiless presence or colossal sculptural proportions of the African figures. The features are clearly outlined, as is the apparel, and it was conceded by even the earliest investigators that this was, to use art historian Miguel Covarrubias' phrase, "a visitor." When it was finally recognized that there was some relationship between this figure and the African-type figures standing beside it on the ceremonial plaza at La Venta, the African types were seen as "mercenary troops" of the Phoenician,[17] or "a cargo of captured blacks."[18]

Let us look closely at this figure. He has been identified as Phoenician by Irwin and others by reference to several details on the stele (engraved stone slab)—his turned-up shoes from a type diffused from the shattered empire of the Hittites in the flight of their upper class to Phoenician capitals; the conversational posture struck by him and his companion on the same stele; the curious figures tilted above him, a floating doll and a man pointing his forefinger down at him—all of which have been shown to correspond to elements in Phoenician culture. Von Wuthenau has presented us with clay representations of figures of this type from several sites in the Olmec world. The Phoenician traveling mascot, Melkart, has turned up at an Olmec site, Rio Balsas. We have no reason, therefore, to question this identification.

There is nothing more natural in this period of history than the association of Nubians, Egyptians and pale-skinned Phoenicians. The Phoenicians became progressively darker and Africoid in the North African civilization of Carthage, so that by the time of Hannibal, the coins and skeletal remains of Carthage show the virtual disappearance of the Semitic Phoenician type as found in their home bases in Tyre and Sidon. An examination of the relationship between the Phoenician and the African is crucial to our understanding, not only of how they could be associated on the same ceremonial plaza at La Venta, but how and why they could find themselves so far away from home.

The relationship between these peoples, their common interests in the face of a threat from the Western Asiatic power—the Assyrian—is an important factor in this period. It helps to explain how this figure with flowing beard, Semitic nose and turned-up shoes appears in association with the African figures in ancient

Mexico and how certain Phoenician elements (including Punic inscriptions, a traveling mascot, and a type of mummy mask) have been unearthed in America in archeological contexts related to the Afro-Egyptian or Egypto-Nubian presence.

Egypt had been trading with the Phoenicians for centuries. These people had once been nomads of the desert but had eventually settled in city-states on the edge of the Mediterranean Sea, colonized islands or built settlements on them. They were, however, a people of nomadic urges and soon made of the sea what they had once made of the desert, a field for their restless wanderings. In the 9th century B.C. (circa 814 B.C.) hundreds of them sailed to North Africa and built a city together with the Africans, which was called Khart Hadast—The New Town—later known by westerners as Carthage.

They trafficked in metals, among other commodities, and their maritime trade in copper, silver, gold and tin took them to Hatus, a Hittite seaport, to an island called Cyprus for its copper, to the Iberian peninsula for silver, to Egypt for silver and for Nubian gold dust, and as far as Cornwall in the British Isles, right out into the North Atlantic, for tin. Although their boats were smaller than those of the Egyptians, 70 feet long was the average, they were extremely maneuverable and were equipped with both sail and oar.

From their settlements they carried linen cloth and wool, fine jewelry, cedar (from which some of the Egyptian ships were made), perfume and spices; and from their major seaports, Tyre, Sidon and Byblos, they exported things that were rare and treasured in the ancient world, particularly a purple dye that came to be known as Tyrian purple, which was reserved for royalty in the Mediterranean basin. It is remarkable that purple, made sacred by the Egyptians and spread by the Phoenicians, was also reserved for royalty and the upper class among the ancient Mexicans as the *Nuttall Codex* (a surviving American book) shows.

The Egyptians, Herodotus tells us, even when they made vassals of the Phoenicians, did not stifle their maritime trade. It was as vital to Egypt as it was to them. The more riches they amassed from trade, the more tribute they could pay to Egypt. A lot of Egyptian trade, particularly the metals so badly needed for the bronze weaponry of their armies, was transported in Phoenician ships. Although merchants in their own right, the Phoenicians were often mercenary seamen for the Egyptians.

During the period under study we have indisputable evidence that Phoenician ships were moving in the waters of the North Atlantic and any examination of the Egyptian or Phoenician navies, from the time of the Ramessids down to the reign of the Nubians, reveals a multi-racial complex and a close relationship between blacks and Phoenicians. Black soldiers, similar to the helmeted ones we find in the Olmec world, were, as indicated above, powers behind the Egyptian throne since 1085 B.C. and they remained so until they established total military and political supremacy over Egypt, circa 720 B.C., under the Nubian king, Piankhy, of the House of Kush.

During this period, corresponding to the middle pre-Classic period in ancient America, the Phoenician was in the position of mercenary, or vassal, in relation to the black power in the Mediterranean. The Phoenician had been cowed by the Assyrian forces of Western Asia, which later threatened Egypt, and, in the cold and hot wars between Egypt and Assyria, which ran right through the 25th dynasty, they were protected allies and mercenaries of the Nubian-Egyptian. This is not to belittle the Phoenician, but to give the lie to speculation that, because the two were found in association on the La Venta site, the Phoenician was the master and the black his mercenary or his slave.

But why should Egyptians, Nubians or Phoenicians cross the Altantic to America? Some have claimed that this voyage was intentional, that the Egyptians had concrete knowledge of a land beyond the western sea. This is not necessarily true. As a result of their astronomy, the Egyptians knew the circumference of the earth. But then there was no way of telling that the missing bulk was not totally covered by water. The evidence points to an accident at sea. But the question arises, could an ancient fleet blown off course, driven toward America by wind and current power, survive the Atlantic crossing?

All the world knows of Thor Heyerdhal's Egyptian papyrus boats, Ra I and Ra II, the former built by Africans, the latter by Americans. Both boats navigated the Altantic successfully, though the first model got into trouble after fully proving itself by drifting on currents off the North African port of Safi to Barbados in the Caribbean. But while Heyerdahl proved that such a journey had been possible from the very earliest of the Egyptian dynasties when papyrus boats were in use, the sophisticated Egyptian and Phoenician galleys of the first millenium B.C. were superior to those earlier models.

We know for certain that the Phoenicians were circling Africa in ships under the orders of the Egyptian king, Necho II, circa 600 B.C. These documented journeys, though occurring later, lend validity to the contention that such journeys were eminently possible in the period under review when similar ships were moving down the Mediterranean into the North Atlantic. Archeology has confirmed that tin was being heavily mined in Cornwall in the British Isles, just 25 miles away from the Scilly Isles, where there are records of Phoenician visits circa 800 B.C. It is only logical to infer that they were in that area in pursuit of their metal trade. Tin was a vital alloy in the manufacture of the bronze weaponry of their allies and sponsors, the Egyptians.

If one looks at the Atlantic currents off Africa and the way they move like conveyor belts to the Caribbean, the northeastern corner of South America and the Gulf of Mexico, one appreciates how easily an expedition into North Atlantic waters could be blown off course into the Gulf of Mexico. According to the later Quiche' Maya people, in whose book the *Popul Vuh* records oral traditions going back to very ancient times, ''black and pale-skinned people'' appeared from the east in boats.[19] The historian Bernardino Sahagun cites one report, common among the natives, that ancient visitors came by sea from the east: "It is certain that they came in vessles of wood . . . they came out of seven caves and these caves are ships or galleys."[20]

The clear feasibility of the trans-Atlantic crossing to America in this ancient period is of the greatest importance. The winds and currents of the Atlantic have not changed appreciably in this brief span of geological time, less than 3,000 years. Just 28 years ago, Dr. Alain Bombard, a medical doctor in Liberia, crossed the Atlantic in a boat that was far inferior to those used by the Egyptians and Phoenicians in the Bronze Age. In an African dugout, without oar and sail, with little food or water, with only an African fishing kit and an implement to squeeze juice **from fish to supplement his supply of liquid in case the rains failed, Lindemann** completed the journey in 52 days, in less time in fact than the first caravels of **Vespucci and Columbus. Current power was his sole source of locomotion. Lindemann not only proved the feasibility of the journey in the most primitive of** vessels but also that it could have been an accident (as was Cabral's later "discovery" of Brazil), and that such an accident was not only repeatable but that even a crew, unprepared for such an emergency, feeding on the billion-finned life of the ocean, could still survive the crossing.

It is my contention that a small but significant number of men and a few women, in a fleet protected by a military force, moved west down the Mediterranean toward North Africa in the period 948-680 B.C., probably on the usual metal run, and got caught in the pull of one of the westward currents off the North African coast, either through storm or navigational error. A map showing the flow of these Atlantic currents illustrates how easily such a crew blown off course could land in the Olmec heartland. A study of the same map, however, would show how difficult it would be for them to retrace their course and return to the Old World, unless they were also fully aware of the circular distribution of the currents in the Atlantic. Africans became aware of this circular return route but much later. We are not discussing these later pre-Columbian journeys here. Ignorance of this unknown sea in an ancient time, therefore, not navigational expertise or geographical knowledge, would explain both their unexpected arrival in this area as well as their inability to return home.

But proof of contact is only half of the story. What is the significance of this meeting of African and native American? What cultural impact did the outsiders have upon Olmec civilization.?

A study of the Olmec civilization reveals elements that so closely parallel ritual traits and techniques in the Egypto-Nubian world of the same period that it is difficult to maintain all these are due to mere coincidence. While it is possible to find a cultural trait or a technique in one place which is similar to that in another, *without any contact having taken place*, there is a method by which we can examine a parallel or a series of parallels to determine with relative certainty when something is purely coincidental or whether it is strongly suggestive of contact with, and influence from outsiders.

Let us first look at the monarchic traits, that is, the royal and priestly dress and emblems of power among the Olmecs and the Egyptians. We can point to a cluster of half a dozen royal traits shared by ruling circles in both civilizations that are functionally related and appear in a combination too arbitrary and unique to be independently duplicated.

The double crown. This grew out of special historical circumstances in Egypt, the joining of the "two lands," Lower and Upper Egypt, by the African Pharaoh Menes.[21] The Nubian pharaohs donned the double crown of the two lands in the 8th century B.C. when they regained their power over the north. The double crown appears on an Olmec dignitary at Cerro de la Piedra. He is seen offering a glyph (symbolic object) with the Egyptian cross motif to a seated figure that has African features and African-type hair.[22]

The royal flail. This was part of the ceremonial regalia of the pharaoh. It has one or more pendants hanging from a staff and is usually represented resting on the king's shoulder. In an Olmec painting at Oxtotitlan, the Olmec personage seated on the throne has this type of flail, and it is in the same position behind the head.[23]

The sacred boat or ceremonial bark of kings. This not only appears in both civilizations with the same function and curved shape but it also carries the same name (Mexican *cipac*; Egyptian *sibak*).

The use of purple. The religious value of purple and its use to distinguish priests and people of high rank had its origin among the Egyptians. Sanctity was attached to shell purple because the murex shell, from which it was extracted, revealed, by the sequence of colors through which it moved before acquiring its final fixed purple, a parallel to color changes of the Nile in flood. The Egyptians therefore, considered purple a noble and sacred color,[24] and, through the Phoenicians, who adopted the purple industry, the association of purple with royalty, the priesthood and the high-born spread throughout the Mediterranean.

We find purple having the same value in the Olmec world. Professor Zenil Medellin has noted that a patch of purple dye appears on one of the African monumental heads at San Lorenzo. He claims that these stone heads were originally painted but that the paint faded over time.[25] In the *Nutall Codex* (one of the few surviving documents of ancient America), Zelia Nuttall, the discoverer of the codex, notes "pictures of no fewer than 13 Mexican women of rank wearing purple skirts and five with capes and jackets of the same color. In addition, 45 chieftains are figured with short, fringed, round, purple waistcloths, and there are also three examples of the use of a close fitting purple cap."

The artificial beard. Another sign of royal or priestly office is the beard. A study of Olmec sculptures, carvings on stelae and paintings sesms to suggest that the beard is alien to the usually hairless American chin. When it does appear on the native American chin, it looks like an appendage, artificially tapered and attached. When found on men with the air and poise of authority, it also functions as a badge of high rank. The use of highly stylized chin stubs as a mark of distinction is a custom of the Egyptian pharaohs.

Feathered fans or sunshades. The Egyptian pharaohs bore feathered fans that are almost identical in shape, style and color to those found in ancient Mexican paintings in the pyramid of Las Higueras. These fans were painted in an Olmec area and in a culture influenced by the Olmec, even though this culture (Totonac) is of a slightly later period. The fans are made of feathers arranged in concentric circles of blue, red and green. In Mexico they are blue, red and light blue. The Mexican light blue is the nearest equivalent on the color spectrum to the Egyptian green.[26]

The parasol or ceremonial umbrella. This is another emblem of royalty in the two cultures. Today, the umbrella is so common and has such a utilitarian function (protection from sunburn or the occasional shower), that its unique ritual use and value as an index of rank has been forgotten. Professor A. Varron has demonstrated the use of the umbrella or parasol as an emblem of dignity and power in ancient times.[27] The parasol is one of the items mentioned as being brought into Mexico by foreigners in an oral tradition recorded in the *Titulo Coyoi*. This is a major document of the Quiche Maya. They were touched by the earlier Olmec and their tradition harks back to ancestral visitors of that time. "These things came from the east," goes the tradition, "from the other side of the water and the sea: they came here, they had their throne, their little benches and stools, they had their *parasols* and bone flutes."[28]

It is important to understand what a great burden of proof is required to establish a cultural influence, even when there is a sound case for a physical presence and contact. Any one of the above traits, standing by itself as a single parallel, can be dismissed as coincidence. When such traits appear as an interconnected cluster, performing a single function and duplicated nowhere else in the world, except where the Egyptians traveled or left their influence, then only a dogmatic conservative or a bigot can deny the possibility of both a physical contact and a cultural influence.

The Indian scholar, Rafique Jairazbhoy, in a book on the ancient Egyptians in America, has pointed to many other ritual parallels. (Although we disagree about the date of the visit of the Egyptians, we complement each other in our study of cultural diffusion. I should point to some of these ritual artifacts, themes and practices he has outlined even though I cannot go into much detail in such a short article.)

There are hand-shaped incense spoons found at the Olmec site of Xochipala in Guerrero and depicted also in one of the Mexican books—the *Codex Selden*—that are almost identical with those of the Egyptians. The name for incense is *kuphi* in Egyptian and *copal* (pronounced *ko-pl*) in Mexican.[29] Again, in Egypt, there are several sculptures in which four figures hold up the sky. These

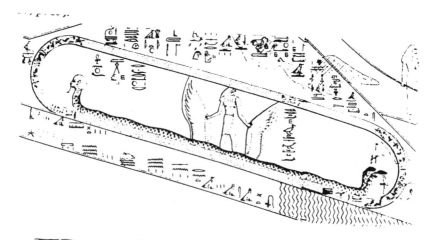

The God Sokar (a), winged god standing on the back of a double-ended serpent in Egyptian papyrus painting of the Underworld, can be compared with the god at Izapa in Mexico. (b) In the Egyptian painting the god stretches out his hands to hold up his wings. The Mexican god does the same. He also stands on the back of the same type of double-ended serpent and wears a foreign beard. (*Ancient Egyptians and Chinese in America*, by R.A. Jairazbhoy)

are known as the *Atlantes*. At the Olmec site of Portrero Nuevo two figures appear in the same posture, holding up the sky. While there are only two in the Olmec relief, the four in the Egyptian sculpture are suggested by the use of four hieroglyphs above the two Olmec figures. These are identical with the Egyptian hieroglyphs for sky.[30]

There is the human-headed bird, Ba, which flies out of the tomb in Egyptian mythology. This bird with the human head appears in a relief from Izapa, Mexico,[31] and Mexican sarcophagi leave an opening in the tomb, as do the Egyptians, for the bird's escape from the dead. The Olmec seem also to have practiced mummification. Although the corrosive humidity of the soil in capitals like La Venta destroyed all skeletal remains (Wiercinski's skeletons were found in the drier area of Olmec civilization), Jairazbhoy cites Olmec sculptures at Oaxaca with rib cages outlined as those of a dead man and arms folded in exactly the same way as some Egyptian mummies—arms crossed

The Egyptian papyrus painting (a) from the Book of the Dead depicting the Opening of the Mouth Ceremony can be compared with wall painting (b) in cave at Juxtlahuaca, giant figure wearing leopard skin. He holds two ceremonial objects, similar to the Egyptian before the kneeling man. Both priests wear skins of beasts whose tails hang between their legs, and both proffer a snake-headed instrument to the seated man. (*Ancient Egyptians and Chinese in America*, by R.A. Jairazbhoy)

over chest, fingers open.[32] Another, in the museum of Jalapa, duplicating this ritual posture, wears an Egyptian-type wig.

Jairazbhoy demonstrates the remarkable similarity between several gods in the Egyptian underworld and Olmec Mexico. Two of these are the most visually striking—the winged god Sokar who stands on the back of a double-ended serpent, and the double-rope swallowing god, Aken, "a serpent without eyes, nose or ears, a non-articulated ophidian." There are at least half a dozen that exhibit an identity in complexity that is hard to dismiss as coincidence. Ritual practices, too like "Opening the Mouth Ceremony" (see illustration) and "Heart-plucking," are common to the Olmec and the Egyptians.[33] It is important to note, however, that whereas this was symbolically done in Egypt the later Mexicans (particularly the Aztecs) made it a literal practice.

Similarities between the two civilizations in terms of certain technologies or techniques they used are even more striking. What makes the technological argument easier to prove is that we are certain there are no antecedents for these technologies in America before this period whereas there is a clear series of evolving steps and stages in the Egypto-Nubian world. There is the burial mound or *mastaba* in Nubia which becomes progressively more complicated with interior rooms and underground passages before the black genius Imhotep uses this as a platform for his technological leap into the stepped pyramid.[34] We see the pyramid evolve from "stepped" to "true," taking on a conical form, the steps being filled in but remaining the core of the structure, even when hidden from view. We see the Egyptians stop building the pyramid in 1600 B.C. but the Nubians returning to this in 800 B.C., although on a miniature scale.[35] They were too involved in political and military problems to repeat the architectural monuments of the earlier Africans but they managed to preserve the structural and functional bases of the pyramid in miniature.

Where do the first miniature step pyramid and the first manmade mountain or conical pyramid appear in America? On the very ceremonial court and platform where four of the African-type heads were found in the holy capital of the Olmec world, La Venta. Even among the Maya, where the American anthropologist Dr. Hammond has found 2000 B.C. villages, no pyramid appears until much later. Of course, the Americans introduced innovations, as they continued to build pyramids long after the Egyptians and Nubians had stopped, even down to the time of the Aztecs. But who can categorically deny the possibility of a stimulus from these outsiders at the beginning? Why would the Americans build a pyramid three and a half million cubic feet in volume beside these colossal stone heads when they had never built one before? Why would they place it on a north-south axis, as all Egyptian and Nubian pyramids are placed, when they had never used this axial orientation in erecting buildings in earlier settlements? Why would their pyramids combine the same double function, tomb and temple, and their own great pyramid in the Olmec-influenced city of Teotihuacan have a pyramidal base almost identical in proportion to that of the base of the Great Pyramid in Egypt? Why should the pyramid at Teotihuacan also serve, as does the Egyptian Great Pyramid, as an astronomical observatory and geodetic marker? Why should some of the Mexican pyramids have movable capstones for this purpose as do some of the Egyptian counterparts? And why should the Mexican be found using the same standards of measurements developed by the mathematicians and astronomers of the Nile Valley?

The reconstruction of the ceremonial court at La Venta to accommodate the colossal sculptures, the carving of these and the equally monumental stelae, the erection of th pyramid that took 18,000 men one million man-hours to complete, the planning of all these on the same axis, with the same ritual orientation, called for a new organization, a new technology. It required skills in the quarrying and transportation of massive blocks of stone, a building material rarely used before among the Olmec. It also called for great mathematical precision in the laying, leveling and fitting, all of which had reached a high level of sophistication in

Plan of the La Venta ceremonial platform, showing true pyramid, the first of its kind in America, as well as the miniature step-pyramid.

Egypt but were being attempted for the very first time in Middle American civilization. The slipshod, poorly planned and highly irregular or uneven architecture at San Lorenzo, an earlier Olmec site, is clear proof of the enormous and sudden leap forward in Olmec technology. At the San Lorenzo site none of the structures observes any regular orientation.[36]

The four sides of the pyramidal base at La Venta describe an almost perfect circle. Complex measurements were involved in the erection of a palisade of basalt columns in subsiding sand. Since the sand sank, the builders had to take into account varying degrees of subsidence and so devise a scale of varying heights. Yet they all match evenly at the upper extremities. Apart from this mathematical skill, some of the problems confronting the builders involved the transportation of between 2- to 50-ton blocks of uncut stone from quarries 60 to 80 miles away by way of rafts down the rivers to the island of La Venta. The transportation of massive stones down the Nile by the Egyptians to the sites where they built their pyramids raised problems that would daunt even the best of modern engineers. Vast monuments had to be abandoned recently to the rising waters behind the Aswan dam because of the difficulty even modern technology faces in moving the colossal monuments of the Egyptians who had devised the most ingenious methods for transporting heavy stones. R.F. Heizer has noted startling similarities in the heavy transport techniques used by the ancient Americans and the Egyptians.

This does not mean to suggest that Africans physically built the American pyramids. There were not more than 1,000 Africans in the Olmec world. A substantial number of these, as skeletal studies of the royal graves show, were in the priest caste. What we are speaking of is a stimulus, an influence. The assumption that one can only wield an influence or have a considerable impact on a native population through military conquest or the pressure of great numbers is nonsense. Cabello de Balboa cites a group of 17 Africans shipwrecked in Ecuador in the early 16th century who in short order became governors of an entire province of native Americans. The reason why this African influence is historically significant is because the Olmec civilization was formative. Even Michael Coe has pointed out: "There is not the slightest doubt that all later civilization in Mesoamerica, whether Mexican or Maya, rests ultimately on an Olmec base."

That is why the debate on the African presence among the Olmec is so heated. A whole vision of American history is at stake. When *They Came Before Columbus* was published in 1977, the *New York Times* critic Glyn Daniel launched a savage attack against my thesis.[37] Among the things he said that were downright falsehoods was that I had mixed up step-pyramids with true pyramids and that the American pyramids were temples while the Egyptian pyramids were tombs.

With respect to the first statement, it is clear that this reviewer merely skimmed through the pages of my book since I began my discourse on the pyramids by making this distinction utterly clear. I also pointed out that both step and true pyramids had gone out of vogue until the beginning of the 9th century B.C. when both forms returned in the Nubian renaissance of classical Egyptian architecture. Equally important is the fact that *a true pyramid,* even the Great Pyramid of Khufu at Giza, *has a stepped structure at its core.*

With respect to the second statement, in which Daniel contends there is a clearcut distinction between tomb and temple in the two civilizations, I refer my readers to a letter by Dr. Norman Totten, archeologist-historian, who was site supervisor for the archeological excavation at Deir Alla, Jordan. The following is an excerpt from Dr. Totten's letter, which the *New York Times* would not publish in the heat of a controversy that brought more letters, says *The Washington Post,* than any critique since Robert Frost was attacked:

> Daniel states without qualification, to disprove possible linkage between Egyptian and American pyramids, that "American pyramids are temple platforms; the Egyptian pyramids are tombs." This is news to those of us who have stood inside the tomb chambers of the great pyramids of Cuicuilco and Cholula, Mexico. It disregards the fact that the thousands of earthen mound pyramids across the United States were of two contemporaneous types, temple platforms and tombs. And what of the great stone Maya pyramid with its temple on top and famous tomb with sarcophagus within, the so-called "Temple of the Inscriptions" at Palenque?

> While his understanding of American pyramids is erroneous, his statement about Egyptian pyramids is simplistic and misleading. Certainly the great pyramids at Sakkara, Giza and Dashur were tombs. I have been inside a number of them. There were, however, funerary and valley temples adjoining those pyramids as an integral part of their total plan. The sun temple of Pharaoh Ne-suer-ra (5th Dynasty) at Abusir had a huge kind of obelisk set on a pyramidal platform, and was not a burial chamber but a temple complex. The famous mortuary temple of Mentuhotep I, founder of the 11th Dynasty at Dier el Bahri, Thebes, was topped by a pyramid.[38]

In addition to the evidence in this letter, Rafique Jairazbhoy has cited many pyramids in America which serve the function of both temple and tomb. The superficial face of the pyramid underwent a change as the native Americans introduced their own innovations (they preferred not to fill in the steps and to have a flat top, as in earlier Egyptian and some later Sudanic and West African models), but the structural and functional correspondence remained the same.

Egyptian scripts seem also to have turned up in ancient America. Dr. Barry Fell, professor emeritus of Harvard, has claimed that some ancient American tribes made use of Egyptian hieroglyphs. Fell attempts to show the Egyptian influence on the writing systems of the Micmac. The Micmac are a tribe of the Algonquian Indians inhabiting the eastern provinces of Canada and closely related to various tribes of Maine, commonly called the Wabanaki or Men-of-the-East.

Fell's examination of the Lord's Prayer in Micmac hieroglyphs seems to show that half of the hieroglyphic signs were similar to Egyptian hieroglyphs as rendered in the simple cursive form called "hieratic." He claims also that these signs in Egyptian matched the meaning assigned to them in the English transcript of the Micmac text. A limited but recognizable Egyptian vocabulary is present, probably suggestive of contact with Egyptian (or related peoples speaking Egyptian, such as the Nubian or the Libyan) from whom these words could have been acquired as loans at the same time that the writing system of the natives was affected.[39]

The influence spread out from the Olmec center and basin, affecting other peoples on the North American continent. The black figure left an indelible mark. Not only his color but his stature (the continental African is usually a foot and a half taller than the aboriginal American) was remembered in the oral traditions of the Mexicans.

Nicholas Leon, an eminent Mexican authority, reports on the oral traditions of his people, according to some of whom "the oldest inhabitants of Mexico were blacks. . . . The existence of blacks and giants is commonly believed by nearly all the races of our soil and in their various languages they had words to designate them."

Everywhere, from one corner of the ancient American world to the other, blacks were found. Not only were they here long before Columbus, but they were here, not as slaves, but as free men, even as priest-kings among the Olmecs. As Jairazbhoy has pointed out, "The black began his career in America not as slave but as master."[40]

That fact in itself opens a new historical window from which to view the history of America and of the black race.

Notes

1. Frederick Peterson, *Ancient Mexico*, Putnam and Sons, New York: 1959: p. 50.

2. Ivan Van Sertima, *They Came Before Columbus: The African Presence in Ancient America*, Random House, New York: 1977.

3. José Melgar, "Antiguēdades Mexicanas," *Sociedad Mexicana de Geografrica ya Estadistica Boletin*, 2a epoca 1, 1869, p. 292-297.

4. Orosco y Berra, *Historia antigua y de la conquista de Mexico*, vol. 1, Mexico: 1880.

5. Matthew W. Stirling, "Discovering the New World's Oldest Dated Work of Man," *National Geographic Magazine*, Vol. 76 (August, 1939) pp. 183-218.

6. Idem.

7. Idem.

8. Frans Blom and Oliver La Farge, *Tribes and Temples*, New Orleans, 1926 (Record of expedition to Middle America conducted by Tulane Univ. of Louisiana in 1925)

9. Sterling op. cit.

10. Constance Irwin, *Fair Gods and Stone Faces*, St. Martin's Press, New York: 1963, p. 166.

11. Philip Drucker, Robert F. Heizer and Robert J. Squier, "Radiocarbon Dates from La Venta, Tabasco," *Science*, Vol. 126, July 12, 1957, pp. 72-73.

12. Rainer Berger, John A. Graham and Robert F. Heizer, "A Reconsideration of the age of the La Venta site." Contributions of the University of California Archaeological Research Facility, 3: p. 1-24, Berkeley, 1967.

13. Bruce Williams, "The Lost Pharoahs of Nubia" in *Nile Valley Civilizations* (ed. Ivan Van Sertima), *Journal of African Civilizations*, Vol. 6, No. 2.

14. Coe, who dated occupation phases at San Lorenzo as early as 1500 B.C. has nevertheless concluded in a private communication to Bernal . . ."The sequence would begin with the La Venta heads . . . then the San Lorenzo heads, and finally the Tres Zapotes ones . . ." see Ignacio Bernal, *The Olmec World*, University of California Press, Berkeley: 1969, p. 57.

15. Boyce Rensberger, *Science Digest*, September, 1981.

16. Andrzej Wiercinski, "Inter and interpopulational racial differentiation of Tlatilco, Cerro de las Mesas, Monte Alban and Yucatan Maya," XXXIX *Congresso Internacional de Americanistas, Lima 1970*, Actas y Memorias, Vol. 1, pp. 231-252, Lima: 1972.

17. James Bailey, *The God-Kings and Titans*, St. Martin's Press, New York: 1973, p. 46.

18. Irwin, op. cit., p. 157.

19. *The Popul Vuh of the Quiche Maya of Guatemala* (trans. Edmonson) New Orleans: 1971, 5128 f.

20. John Sorenson, "Some Mesoamerican Traditions of Immigration by Sea," *El Mexico Antiguo*, VIII, p. 429. See also Sahagan, *Historia de los Cosas de Nueva Espana*, 1829. Reprinted Mexico: 1946, pp. 13-14.

21. Chancellor Williams, *The Destruction of Black Civilization*, Third World Press, Chicago: 1974, p. 66.

22. R.A. Jairazbhoy, *Ancient Egyptians and Chinese in America*, Rowman and Littlefield, New Jersey: 1974, p. 29, Illus. 15.

23. Ibid., p. 10.

24. Donald Mackenzie, *Myths of Pre-Columbian America*, London: Gresham Publishing Co., 1924, pp. 104, 105.

25. Alfonso Zenil Medellin, *Monolitos Indeditos Olmecas*. La Palabra y el Hombre, Revista de la Universidad Veracruzana, XVI, p. 86. While Medellin made this suggestion, the purple patch on the head of a colossal Negro at San Lorenzo was first noted by Matthew Stirling in "Stone monuments of the Rio Chiquito, Vera Cruz, Mexico," *Bulletin of the Bureau of American Ethnology*, Washington, 157, 1955, p. 20.

26. For this comparison, see Jairazbhoy, "Further Evidence of Egyptian Intrusion into Pre-Columbian Mexico" in *The New Diffusionist*, No. 18, Vol. 5, 1975, Figs. 19, 20A and 20B, facing page 11.

27. A. Varron, "The Umbrella as an Emblem of Dignity and Power," *Ciba Review* 9, 1942, p. 42.

28. Jairazbhoy, op. cit., p. 8.

29. Jairazbhoy, *Ancient Egyptians and Chinese in America*, page 45, Figs. 29, 30.

30. Ibid., p. 50 (Figs. 41 and 42)

31. Ibid., p. 81 (Figs. 86 and 87)

32. Ibid., p. 78 (Figs. 81 and 82)

33. Ibid. p. 69 (Fig. 68)

34. L. Sprague de Camp, *The Ancient Engineers*, Ballantine Books, New York: 1974, pp. 22-23.

35. For examples of Nubian pyramids at Kurru and Nuri, see P.L. Shinnie, *Meroe: A Civilization of the Sudan*, Praeger, New York, 1967.

36. Bernal, *The Olmec World*, p. 45.

37. The *New York Times*, Book Review section, March 13, 1977.

38. Dr. Norman Totten, private communication.

39. Barry Fell, *America B.C.*, Quadrangle, New York Times Book Company, 1977.

40. R.A. Jairazbhoy, *Ancient Egyptians and Chinese in America*, Rowman and Littlefield, Totowa, New Jersey, 1974.

UNEXPECTED AFRICAN FACES IN PRE-COLUMBIAN AMERICA

Alexander von Wuthenau

In 1966 I was honored by an invitation of President Senghor of Senegal to attend the great Festival of African Art in Dakar as a representative of Mexico. Officially this was, of course, not possible since my research on the presence of Africans in Ancient Mexico went against all the teachings in Mexican schools and universities. To believe that almost three thousand years ago Black people had reached America and had been interbreeding with natives in Mexico was, to say the least, "politically inconvenient."

Nevertheless, I did go to Dakar after the Mexican authorities had informed the Senegalese ambassador that it was now "too late to appoint him for this job." I took the last flight from New York to reach the Festival on time. On the plane was the official representative of the United States, the famous jazz musician, Duke Ellington, with all his musical instruments. Upon our arrival the next morning we were both given a very warm welcome by the Senegalese government. The cultural representative of the Foreign Office in Dakar, an extremely amiable person with a Ph.D. from the Sorbonne in Paris, took excellent care of me. I asked him where I could exhibit the many big photographs and 25 archeological pieces, depicting African features, which I had brought with me. He told me that the official exhibition of the Festival in the *Musee Dynamique* was already complete, but that he would arrange a place for me in the library of the Chamber of Commerce of Deputies, where everybody could see my interesting material.

As a matter of fact, the first people to see my pieces was the *Corps Diplomatique* accredited to Dakar. They were so interested in my display that they insisted on having me included in the list of speakers at the general assembly of the Festival. Finally, my slide show of African Art in Ancient America was squeezed into the program. Addressing the illustrious gathering in the Congress Hall, I told them that up to a certain point we had listened over and over again to the story of the deportations of African slaves from Dakar, but that I, on the contrary, was showing them the nobility of Black rulers who had their portraits carved in colossal stone monuments on American soil. Furthermore, these distinguished overlords had a tremendous cultural impact on the New World almost three thousand years ago. In spite of the adverse opinions of academic circles against diffusionism I was proud to be in such an illustrious company of diffusionists as the famous Baron Alexander von Humboldt and the eminent explorer of Africa, Leo Frobenius, whose books were on display in Dakar, arranged by the Frobenius Institute in Frankfurt, Germany.

My address was received with enthusiastic applause by the members of the Festival. Afterwards, I was even embraced by a distinguished lady who congratulated me on my exposition and expressed her satisfaction that I was the first and only one to mention the name of the great explorer Frobenius at the Festival. She was a member of the Academy of Science of Moscow and had been sent as a representative of Russia to Dakar.

I disclose this significant happening in Senegal on African soil so that the people of the United States and especially the Black communities will know something about it. Besides, I wish that the latter should take this as an incentive to think less and less about slaves and more and more about the glorious past of African lords in Ancient America. For this reason it is also indispensable to acquire a correct concept of the ancient history of the African continent which up to now has been distorted, in many cases, by white historians. I begin with one of the most conspicuous treasures of world history represented by the colossal Sphinx near Cairo. While visiting Egypt in 1966 I walked around this monument three times and got the vivid impression that this *is* the voice of Africa. How right I was is amply confirmed by the picture included in this book, an early 19th century engraving, which shows the Sphinx, in the time of Napoleon, before its mutilation. What a sad story this is. To destroy the nose of a Black woman for some idiotic reason, the worst of which would be a vicious racist complex.

It is about time that the black communities in the United States insisted that, in schools and universities, even if only one member of their community is attending them, the true picture of Ancient America and a reformed concept of Ancient African history, beginning with the earliest Nubian Kings, should be revealed!

From around 1000 B.C. until the Post-Classic era in the 16th century we have an abundant testimony of African portraitures in clay, stone and jadite on the American continent. The concept that all the African faces shown in this book could be "casual creations" of the many artists in Pre-Columbian America is absurd. I definitely claim that nobody can "invent" a Negroid face if he has not seen one, on a continent where Africans were never native. Since they could not swim over the Atlantic (or Pacific) Ocean, they could only arrive by ships, canoes or rafts. I refuse to accept any other explanation.

Besides that, all the figures, big and small, were works of art produced to commemorate or accompany the dead, who were loved and venerated by their communities. Certainly all the artists made a great effort to portray the contemporaries of the deceased so they should not make their trip to the underworld alone. It is nonsense to believe that they would create somebody the dead never knew or could not recognize as a member of his community.

1A

1C   1B

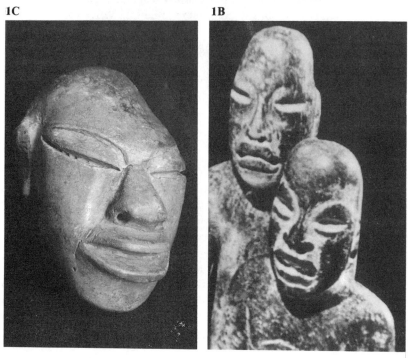

And if by chance an African-looking person was among his friends, no doubt this black portrait was put next to him in the tomb.

Some of the most convincing archeological items of Ancient America are two Jadite Figurines (see picture 1B) in the famous "Ofrenda" No. 4, still on exhibition in the National Museum in Mexico City. Analyzing the faces of this group of 17 burial pieces, we come to the conclusion that not only Africans were portrayed at this ceremony but several Asiatics, at least one white and several mixed types as well. Yet the two African ones have the most definitely designed features and bodies which defy any doubt of their Negroid origins. In the same picture we show (1A) a fragment of an Olmec stone head, slightly more primitive in execution, and last, but not least, a clay head which exquisitely combines the Negroid and Asiatic features, so characteristic of this mixed race of our continent three thousand years ago.

Most convincing of the presence of Africans in the New World is, of course, the famous colossal stone head of Tres Zapotes No. 2 not only on account of its purely negroid features, but even more so by its typically Ethiopian braided pigtails, ending in rings and tassels. This head first reappears in recent times in *Nile Valley Civilizations*, edited by Van Sertima. It has been seldom displayed among the other Olmec heads.

Side-view of the Tres Zapotes head. This is left side of Fig. 2.

Fig. 2 (right side)

Chalcalzingo, a late Olmec site in the state of Morelos, Mexico, gives us another irrefutable clue. A large African head was sculptured on the living rock hundreds of feet above the archeological site below. The head was reproduced in color in my book *Unexpected Faces in Ancient America* (Crown) in 1976 with an excellent photo by the famous New York photographer Herman Emmet, who almost collapsed dragging up the equipment to this elevated site.

It is interesting to note that the head is looking directly over the Morelos plains, towards Mexico's highest snow-capped volcano Popocatepetl. According to my research, the crater of this mountain was possibly considered the highest entrance to the underworld by the Olmecs. After all, it seems to have been the reason for sending the Nubian expedition to the West over the Atlantic by Ramses III. Another detail for this interpretation is the fact that the Black head is wearing a helmet with a round knob identical with a helmet worn by a member of the Sherden bodyguard of the Pharoah depicted on his tomb.

Of equal importance is a large stone slab preserved in Chalcalzingo repre-

Fig. 3

Fig. 4
(Girl of Las Bocas)

5A

5B

senting what seems to be a Black priestess. She is showing a panel with several *empty* Egyptian cartouches, a procedure which, according to Professor Cyrus Gordon of New York University, means that she is showing something that has to be kept a secret. (See Fig. 3.)

To the late Pre-Classic Olmec period belongs a beautiful black clay figurine from Las Bocas, Mexico, near the Puebla-Guerrero dividing line. Not only the face but the modelling of the whole body is one of the most sensitive representations of an African girl on American soil more than two thousand years ago. (See Fig. 4.)

Geographically speaking, many Black representations are found all over the middle zone of Mexico, from the east coast of Tabasco, over the high plateau of Mexico City, to the west coast of the Pacific. Picture 5B shows one of the best African heads produced in the Pre-Classic site of Tlapacoya, north of Mexico City. I challenge any artist to equal the depiction of kinky hair, unique for the African race, with such minute perfection. The strange Black slip figurine on the left side, also excavated in Tlapacoya, one might possibly connect with someone recalling the corpulent Queen of Punt of Solomon's time.

Proceeding further west we arrive at one of the most important archeological regions of the American continent. Guerrero stretches out towards the coast of the Pacific Ocean. Amongst the innumerable small clay heads produced there from the Pre-Classic time on, a considerable number show African features. *6A* was found in the region of Acapulco with stylized kinky hair. *6B* is an extremely interesting item. It was excavated at the border line between Morelos and Geurrero. It shows not only a nose ring, but undeniable black features and a typical hair formation. *6C* is an Ethiopian type and, in this case, a mixture between Black and Semitic. *6D* is the smallest piece in my collection "Humanitas Americana" in Mexico City. It is almost spooky how a little ball of clay, the size of less than half an inch, can become, through an acute visual insight, important historical testimony in Ancient America.

In the Televisa Pre-Columbian Collection in Mexico City is a stone head on display from the Mezcala region of Guerrero. The stylization of this piece is quite unusual for a Mezcala sculpture. Nevertheless, it is obvious that the artist tried to portray a Black person he apparently was interested in, giving us another hint of the presence of such a racial type of Ancient America.

The state of Veracruz is one of the richest regions in archeological portraitures, especially during the Classic epoch. However, we shall begin with two items which might well go back to the late Pre-Classic time. Particularly the very strong sculpture No. 9 which, with its protruding thick lips, shows a definite Olmec influence, on an archaic level.

No. 8 seems to depict a sick person who lost one eye. There is nothing remotely "Indian" about him. All his characteristics are those of the African race.

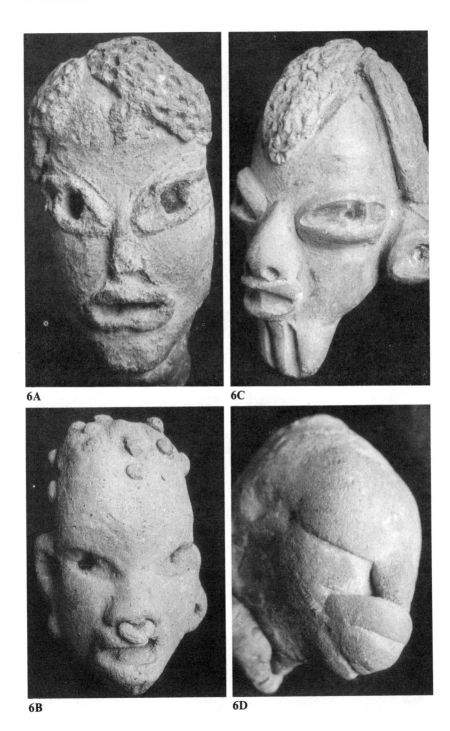

6A

6C

6B

6D

Figs. 7, 8, 9

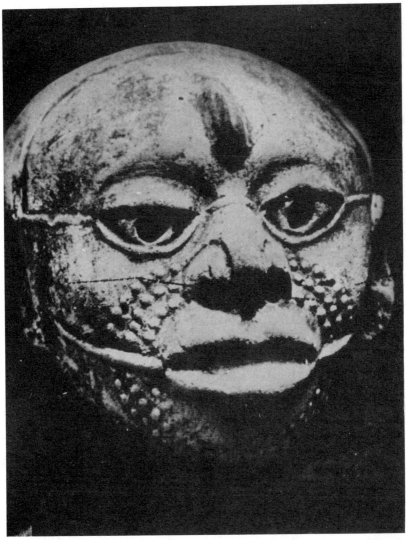

Fig. 10

The first classic terracotta head we show in No. 10 is kept in the Museum of the State of Veracruz in Jalapa. Like all other pictures in this book, its features speak for themselves. However, specially important in this case is the splendid tattoo sculptured in the face, a procedure which can only be performed successfully on the skins of Black people. Another item is worth mentioning. The way the eyes are depicted reminds us of the ancient terracotta artifacts in Nigeria belonging to the Nok period (about 500 B.C.). That this tradition was somehow carried over to America in early times is not impossible.

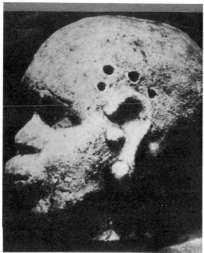

Fig. 11   Fig. 12

People living in New York might still remember the splendid exhibition of Nigerian archeological treasures in the Metropolitan Museum, where amongst the beautiful Black terracotta heads, belonging to the Nok period, some excellent Jewish heads were on display. The dating of the artifacts dovetail perfectly with the time of the Cambyses invasion (525 B.C.) in Egypt and the destruction of Memphis. The Jews, remembering the appalling fate of their compatriots in Jerusalem, could not escape via the Nile, guarded by the Persian soldiers. So they tracked through the whole African coast. It stands to reason that, on this trip (Vasquez mentions several African kingdoms the migration had to cross) they had contacts and friendships not only with the Nigerians but also with the experienced Black river navigators.

This (Fig.11) shows an excellent sample of a negroid head. This piece would have been the delight of the Polish anatomist, Andrzej Wiercinski, who had found a number of skulls from Olmec sites, with a clear prevalence of the total negroid pattern. I still regret that I missed showing this piece, which was in the collection of the late Kurt Stavenhagen, to Wiercinski while he was in Mexico City. I hope that this significant archeological piece has now found its way into the collection of the State Museum in Jalapa, Veracruz.

Another smaller classical Veracruz head (No. 12) has a special story to reveal. It was precisely this head I took with me to show it to President Senghor in Dakar. As a matter of fact, I had decided to show my specialized collection of archeological artifacts with negroid features, first of all to the Africans. I believe that they were more fit to decide if my personal observa-

Fig. 13   Fig. 14

tions and conclusions were correct or not. Everybody admitted unanimously that the 24 pieces I had brought with me, were obviously portraits of African people. The head in picture 12 would spark a discussion, concerning the three wounds shown on the head. Some considered that the cuts on both cheeks could be tribal marks, but that the deep cut on top of the head suggested that this was a representation of a sacrificed Black person, especially taking into consideration the painful expression of the face.

Picture 13 was photographed in the archeological collection of Princeton University. It shows, in a realistic and very subtle way, the pensive mood of a Black person in America many hundreds of years ago.

Apart from the Olmec figures of the La Venta burial (Plate No. 1) and the small Maya head from the Island of Jaina (No. 26A) this is the only other specimen with African features exhibited in the National Museum in Mexico City, a classical Totonacan head from Veracruz. It shows, in addition to the sacrification tattooing, a typical African hairdo with strips rolled up.

Apart from the sacrification tattooing (Plates 10, 14, 19, 26A) and hairdos (Plates 2, 6, 14) we find another typical custom of some African tribes, the stretched out lips, depicted in a Pre-Columbian sculpture. To claim that all these aspects happened by chance in America, about a thousand years ago, is absurd. The real facts of history are sometimes very slow to surface. Yet

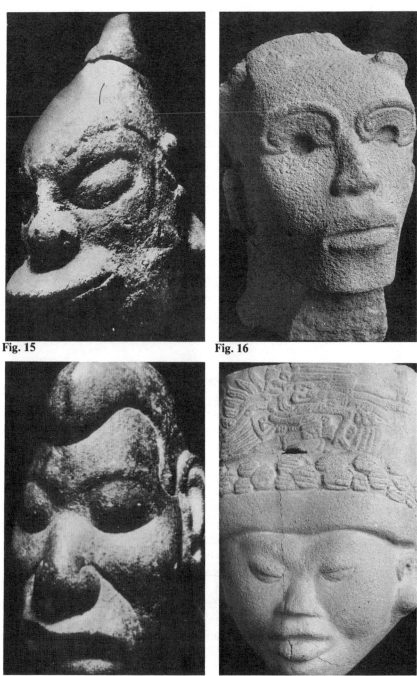

Fig. 15

Fig. 16

Fig. 17

Fig. 18

something should be done to accelerate this process. Thousands of Pre-Columbian artists stretch out their hands to help us in this endeavour. (See Fig. 15.)

Here is a helpful artist mentioned in the previous picture: a Totonac "Palma" carved in stone during the Classic epoch in Veracruz. I believe that a number of white people left their mark on the Totonac population. The elongated face of this precious sculpture shows it. Yet the treatment of the eyebrows proves an ancient Olmec influence and the mouth reveals the subtle undertone of a negroid ingredient in this racial mixture. (Fig. 16.)

One of the best concepts of a powerful Black man comes to light in this Veracruz terracotta sculpture belonging to the Natural History Museum in New York. I do not understand how anybody can doubt the racial affiliation of this Pre-Columbian personage. (Fig. 17.)

Well known are the many representations of the Totonac dancers produced in Veracruz. Usually they depict Asiatic and other women in various positions. Here is a lovely negroid face to prove that all racial types mixed in the composition assembly of Pre-Columbian ballerinas. (Fig. 18.)

We have spoken already of the importance of sacrification tattooing in Ancient America. Here is an excellent sample. I believe the person depicted belongs to the Post-Classic period, and might be considered an immigrant from Mali, considering his Moselm turban. Thus this figure would be a good confirmation of the splendid research carried on by Professor Ivan Van Sertima concerning African contacts in this epoch. (Fig. 19.)

This head is not from Mexico but from Costa Rica. I show it here on account of its obvious affinity with classic Veracruz terracottas. The face is very expressive. A number of people have observed his likeness to a well known Black writer in the U.S.A. In any case it is a human document of a person living on American soil and being used as a model for a contemporary artist in Pre-Columbian times. (Fig. 20.)

For the two heads from Chiapas, Mexico we have to go back to the early Classical period. (Fig. 21.)

No special commentary is necessary for the piece on the other side, which is considerably older. I repeat my claim that nobody could "invent" a little face like that in America without having seen a Black person.

Three pieces from the Northern region of Mexico, the Huasteca. According to Sahagun, the Panuco River in the Hausteca was the entrance gate of foreigners. Here we have some representations of a negroid type. On the top is the most African-looking one. On the lower right is a sensitive face directly staring at you, whereas the charming girl on the lower left side, with her elegant head-dress, is already on the way to join the incredible early racial mixture of America. I call this (using the term of the Mexican philosopher Vasconcelos) the Cosmic Race. (Fig. 22.)

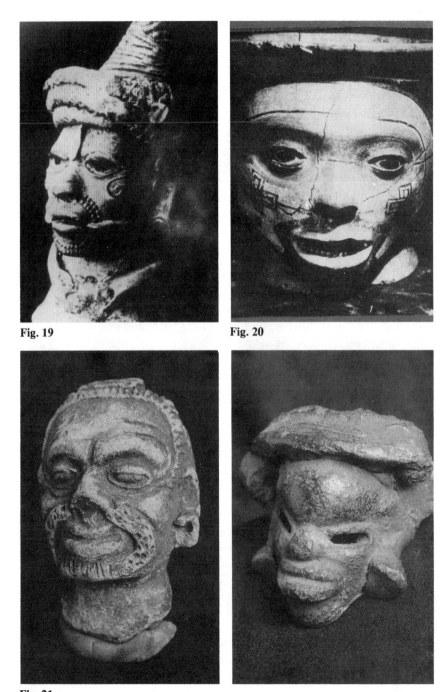

Fig. 19   Fig. 20

Fig. 21

Fig. 22

Two representations of South America, one above from Peru and the one below from Ecuador. The Peruvian belongs to the early classical Mochica culture. It is one of the best Black representations in all of South America. The Ecuadorian sample has enough Negroid traits to single it out from other racial types. (Fig. 23.)

Fig. 23A

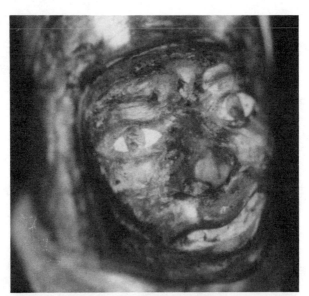

Fig. 23B

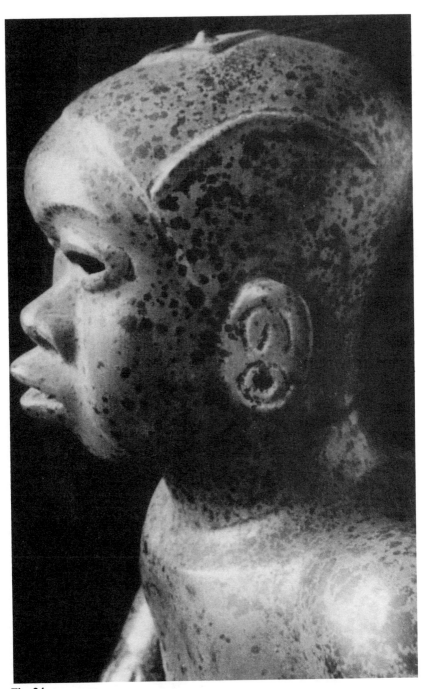

Fig. 24

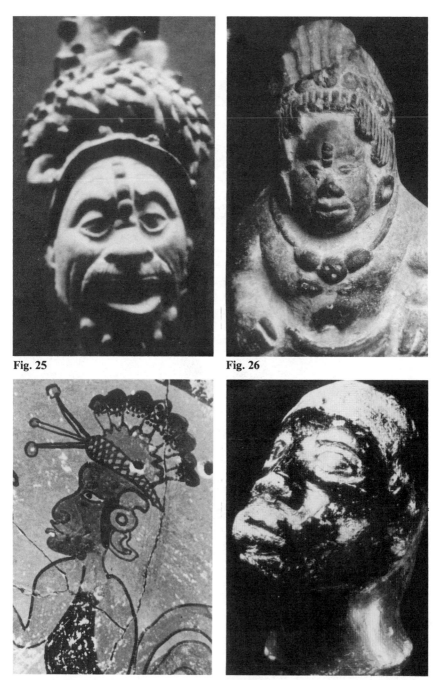

Fig. 25   Fig. 26

Fig. 27   Fig. 28

Both items are important witnesses. There is no doubt that the evolution of American man took place between Peru and Arizona. Both the northern and the southern tip of our continent mostly contain very late newcomers who practically exterminated what was there before.

Describing a previous picture I mentioned "the Cosmic Race." Well, it is precisely between the northern and the southern tip of our continent where the Cosmic race has been forming, which sooner or later will engulf our so called New World. Nobody will stop it. What about the greatest cosmopolitan city in the world, New York, and the overpowering Black population in the United States capital, Washington? We have to learn to live together, in understanding, as a Cosmic Race. By this time everybody should be ready to curb, combat and finally eject the greatest disease on our planet which is still the dormant virus of racism.

A very human touch is given by this terracotta figure from Colima, Mexico. The boy involved has nothing to do with the so called "Indian" native. He certainly could trace his ancestry to Africa. (Fig. 24.)

Two late classic figures from the island of Jaina, Mexico. They decidedly contrast with the aspects of the people portrayed by the contemporary artists in the Maya region, especially the male head which has irrefutable negroid features in addition to his sacrification tatooing. Besides that, this is only one of the negroid artifacts publically exhibited in the National Museum of Mexico City. (Fig. 25.) The female figure on the right side is a well-suited companion of the masculine one on the left. (Fig. 26.)

Also of the Maya region of Campeche and of the Late Classic period is this elegant girl painted on a plate which formerly belonged to the M. Barbachano collection in Merida. The African look of the beguiling girl makes her a delightful little star in our extensive gallery of African Pre-Columbian figures. (Fig. 27.)

We shall end our exhibition of Black people in Ancient America with this Post-Classic figure of Mixtec origin. This piece is in the store room of the National Museum in Mexico City and, as far as I know, was never exhibited publicly. This is a great pity, because one cannot imagine a better portrait of a Black inhabitant in Ancient America. (Fig. 28.)

Let's hope that times will slowly change narrow concepts. This figure and the all important historical Stela from Izapa, Chiapas, Mexico, should sooner or later be given an honorable place in the National Museum of Mexico City. One is buried in a store room and the other has long been exposed to the destructive elements of the open air.

THE AFRICAN PRESENCE IN ANCIENT AMERICA: EVIDENCE FROM PHYSICAL ANTHROPOLOGY

Keith M. Jordan

The evidence for an African presence in the pre-Columbian New World has been gathered from the results of research in many disciplines—from art history to botany, linguistics to comparative religion. But perhaps the most compelling data supporting the theory of pre-Columbian contact between Africans and native Americans comes from the field of physical anthropology, data drawn from the painstaking measurement of the skeletal remains of ancient American populations. This line of inquiry has produced strong support for the diffusionist case with its indication that a negroid element was present in Preclassic Mexico, in the same time and place of Van Sertima's[1] proposed Egypto-Nubian contact with native American cultures, as well as in the prehistoric Carribean and southwestern United States.

Such material is of supreme importance to the argument for a lasting and substantial impact of African visitors on the ancient New World, and bolsters the theories built upon other material (e.g., artistic representations) which has been more open to interpretation and thus to criticism from theorists hostile to the notion of interhemispheric contact before Columbus. This is not to say that the skeletal material has not itself come under attack. There have been attempts (as will be shown below) to discredit or explain away anatomical data suggestive of an African presence. But, as a commentator at the 1964 International Congress of Americanists in Barcelona observed, the only thing needed in addition to the record in early American art to confirm the presence of Africans in ancient America are negroid skeletons. The data drawn from varied fields thus converge to provide verification of the African presence.

The material in question, as cited in the writings of Von Wuthenau,[2] Van Sertima,[3] and Jairazbhoy,[4] consists of (a) the data obtained by the Polish craniologist Wiercinski from analysis of human remains from the Mexican sites of Tlatilco, Monte Alban and Cerro de las Mesas (b) remarks made by archaeologist Frederick Peterson in his book *Ancient Mexico*[5] regarding negroid skeletal material associated with the "Magicians" (meaning the Olmec) (c) the examination by the noted physical anthropologist, Earnest Hooton, of skulls from Pecos Pueblo in New Mexico, indicative of negroid traits in the prehistoric inhabitants of this area and (d) the controversial find of two skeletons at Hull Bay in the Virgin Islands of an African morphological type with an African ritual dentition, in an ostensibly pre-Columbian strat-

Burial at Tlatilco. From *The Jaguar's Children* by special permission of Michael Coe

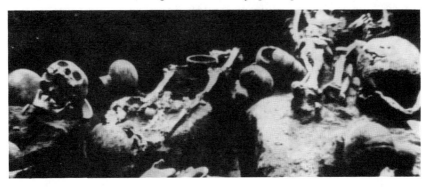

Burial at Tlatilco. From *The Jaguar's Children* by special permission of Michael Coe

igraphic context. This was reported by the Smithsonian in early 1975. The Smithsonian has since disavowed the implications of pre-Columbian contact originally drawn from these remains, and further investigation of these skeletons by other researchers has not been permitted.

This paper will focus on the first two links in this chain of evidence, the Mesoamerican discoveries. It is an attempt at an overview and analysis of the subject using Wiercinski's original report,[6] an attempted critique of Wiercinski's conclusions by Comas,[7] Peterson's book and the writer's correspondence with Peterson. It seeks to further elucidate the significance of the skeletal evidence in each archaeological context by recourse to Van Sertima's theory of an African contact with the Olmec. In all three sites from which Wiercinski drew his material, there is other evidence suggestive of an Egypto-Nubian influence. This evidence, when combined with the anatomical data, affords a further demonstration of the validity of Van Sertima's reconstruction of the ancient past. The Hooton and Hull Bay finds will be dealt with in a more summary fashion, due to the uncertainties surrounding the interpretation of the former and the information blackout that has obscured the emergence of further revelations from the latter.

African Skeletons in Mesoamerica

The earliest reference to an African element discernible in skeletons excavated from pre-Columbian Mesoamerican sites comes from Frederick Peterson's *Ancient Mexico*. This reference is quoted by Van Sertima in *They Came Before Columbus*.[8] On page forty of his book Peterson remarks that "A substratum with Negroid characteristics that intermingled with the Magicians leads some anthropologists to speculate on Negroid immigration into Mexico." The basis for this statement is given in an annoyingly non-specific fashion as "Studies of the skeletons of the Magicians." Later in the text, we find "We can trace the slow progress of man in Mexico without noting any definite Old World influence during this period, except possibly a strong Negroid substratum connected with the Magicians."[9]

"This period" is the Preclassic, and "Magicians" is a term used by Peterson to refer to the Middle Preclassic inhabitants of central Mexico, particularly the inhabitants of Tlatilco during the period of Olmec influence at the site. "The Preclassic period is divided into three stages of human progress . . . I find it convenient to distinguish the three stages by outstanding or peculiar characteristics of the population . . . some weird individuals called Magicians became dominant in the second stage . . ."[10] Peterson wrote at a time when there was still controversy about the nature and antiquity of Olmec civilization; thus he discusses the great Olmec centers of the Gulf Coast in his chapter on the Classic period although he cites radio-carbon dates placing La Venta within the Preclassic range, and he disputes the role of the Veracruz Olmec as the first Mesoamerican civilization.[11] With regard to the Olmec presence in the Valley of Mexico, he is also uncertain. "The strange, shamanistic Magicians have been called Olmecs; but the term is grossly misused . . ."[12] But there is of course no longer any controversy in the academic community as to the Olmec identity of the priest-rulers of Middle Preclassic Tlatilco.[13]

To find the sources for Peterson's statements on negroid skeletal material, I wrote to him in the spring of 1985. In his reply, he claimed that his information on this matter derived from "a symposium on the Preclassic (essentially Tlatilco) held in Mexico City, sometime in the 1950s—I am not sure who mentioned it, although I think it was Dr. Davalos, then head of the National Institute of Anthropology—it could have been the brother of Miguel Covarrubias, Luis, or it could have been (and here I have a mental block—can't recall his name)—the head of the Physical Anthropology Section of the National Museum of Anthropology of Mexico. There is a short mimeographed pamphlet on this symposium, but I cannot find it among my thousands of books and reprints.—"[14]

Burial at Tlatilco. From *The Jaguar's Children* **by special permission of Michael Coe**

Peterson goes on in his letter, however, to disavow the whole thing: "I am not at all sure that I should have presented this view as strongly as it appeared—I am not at all convinced that there was any such 'negroid' element . . . I have since found not a shred of evidence for this 'negroid' view. My book . . . was written in 1958 (so the symposium must have been prior to this date) and certainly needs updating—one of the errors is the 'negroid' comment . . .":[15]

Despite this about-face on Peterson's part, which displays a lack of knowledge of other research which would lend more than a shred of evidence in support of his "error," several things are worth noting. First, all of the people he mentions as possible sources were highly reputable scholars connected with equally reputable Mexican institutions. This puts some impressive weight behind Peterson's original statements. Second, the skeletal material studied came from Tlatilco, where Wiercinski has *independently* determined the presence of an African element in the preclassic population from his own anatomical analyses. We thus have the testimony of two independent authorities as to the reality of such a component in the prehispanic population, an impressive piece of evidence indeed. Third, the skeletons came from a context linked to the Olmec civilization, the host culture to Van Sertima's postulated Egypto-Nubian visitors. A search should be made for the pamphlet alluded to by Peterson; it would be a valuable research tool for modern investigators.

Turning now to Wiercinski, his work has been cited by a number of writers on the subject of pre-Columbian voyages. Von Wuthenau[16] writes: "It is strange that some people still believe that all the Negroid images . . . were accidental creations of the American 'Indians.' A severe blow to this erroneous belief was given during the XLI International Congress of Americanists in Mexico (September 1974) by Andrzej Wiercinski, the well-known craniologist from the University of Warsaw. Dr. Wiercinski was kind enough to lend me the manuscript of his contribution to the Congress, which I included in my paper also read at the Congress. Wiercinski says: 'It appeared that some of the skulls from Tlatilco, Cerro de las Mesas and Monte Alban (all preclassic sites in Mexico) show, to a different degree, a clear prevalence of the total Negroid pattern that has been evidenced by the use of two methods: a) multivariate distance analysis of average characteristics of individual fractions distinguished cranioscopically; b) analysis of frequency distributions of Mean Index of the position between combinations of racial varieties.'" The same Wiercinski quote is used by Van Sertima,[17] who makes clear the differences between the African type of Wiercinski and the "proto-negroid" type found in other prehistoric New World populations, which represents a genetic strain among some of the earliest migrants across the Bering Strait. Such "proto-negroid" tendencies in the native American gene pool cannot, Van Sertima points out, be used to explain the Wiercinski data, as "they had mixed and melted into the billion-bodied Mongoloid gene pool for at least 20,000 years,"[18] far too long to emerge again with such dominance in Olmec-era Mesoamerica. Van Sertima cites Jairazbhoy who in turn draws on Wiercinski, to reinforce this point: "The new light Jairazbhoy sheds on the skeletal evidence of the Polish craniologist Wiercinski is of great importance in clearing up confusions over the Atlantic origin of the Negroid population among the Olmecs. He highlights the fact that 13.5 percent of the skeletons examined in the pre-Classic Olmec cemetary of Tlatilco were Negroid, yet later at Cerro de las Mesas in the Classic period, only 4.5 percent. This indicates that the Negroid element intermarried until it almost fused with the native population. The female found in the graves in the pre-Classic period next to the Negroid male is very distinct from the male (native female, foreign male) but becomes similar to the male in the later Classic site, indicating progressive intermixture and the growing absorption of the foreign Negroid element into the largely Mongoloid American population. This evidence makes it very clear that the Olmec Negroid element was a distinctive outside element that came, conquered and crossbreeded in the Olmec time period, rather than proto-Australoid or proto-Negroid aborigines who may have trickled into America from the Pacific in the very ancient glacial epoch."[19]

I have succeeded in procuring a copy of Wiercinski's original report from the library of the American Museum of Natural History[20] in the summer of 1985. The main thrust or topic of the paper is not to make the argument for an African presence in ancient Mesoamerica (Wiercinski has no theoretical stake in this matter) but is simply an attempt, with review of previous attempts, at a taxonomy of native American physical types. The analysis indicative of a negroid element is presented in a matter of fact fashion as simply an aspect of Wiercinski's work in creating a "typology of human groups"[21] among native Americans. The occurence of the references to negroid skeletons in this objective report lends strong support to their veracity.

Wiercinski refers back to two of his earlier publications "An anthropological study on the origin of the 'Olmecs'" (Swiatowit, Warsaw, 1972, v. 33, pp. 143-174) and "Inter- and intrapopulational racial differentiation of Tlatilco, Cerro de las Mesas, Teotihuacan, Monte Alban and Yucatan Maya" (Swiatowit, Warsaw, 1972, v. 33, pp. 175-197) where his original analyses indicative of negroid traits in Mesoamerican skeletons appeared. Here again, a search should be undertaken to procure copies of these, which will be no easy task considering the present state of affairs in Poland (attempts by Van Sertima to locate Wiercinski himself have been unsuccessful). Wiercinski summarises in his 1974 paper the criteria employed for determining race in his earlier work: "the present author (A. Wiercinski 1972-1972b) has assessed positively the presence of Negroid pattern of traits on the basis of the detailed multivariate analysis of a larger set of diagnostic, cranioscopic traits which differentiate between Black, Yellow and White racial varieties. They run as follows: degree of prognathism, prominence of nasal bones, profile of nasal bones, frontal shape of nasal bones, height of nasal roof, width of nasal root, shape of nasal aperture, lower margin of nasal aperture, position of nasal spine, prominence of nasal spine, shapes of orbits, depth of canine fossa and depth of maxillary incisure."[22] This statement is followed by the one quoted by Von Wuthenau above. To simplify Wiercinski's point, which is couched in the jargon of craniology, the statistical analysis showed the skeletons to display African traits (i.e., prognathism, broad noses, etc.) in skull and facial structure.

Wiercinski mentions the issue he had dealt with in his earlier writings in order to reply to an attempted critique of the latter by Comas, which appeared in a book *Hipotesis Transatlanticas SobreEl Poblamiento de America* (Instituto de Investigaciones Historicas, Mexico, 1972) as well as in a paper, "Transatlantic Hypotheses on the Peopling of America: Caucasoids and Negroids," *The Journal of Human Evolution*.[23] Comas attacked Wiercinski's conclusions on the grounds that the skulls classified by the Polish scholar as negroid in type showed a wide range of skull shapes: "This evident cra-niometric variability would not seem to justify conclusions in favor of the presence of a Negroid type in these prehistoric Mesoamerican populations."[24] He called the whole idea of pre-Columbian African visits to the New World "utopian."[25] Wiercinski counters Comas, calling into question the latter's methodology: "The objection of Comas . . . consisted of simple comparison of means of the total series from Tlatilco and Cerro de las Mesas calculated for several, classic craniometric indices (with erroneous attribution of nasal index equals 56.5 to leptorrhinyl). However, any of these means of indices cannot serve as indications for the presence or absence of any of the great racial varieties since (a) these . . . craniometric indices are not diagnostic features . . . for distinguishing between varieties' affinities . . . and (b) this set of arithmetic means of total series of crania only after a very detailed analysis may provide some information about their racial composition." He then demonstrates how some of Comas' measurements support his own conclusions. "If so, nothing remains from this objection of Comas."[26]

Comas had also attacked Wiercinski's work by seeking to deny the negroid character of the Olmec colossal heads, which had apparently been cited by Wiercinski in support of his extrapolation from the skeletal material. But, in making this criticism, Comas contradicts himself; in Wiercinski's words: "there was advanced by him another objection based on Aguirre Beltran's statement that the Colossal Olmec Heads do not represent a real Negroid pattern but only the stylized physiognomy of the Jaguar God. And imme-diately after this, Comas quotes the rather contradictory opinion of Bernal that the Heads cannot represent true Negroes because of a combination of epicanthic fold with Negroid physiognomy. Thus, are these excellent pieces of the Olmec art true realistic portraits or not?"[27] Wiercinski affirms that they are, citing authorities like Stirling, Coe and Wicke in support. The epicanthic fold argument of Bernal is dealt with by Wiercinski as follows: "it was no-where written by the present author that the Colossal Heads represent classic Negroid type but only its strong influence in combination with the compo-nents of the White or Yellow Varieties,"[28] e.g., the Olmec colossi represent individuals with negroid traits predominating, but with an admixture of other racial traits as well (presumably through marriage with members of the native population). This is a little less than the pure African pedigree that is claimed by Van Sertima for the members of the Olmec ruling class represented by the great stone heads, but nonetheless is strongly supportive of his theories.

Comas makes the erroneous claim that no Mexican sculptures are extant which show "wooly hair"[29] or other such characteristically negroid traits (he is obviously unfamiliar with Von Wuthenau's work) to which Wiercinski replies: "true Negroid . . . racial types appear in undoubtedly realistic human repre-sentations on the Olmec stellas (sic) and other reliefs . . . for example . . . Monument F from Santiago Tuxtla, stellas from Alvarado and La Venta."[30]

The Colossal Heads, in contrast to these "true Negroid" portraits, he sees as depicting "intermediate types between Black and Yellow Varieties,"[31] as noted above. He concludes his rebuttal of Comas: "And so, the presence of Negroid pattern of traits both in skulls and artistic representations is a simple morphological fact, especially in connection with the Olmec culture."[32]

As to how this fact is to be explained, Wiercinski is less clear. He refers to the Tlatilco skulls as "showing Equatorial component"[33] as well as "Bushmenoid"[34] elements, alluding to continental African physical types. He is uncertain, however, whether this should be interpreted "in the frame of local microevolution or a hybridisation by migration."[35] In connection with this question, he draws attention to the work of A. Vargas Guadarrama, whose independent analysis of Tlatilco crania revealed that those skulls described by Wiercinski as negroid were radically different from the other skulls from the same site; there were more similarities between the native and the skulls from distant Peru than between the native and the negroid remains. Guadarrama also noted similarities in skull traits between specimens from Peru, West Africa, and Egypt. Do all these data "reveal more remote connections"[36] for the New World material? Wiercinski, although noncommittal, remarks that "as regards the origin of racial differentiation of Amerindians, there definitely prevails, at present, the autochtonic concept which tries to interpret . . . in terms of only microevolution and metisation. This isolationistic view seems to be supported more by some other factors than the purely scientific reasons . . ."[37]

Certainly, Wiercinski's work is strongly supportive of Van Sertima's theories of African diffusion, and Van Sertima's critique of the genetic drift explanation would appear to negate for us any doubts Wiercinski may have had about an Old World origin for the negroid characteristics of his skeletal material. The case becomes more convincing when that material is seen in archaeological context. All of the sites in question have connections with the Olmec.

At Tlatilco, the Preclassic village culture was taken over by an Olmec ruling class. Miguel Covarrubias, one of the first and greatest authorities on Olmec civilization, referred to the Olmec at Tlatilco as "'invaders,' and concluded that they must have been a theocratic elite."[38] Coe calls them "warrior-traders,"[39] analogous to the later Aztec pochteca. Either way, they belonged to the Olmec aristocracy, which in Van Sertima's reconstruction had intermarried with the Egypto-Nubians. (It is of relevance to note here that the post-Classic Mesoamericans saw the god of traders as black, which Van Sertima attributes to Mandingo contacts in the medieval period. If Coe's insight noted above is correct, this tradition may have its roots in the Olmec period.) The intruders introduced the distinctive art and ceramic styles of the Gulf Coast Olmec to the Valley of Mexico, along with a ritual complex (Peterson's "Magicians") associated with the jaguar god. Wiercinski's figure of 13.5 percent for skulls showing negroid traits fits well with the other evidence—a foreign mi-

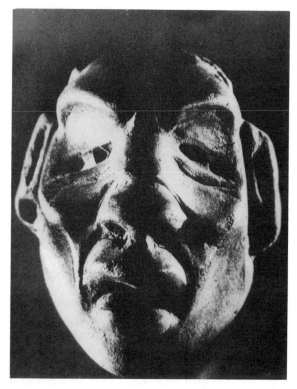

Mask from Tlatilco. From *The Jaguar's Children* by special permission of Michael Coe

nority ruling over or trading with the local population. Coe refers to the Tlatilco skeletons as showing "the werid, front-and-aft cranial deformation favored by the Olmec,"[40] a practice Van Sertima traces back to Egypt, where it was a mark of ruling class status.[41]

Artistic representations from this time period at Tlatilco show negroid types, confirming the conclusions from the skeletal material. Coe[42] illustrates a very negroid-looking mask, and while of course he does not interpret it as such, nonetheless refers to its "prominent cheekbones and full lips."[43] Von Wuthenau[44] illustrates a Tlatilco figure depicting a negroid girl, a ceramic head of a "charming Nubian 'Nilotic' girl" (with cranial deformation) from the Middle Preclassic at the site,[45] and a mask of a bearded African.[46] Van Sertima shows three Tlatilco terracotta heads of blacks.[47] When artistic representations of Africans and skeletons of Africans are found at the same site, the logical conclusion is that Africans were present at that site, the racist bias of academic archaeologists notwithstanding.

Coe[48] cites two C-14 dates from Middle Preclassic burials at Tlatilco, 982 BC plus/minus 250 years and 567 BC plus/minus 250 years, "coeval with the apogee of Olmec civilization in the Veracruz-Tabasco lowlands."[49] In a later work, he cites other dates in "the twelfth century BC, and therefore coeval with the height of San Lorenzo."[50] The first dates would coincide with the time of Van Sertima's Egypto-Nubian contact, the second with Jairazbhoy's date for his postulated Egyptian discovery of America. Bernal[51] observes that "comparison of C 14 dates from Tlatilco with those obtained in La Venta show that they are strikingly similar."[52] In any event, the occurrence of African traits at Tlatilco corresponds well with the diffusion models of Van Sertima and Jairazbhoy.

Preclassic Monte Alban is noted for its "Danzantes," the negroid character of which has been remarked upon by Von Wuthenau[53] and Van Sertima.[54] The Olmec presence at the site, however, predates the period of the Danzantes (although encompassing it), with the first traces being dated to 1100-900 BC by radiocarbon methods.[55] But the time of the Danzantes, the Monte Alban I Phase, is more likely to have been the time of African contact; this would appear to be supported by the famous reliefs as well as by C-14 dates of c. 649 BC, coeval with Egyptian contact in Van Sertima's model. It is tempting to speculate that some of Wiercinski's Monte Alban skeletons were the physical remains of the slain negroid figures depicted in the Danzantes carvings. Bernal comments that the population of Monte Alban remained basically morphologically constant from Olmec times onward, and in connection with this it is interesting to note the Postclassic Mixtec representations of blacks from the same area that are reproduced by Von Wuthenau[56] and Van Sertima.[57] These are attributed by Van Sertima to the later medieval Mandingo influx, but perhaps they depict a racial type that had been established in the area since Olmec times.

Cerro de las Mesas, in Veracruz, is where the percentage of skeletons with negroid traits is the lowest, indicating a sort of dilution of the original strain through intermarriage with the Amerindian majority. This is not surprising, considering they occur in Classic period strata. Significantly, the archaeology of Cerro de las Mesas reveals links between the Classic culture there and the earlier Olmec. There are Preclassic Olmec monuments at the site, but some traits of the earlier culture persisted down into Classic times. Jade objects of Olmec origin were buried by the Classic period inhabitants as part of the rituals surrounding in the dedication of a temple. It is believed that the more ancient pieces might have been heirlooms, passed down from the Preclassic. The cultural continuity shown at the site corresponds well with the racial links discerned by Wiercinski.

In conclusion, it would seem that Wiercinski's data, especially when viewed in total archaeological context, is strong evidence for an African presence among the Olmec.

The Pecos Material

Far less satisfying as good evidence for pre-Columbian African voyagers is the skeletal material examined by Earnest Hooton from Pecos Pueblo and environs and adjacent parts of west Texas. This material is cited by Van Sertima in *They Came Before Columbus*: "Skeletons have also been found in pre-Columbian layers in the valley of the Pecos River, which, flowing through Texas and New Mexico, empties via the Rio Grande into the Gulf of Mexico. Professor Hooton, a physical anthropologist, reporting on these finds, said of the skeletons: 'The Pecos skulls resemble most closely crania of Negro groups coming from those parts of Africa where Negroes commonly have some perceptible infusion of Hamitic blood:'"[58]

The Pecos skeletons were first used as evidence for an African presence in pre-Columbian America, however, by M.D.W. Jeffreys in a 1953 article in the Journal *Scientia*.[59] In response to Jeffreys, Comas, in the same article in which he attempts his critique of Wiercinski, quotes another Hooton publication, *Indians of Pecos Pueblo*: "We have no record of the invasion of any Negroid people into the New World during the pre-Columbian period . . . I do not for a moment suppose that any large body of Negroes or Negroids ever migrated to America in pre-Columbian times. But I do think that the earlier invaders who worked their way up to Northeast Asia, across the Bering Straits and down the New World carried with them some minor infusion of Negroid blood which had trickled in from the tropical parts of the Old World."[60] Comas prefers to call the Pecos material "Pseudo-Negroid."[61]

The available data are not sufficient to permit judgement of Hooton's and Comas' comments, but two points may be noted. First, the work of Van Sertima, Von Wuthenau, Jairazbhoy, et. al., does seem to have unearthed some "record of the invasion of . . . Negroid people into the New World during the pre-Columbian period" into Mexico, the civilizations of which had contact with the cultures of the American Southwest. Second, Hooton's explanation is the same genetic drift and variation model refuted by Van Sertima. And Van Sertima is not alone in calling this idea into question. Eugene Fingerhut, a skeptical and judicious researcher of the question of pre-Columbian voyages to the New World, concludes his discussion of the Hooton material with his note: "One may wonder for how many generations inbreeding can account for the maintenance of such traits. Proto-Indians have been in the New World for dozens of thousands of years, certainly enough time for traits to have been disseminated among the many tribes and groups."[62] Much more research needs to be done on the Pecos question.

The Hull Bay Skeletons

The find at Hull Bay in the Virgin Islands consisted of the remains of two African males. According to the original reports, the skeletons were found in a context dated by radiocarbon analysis to AD 1250, and a pre-Columbian Carib ceramic vessel was clamped around the wrist of one of the bodies. The teeth were said to have displayed signs of the dental mutilation favored by some early African cultures. But later, the Smithsonian changed its mind about the discovery. It was said that the bones had been in contact with sea water, which might have altered the amount of C-14 present, making dating unreliable. And an iron nail was said to have been found in the same context, indicative—or so it is claimed—of a post-Columbian date. Van Sertima[63] has pointed out that African cultures knew of the use of iron thousands of years before AD 1250, so that the presence of an iron object does not necessarily rule out a pre-Columbian date. In any event, the issue has been closed by the Smithsonian, which has not been very helpful to Van Sertima in his attempts at follow-up. Van Sertima has, however, found further evidence of the antiquity of the skeletons in the form of pre-Columbian African designs carved on rocks near the burial site. In the absence of further information on the Hull Bay skeletons, nothing more can be said at this stage.

Conclusion

It would appear that the craniological material of Wiercinski provides the most support for theories of African contacts with the New World before Columbus. The materials referred to by Peterson are also very important as evidence and should be tracked down. Further research is needed for drawing conclusions about the Pecos and Hull Bay finds. Physical anthropology is a promising avenue of research for those seeking to retore the African to his rightful place in the history of world civilization.

Notes

1. Ivan Van Sertima, *They Came Before Columbus* New York, Random House 1976; Nile Valley Presence in America B.C. *Journal of African Civilizations* November 1984 Vol. 6 No. 2 pp. 221-246

2. Alexander Von Wuthenau *Unexpected Faces in Ancient America* New York, Crown Publishers 1975

3. Van Sertima 1976; 1984

4. Jairazbhoy, R.A. *Ancient Egyptians and Chinese in America* Totowa, NJ, Rowman and Littlefield 1974

5. New York, G.P. Putnam's Sons, 1959

6. *Proceedings of the Forty-First International Congress of Americanists* 1974 pp. 116-126

7. J. Comas, Transatlantic Hypotheses on the Peopling of America: Caucasoids and Negroids. *The Journal of Human Evolution* 2, 1973 pp. 75-92

8. Van Sertima 1976 p. 31, 142

9. Peterson 1959 p. 50

10. ibid. p. 34

11. ibid, p. 58

12. ibid. p. 39

13. see Michael Coe *The Jaguar's Children: Preclassic Central Mexico* New York, The Museum of Primitive Art 1965

14. Peterson, personal communication, July 8, 1985

15. ibid.

16. Von Wuthenau 1975 p. 136

17. Van Sertima 1976 p. 31

18. ibid. p. 264

19. ibid. p.p. 269-270

20. Not without some difficulty. I had to wait a long time while the library attendants tried to find it, and at one point I was told that the Museum owned no such volume. The copy of Jairazbhoy *Ancient Egyptians and Chinese in America* had been taken out by the anthropology department. Let the reader make what he will of that.

21. Wiercinski 1974 p. 117

22. ibid. p. 122

23. Comas 1973

24. ibid. p. 84

25. ibid. p. 85

26. Wiercinski 1974 p. 122

27. ibid

28. ibid. p. 122-123

29. Comas 1973 p. 85

30. Wiercinski 1974 p. 123

31. ibid. p. 124

32. ibid.

33. ibid. p. 122

34. ibid.

35. ibid. p. 124

36. ibid.

37. ibid. p. 117

38. Coe 1965 p. 122

39. Michael Coe, *America's First Civilization* New York, American Heritage, 1968 p. 96

40. ibid. p. 98

41. Van Sertima 1976 p. 170

42. Coe 1965, photo 78

43. ibid. p. 25

44. Von Wuthenau 1975 color plate 8

45. ibid. Fig. 98, 178-179

46. ibid. fig. 100, p. 181

47. Van Sertima 1976 Plate 2, a,c,f

48. Coe 1965 p. 13

49. ibid. p. 14

50. Coe 1968 p. 96

51. Ignacio Bernal, *The Olmec World* Berkely, University of California Press p. 136

52. This would tend to favor Van Sertima's chronology.

53. Von Wuthenau 1975 p. 125

54. Van Sertima 1976 p. 148

55. Bernal 1969 p. 152

56. Von Wuthenau 1975 Color plates 22-23

57. Van Sertima 1976 Plate 5

58. ibid. p. 32

59. July-August 1953 pp. 1-16

60. Comas 1973 p. 82
61. ibid.
62. Eugene Fingerhut *Who First Discovered America: A Critique of Pre-Columbian Voyages* Claremont, California, Regina Books 1984 p. 86
63. Van Sertima 1976 p. 263

Appendix: African Voyagers and American Mounds

The Hooton material discussed in the preceding paper raises the question of an African presence in what is now the United States in Pre-Columbian times. In connection with this question, Van Sertima, following Wiener, addresses in *They Came Before Columbus* the issue of the prehistoric burial and platform mounds of the eastern United States, attributed by almost all archaeologists to native American cultures but seen by some as evidence of foreign visitors to ancient America, being attributed to everyone from Vikings to Africans. Unfortunately, the writings of Wiener drawn upon by Van Sertima to argue the case for an African settlement in the mound areas of the United States suffer from the lack of accurate dating techniques at the time of writing, as well as from the relative lack of archaeological information on the mound building cultures. Much has been learned since Wiener's day, making his ideas about North American mounds invalid. The purpose of this appendix is to present the modern archaeological picture of the mound builders of eastern America in brief, with some bibliographic pointers for students wishing to pursue the subject further, and thus provide a solid background for any attempt to demonstrate an ancient African presence in North America.

The so-called Mound Builders of North America actually were several discrete American Indian cultures, separated from each other by time as well as key artifactual and ideological distinctions. The first mound-building culture was the Adena, which appeared in the Ohio River Valley around 800 BC. This complex produced low conical burial mounds. The dead interred under the mounds were accompanied by grave goods including native copper beads, slate gorgets (a form of pendant-like ornament), stone tube smoking pipes (Wiener was very wrong in his assertion that smoking pipes were unknown to pre-medieval America and were introduced by African visitors; they were known in pre-Adena time) antler crowns and powdered red ochre. Initially, in the earlier days of the Adena phase, the bodies were interred in simple pits under the mounds, but later the dead were deposited in log-built burial vaults. Outside of the mortuary complex the Adena culture is represented by a distinctive stemmed stone projectile point type, a form of pottery called Fayette Thick by archaeologists and other domestic artifacts. While most scholars believe that Adena developed from indigenous roots, others suspect a Meso-american influence, in particular an Olmec influence. This is basd on anatomical similarities of Adena skeletal material with preclassic Mexican remains, the practice of artificial cranial deformation in both areas, the similarity of Adena log tombs to Olmec basalt column tombs, and a mysterious Louisiana site called Poverty Point, dated around 1500 BC, a mound complex resembling Olmec earthworks which might have represented a stopping-off point of an Olmec cultural influx into the Ohio Valley.

The second major phase of mound-building in North America was the Hopewell, which succeeded and was partly derived from the Adena in the Ohio Valley. Among its products are the forts and earthworks mistakenly ascribed by Wiener to the medieval period. The Hopewell culture flourished c. 300 BC-AD 500. It was centered in southern Ohio, but expanded over and influenced a wide range of territory from New York to Iowa and south to Louisiana. The dead of the culture were buried in mounds in log tombs accompanied by abundant and exquisite grave goods of copper, freshwater pearls and carved stone. Examination of skeletal material revealing persistent genetic defects (e.g. ear exostoses) in high ranking individuals hints at the existence of a hereditary leadership. While the core of the Hopewell complex seems to have been an indigenous development, influence from Mexico is also considered possible by some archaeologists. In particular, there appears to be a link between Hopewell and the Crystal River complex in Florida, which is of definite Mexican derivation. The Crystal River site has earthworks and platform mounds closely resembling those of the Olmec, as well as artifactual affinities with this Mesoamerican culture. It is coeval with the last stages of Olmec civilization (c. 500 BC-AD 1). A Mexican-style column dated 400 AD also occurs at the site. Hopewell artifacts have been found in Crystal River contexts, indicating trade linkage of the two cultures.

The third great epoch of mound construction in North America was the Mississippian phase of the Southeast, which was definitely Mesoamerican in inspiration. The mounds constructed by this culture were mostly temple platforms with stairways, earthen copies of the Mexican pyramids, rather than burial mounds. The pottery forms of the Mississippian bottles, effigies, tripod vessels, were copied from Mexican styles. The phase began around AD 700 and is believed to have been a result of Mexican influence moving into the Southeast from the Huastec area through Texas, where the oldest Mississippian site, dated c. AD 500 is located. Around AD 1200, a complex called the Death Cult or Southern Cult appeared among the Mississippian areas, represented by religious motifs executed in Mexican style-feathered serpents, circled crosses, etc. Wiener has pointed out the similarities of these designs with Mandingo iconography. In passing we may note that the object in plate 15b of *They Came Before Columbus* (reproduced from Wiener) is in fact North American Mississippian and not Mexican as Wiener's original caption says. The timing would certainly be correct for African correlations here.

But the hunter for African links to North American archaeology must be wary. For example, the famous Davenport Stela, used by Fell as evidence of an

Egypto-Libyan presence in early Iowa, is a proven fake. Researchers should always consult original sources on the American finds before making judgements about secondary sources like Wiener's.

On the mounds, some good works to consult are:

Hopewellian Studies ed. R. Caldwell and R. Hall Illinois State Museum 1964.

Sun Circles and Human Hands ed. Fundaburks and Foreman; published by Fundaburks 1957.

Hopewell Archaeology ed. Naomi Greber, Kent State University Press, 1980.

The Mound Builders Robert Silverberg, Ballantine, 1970.

The Archaeology of North America Dean Snow Thames and Hudson, 1976.

On the Davenport stone see:

The Davenport Conspiracy Marshal McKusick, University of Iowa Press 1970.

AFRICAN SEA KINGS IN AMERICA?
EVIDENCE FROM EARLY MAPS

Joan Covey

Were some striking, early maps of North and South America used by African Sea Kings to go to America? In the sixteenth century some maps were made of North and South America which seem to be based on ancient maps. They could not have been drawn by the Greeks or by the Renaissance explorers because they appear to be remarkably accurate. The maps are the Hamy-King (1502-04), Piri Re'is (1513) and Mercator (1538) maps of South America, and the Hadji Ahmed (1559) map of South and North America.

Who could have drawn these maps? Who could not only sail to North and South America, but while there, know exactly where they were, make maps, and then return home with their treasure? Making accurate maps requires skills which the Renaissance explorers did not have. It was not only impossible for them to find longitude, they also had great difficulty transferring their geographical knowledge to maps. This would have required advanced mathematical skills which they did not have. A mapmaker needs trigonometry to transfer points on the spherical surface of the earth to a flat plane in such a way as to preserve correct distances and land shapes. For this, the curvature has to be calculated and transferred to a plane by trigonometry. (3:98)

We shall try to show that neither the Greeks of Alexandria, nor the Renaissance explorers were in any way capable of drawing these maps of America. To draw a map of America, a mapmaker would need to know the latitude as well as the longitude of the coastlines, rivers and other features he would plan to record.

Latitude tells how far north or south of the equator one is. It is defined as the angular distance of a place on the earth's surface from the equator. The equator is latitude zero degrees, the poles are latitude 90 degrees north or south. Parallels of latitude are circular lines drawn around the earth parallel to the equator.

Longitude indicates how far east or west of the meridian one is. It is defined as the angular distance between the meridian passing through a given point on the earth's surface and the poles, and the prime meridian. This prime meridian, the line of zero longitude, can be almost anywhere, and at one time or another, it has been many places. Ptolemy had chosen the Canary Islands for the prime meridian. France later chose Paris, and Spain chose Cadiz. "In 1881 there were still fourteen different prime meridians being used. . . ." (14:220)

Finally, in 1884 the meridian of Greenwich near London was accepted as the prime meridian.

The Greeks of Alexandria

There is not even a hint of America on "World Maps" made by the *Greeks of Alexandria*. They knew a lot about the earth. They knew that it was round. Eratosthenes (c̄ 274-194 BC) calculated the circumference of the earth and arrived at a figure that was only 4½% greater than it actually is.

Ptolemy (c̄ 140 AD) overestimated the size of the *known* world, which did not leave enough room for the *unknown* world (America, the Atlantic and Pacific Oceans). He placed the prime meridian at the Canary Islands, off West Africa, because that was assumed to be the westernmost part of the world. It seems he never wondered what would happen if a ship sailed west, past the Canary Islands. Ptolemy ignored the writings of Plato (c̄ 428-348 BC) and Diodorus (c̄ 20 BC) who wrote that there was a large continent in the Altantic Ocean. They wrote that this country had been found long ago by the Phoenicians, who had tried to keep its existence a secret. It is clear that the great Greek geographers of Alexandria did not make maps showing America.

Even their maps of Africa itself were rudimentary.

Ptolemy assumed that the Indian Ocean was bordered on the south by an unknown continent which united southern Africa with eastern Asia. This made the Indian Ocean into a large inland sea. He again ignored the writings of other Greeks who believed that it was possible to sail around the southern tip of Africa. According to Herodotus (c̄ 485-425 BC) the Egyptian Pharaoh Necho had sent a fleet of Phoenician ships around Africa c̄ 600 BC. The Phoenicians started at the Red Sea and after three years and about 13,000 miles, returned to Egypt via Gibraltar. Herodotus wrote that the Phoenicians claimed that the sun was on their right hand as they sailed west. That would mean that the sun was in the north. Of course this proved that they had crossed the equator and had really been in the Southern Hemisphere. But to Herodotus this proved that he could not believe their story. Since he was born and raised in the Northern Hemisphere, he believed the sun should always be in the south (5:211-12).

Ptolemy apparently also doubted that the Phoenicians had really sailed around Africa. As a result the Indian Ocean was thought of as an inland sea for over a thousand years until 1498, when Da Gama sailed from Portugal to India around the south of Africa.

The Middle Ages

During the middle ages two different kinds of maps existed side by side. The

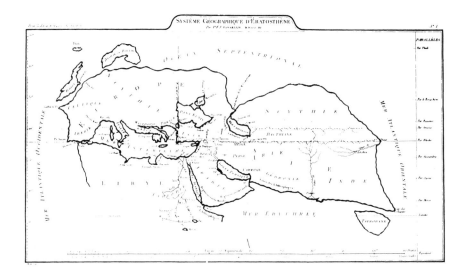

The World Map of Eratosthenes (3:12)

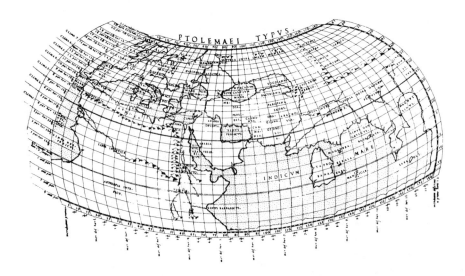

The World of Ptolemy as rendered in the sixteenth century (14:27)

men of learning, the academic geographers, consulted maps based on Ptolemy. The navigators used *portolanos* to find their way around the Mediterranean and Black Seas. These portolanos were masterpieces. The portolanos ("from port to port") were sea charts, intended as guides for mariners and merchants. They showed only coastlines and the towns near the sea, or near the mouths of larger rivers. The mariners were not interested in the interiors. On the Ibn ben Zara portolano of 1487 and the Dulcert portolano of 1339, places from Ireland to Russia are in accurate longitude. Nordenskiold, one of the leading scholars in the field, compared the Dulcert Portolano with Ptolemy's map of the Mediterranean—the difference is obvious:

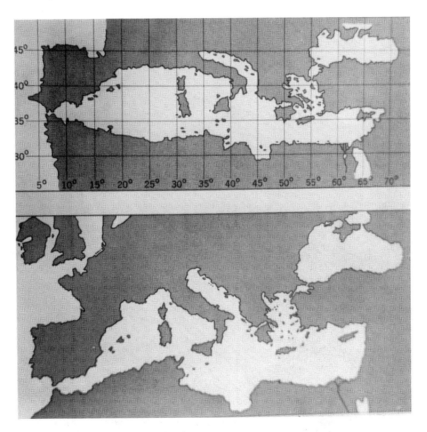

Nordenskiöld's comparison of Ptolemy's Map of the Mediterranean (top) with the Dulcert Portolano. (3:8)

The Dulcert Portolano was just one of the many portolanos circulating in Europe in the Middle Ages. No one is sure where the original portolano came from—it may have been found in Constantinople by Venetians, who captured

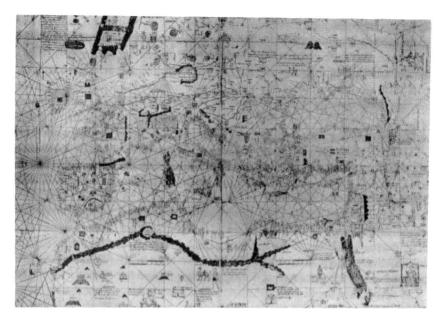

The Dulcert Portolano of 1339. (3:6)

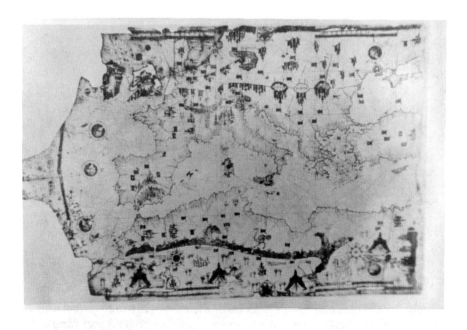

Portolano of Ibn ben Zara 1487 (3:142)

the city in 1204 during one of the crusades. (3:48) The portolanos were much too accurate to have been drawn by medieval sailors, and successive portolanos showed no signs of improvement.

Age of Exploration

During the great age of exploration navigators were severely handicapped because they had no instrument by which they could find longitude at sea. The chronometer was not developed until 250 years later. Latitude could be determined by astronomical observation, but without proper training and equipment, many errors were made.

Admiral Morison, in his book about Columbus, wrote that Columbus made serious mistakes on his First Voyage ". . . we have only three latitudes (all wrong), and no longitude for the entire voyage." (6:157) In the sixteenth century the only way to find longitude was to time an eclipse, but that was hard to do correctly. "At Mexico City in 1541, a mighty effort was made by the intelligentsia to determine the longitude of the place by timing two eclipses of the moon. . . ." (6:186) Scholars in Toledo, Spain and in Mexico City noted at what time the eclipses occurred. They were off by 1450 miles, about 25½ **degrees longitude! (3:36)**

This was hardly an isolated case. For instance:

1. "A pilot in Magellan's fleet proved to be almost 53° off in calculating the longitude of the Phillipine Islands." (14:130)
2. The Solomon Islands east of New Guinea were visited by Alvaro de Mendoza in 1568. The "pilot grossly underestimated the distance they had sailed from Peru—placing their discovery some 3500 miles east of its true position" (1:26-27)
3. Robert de La Salle sailed the Mississippi River to its delta in 1681-82. When he tried to sail from the West Indies to this same delta in 1684, he landed 400 miles to the west of it. Not knowing the longitude of the Mississippi River cost him his life: "Marching north for help in 1687, **La Salle was murdered by some of his disgruntled party"!** (11:222)

One hundred fifty years after Columbus, it was still believed that . . . "Not only is longitude undiscovered, but—it is undiscoverable—." (3:36) In part because of these problems with longitude, the explorers' maps of the sixteenth century were very poor.

The *Hamy-King* map of 1502-04 is based partly on Ptolemy (quite inaccurate) and partly on portolanos (pretty accurate).

Hapgood wrote that the Hamy-King map shows a canal, connecting the Mediterranean and Red Seas. (3:151) This would not be surprising. "According to tradition, the Egyptians dug a canal to link the eastern part of the Nile delta with the Red Sea as early as the 1900s B.C." (15:96) Later the canal was restored

Ptolemaeus Basilae Map of 1540 (3:39) (A sample of 16th century cartography).

by Ramses II (c1290-c1223 B.C.) and again by Persia, after Egypt was conquered by Persia (c1223 B.C.). (3:151) Willem Barentszoon's portolano of 1595 clearly shows a canal there. (7:39, fig.21) He must have copied some map which did show a canal. On further study the "canal" on the Hamy-King map appears to be just a rhumb line. The unknown author of the Hamy-King map drew in two equators, which causes some distortion of the west coast of Africa. But it is still a good map of Africa—obviously not the work of any 15th or 16th century cartographer.

This accurate mapping is not limited to the Mediterranean and Africa. It has been thought that the mapmaker based his information about America on data brought back by Vespucci, but this is very unlikely. Measurements of longitude in Vespucci's time were totally inaccurate. The West Indies are shown in correct longitude. (3:258) On the Hamy-King map the northern and eastern coasts of South America are separated. As Hapgood pointed out: "The blank space represents more than ten degrees of latitude and longitude. If Vespucci or another explorer left the northern coast at 6° N, as the map suggests, how another explorer left the northern coast at 6° S, and how could he have estimated its longitudes and its latitudes so correctly?" (3:164) The answer is, of course, that he could not have mapped this coast.

The mid-Atlantic islands are also shown, with minimal errors in longitude. (3:259) It would seem that this mapping of the coast of Africa and of parts of America was completed in ancient times, by people who could measure longitude with great accuracy. "The width of the South Atlantic Ocean is represented with an error of only 2°." (3:164) Only the Piri Re'is map is more accurate.

The *Piri Re'is* map of 1513, which was rediscovered in 1929 in Istanbul shows information which, according to the history books, was not available in 1513. South America and Africa are in correct relative longitude. How did Piri Re'is have such accurate data?

Piri Re'is wrote that he used twenty source maps; among them were eight maps dating from the time of Alexander the Great, an Arab map of India, four Portuguese maps of the Indian Ocean and China, and a map by Columbus of the western area. (4:18) The eastern part of the Piri Re'is map is missing, i.e., the rest of Africa, Europe, India, China, etc.

At first glance the Piri Re'is map does not seem to be very good. The map is a composite, and while some positions on the map are accurate, others are far off. In most cases the errors are due to mistakes in the compiling of local maps. Hapgood believed that "this long process of combining the local maps . . . had been finished in ancient times." (3:25) There were many fingers in the pie, with the result that we find four different grids, two equators, and even two Norths, which caused some serious errors. The original mapmaker must have found the correct relative longitude across Africa, and across the Atlantic, all the way from the meridian of Alexandria, Egypt, to Brazil. This was obviously not based on knowledge available in 1513. When were these compo-

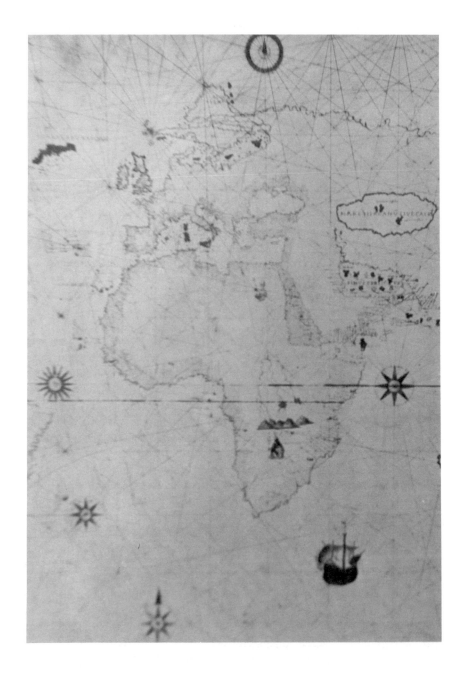

The Hamy-King Chart of 1502-4. (Western half) (3:152)

nent maps made? Who made them? Who had access to them? The Renaissance explorers could not have drawn the Piri Re'is map because *it is very accurate*. Ptolemy was not even aware of America. All we know is that the maps were made a long time ago.

Let us look at some details on the map. The mid-Atlantic islands are shown with remarkable accuracy. According to Hapgood's calculations, the Cape Verde Islands, Madeira Islands and Azores are shown in *perfect* longitude. The Canary Islands are off by 1° longitude. (3:238)

The Andes are shown on this map of 1513. The Andes were not "discovered" until 1527 by Pizarro. The Atrato River (in present day Colombia) is shown for a distance of 300 miles from the sea. Its eastward bend at 5° North latitude is correct. (3:52) Someone evidently explored this river to its headwaters in the western Andes before 1513. Even if some Renaissance explorer went up this river, it would not have been mapped as well. We know that at that time it was impossible to find correct longitude. That *latitude* was also difficult to determine correctly is shown by the fact that for a long time after the four voyages of Columbus, Haiti and Cuba were placed *above* rather than below the Tropic of Cancer. (3:35)

The Amazon River is shown twice, once on the equator of the main grid, and once on the equator of a smaller grid. The Island of Marajo is shown at the mouth of the Amazon only once. This island was not officially discovered until 1543, but is clearly shown on this map of 1513. Hapgood believed that the Amazon without the Island of Marajo may date from a time very long ago when this island did not yet exist; it may once have been connected to the mainland. The mapmaker, seeing a large river without the Island of Marajo, would not have recognized it, and assumed that it was some other river. (3:54) It is also interesting that "Both the duplications of the Amazon suggest the actual course of the river, while all the representations of it in the later maps of the 16th century bear no resemblance to its real course." (3:55) These earlier mapmakers knew their business!

The features shown on the Piri Re'is map (the Andes, the Atrato and Amazon rivers, and the island of Marajo) were obviously shown on the source maps which Piri Re'is consulted. Someone had not only known of South America, but had mapped part of it at least 1700 years before Columbus sailed west.

Some scholars have doubted the accuracy of the Piri Re'is map, because of some of his notations. He wrote on the part of his map which is near the South Pole that these shores are "very hot." (4:25) Why did he write that? The authors of that part of the map, the people who actually went that close to the South Pole, would have been "very cold" on board ship. This sort of inaccurate statement should not be enough reason to disregard the whole map.

Piri Re'is also wrote that "—big snakes are said to be there." (4:25) The constellation Hydra (the Snake) is visible only in latitude 70°-72° South, which is near the South Pole. It is possible that the original mapmakers, who

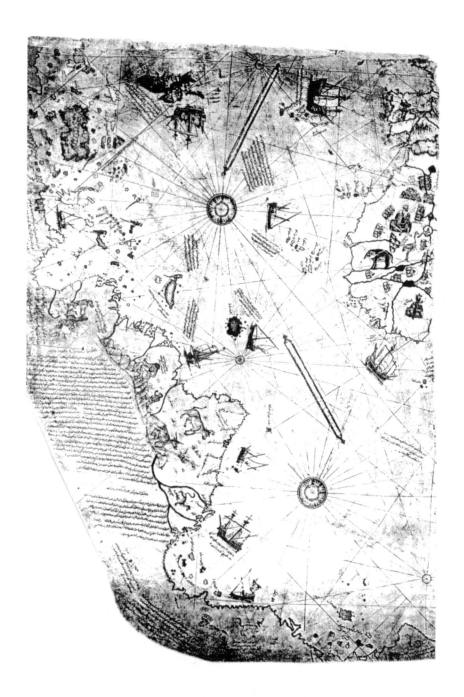

The Piri Re'is Map (4:19)

used the constellations of the stars in the sky to find their way at night, wrote the "snake" on their map when they reached this area. Piri Re'is may not have been familiar with the constellations of the Southern Hemisphere. He was a Turk, at home in the Middle East, in the Northern Hemisphere. (3:224)

Two other interesting maps of America are the Mercator map of South America of 1538, and the Hadji Ahmed map of North and South America of 1559. Mercator is considered to have been the best 16th century cartographer. (3:89) He seems to have realized that the portolanos were far superior to Ptolemy's maps. His 1538 map of South America was based on ancient maps. The coast of Chile is shown at 74° West; the true longitude is 70-75° West! (3:244) Amazing.

It is interesting that he tried to "update" his own map in 1569 using the accounts by explorers. This time the west coast of South America is completely out of shape, and the east coast is poorly done. (3:91)

This clearly shows the superiority of the ancient portolanos over the 16th century maps.

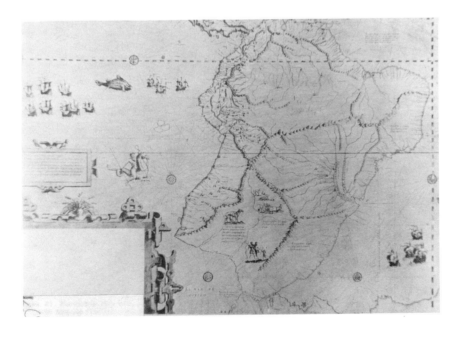

South America on Mercator's Map of 1569 (3:56)
It is distorted principally because in the 16th century there was no means of finding accurate longitude.

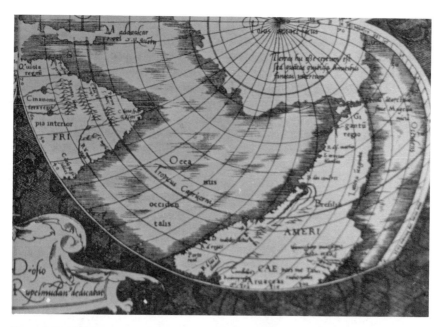

Part of the Mercator map of 1538, showing South America. (3:93)

If we turn the map upside down, South America looks more like the South America we are used to seeing on maps.

The *Hadji Ahmed World map* of 1559 is quite unusual. The eastern hemisphere is done poorly; it was probably based on Ptolemaic sources. In constrast the western hemisphere is mapped so well, it is hard to believe anyone in 1559 could have drawn this map. Only the coasts are shown—is this map related to the other portolanos? "The shapes of North and South America have a surprisingly modern look; the western coasts are especially interesting. They seem to be about two centuries ahead of the cartography of the time,—drawn on a highy sophisticated spherical projection. The shape of what is now the United States is about perfect." (3:84-85)

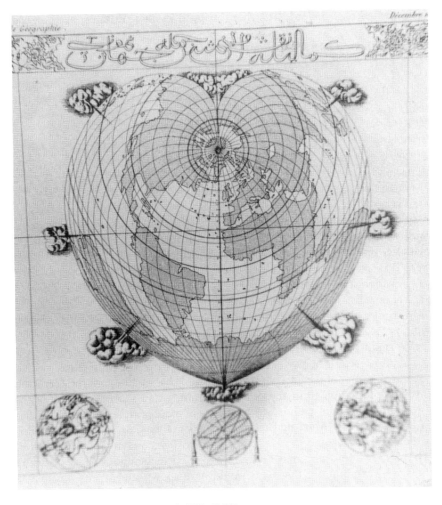

The Hadji Ahmed World Map of 1559. (3:85)

"Both latitude and longitude are surprisingly accurate for places near the meridian—." (3:86) How could the Pacific coasts of America have been mapped so well?? No one in 1559 could find longitude. This must be a very ancient map.

The Greeks of Alexandria had no use for portolanos, and neither did the scholars of the medieval times. They were considered to be "productions of unlearned mariners"! (7:49) Hapgood tried to call attention to these masterpieces, but his work was mostly ignored by the Establishment. But this may be changing. The New York Times recently carried an article by Walter Sullivan concerning ancient mapping. (9) Dr. John Weihaupt, a leading geologist and polar specialist who had never heard of Hapgood, proposed that the outlines of Antartica may, indeed, have been mapped in ancient times, as Hapgood believed. (13)

Some other maps may be found which may help solve this puzzle. The Piri Re'is map was not rediscovered until 1929. Hoye wrote that "In 1955, a cartographer named M. Destombes announced the discovery of Ferdinand Magellan's own chart of his epochal circumnavigation of the world. No one had known it existed, but Destombes found it—in the archives of Istanbul." (4:31)

Istanbul is one of the world's oldest cities. It lies at the trade cross roads of Europe and Asia. It was the Capital of the Byzantine Empire for almost one thousand years, and much ancient culture was preserved there. In 1204 a Venetian fleet, on crusade to the Holy Land, instead captured Istanbul (it was then named Constantinople). For about 60 years they had access to the rich map collection there. It is not surprising that the first portolanos known in the West were made by Italians. In 1453 the Ottoman Turks captured Istanbul, and after that the Turks had the best maps. Both Piri Re'is and Hadji Ahmed were Turks. (3:84)

The Moors and Arabs also played a major role in the preservation of knowledge of ancient maps. "It was the writings of a 12th century Moorish scholar, al-Idrisi, . . . that provided Europeans with one of their first glimpses of what Arab travelers knew. . . ." (11:149) In 1154 he made a 70 sheet world map for the Norman King of Sicily, Roger II. (11:23)

The most beautiful portolanos were produced by the Majorcans. (11:24) "Majorca, center of the great school of Catalan chart-making, was under Arab [Moor] domination until the mid-13th century, and more Arab [Moorish] lore filtered into Europe this way by means of maps such as the Catalan Atlas of 1375." (11:149) "Abraham Cresques, compiler of the Catalan Atlas, was called to Portugal to become the leading adviser to Prince Henry the Navigator" (11:24) (1394-1460) This may explain why the Portuguese took the lead during the age of exploration: the maps would have shown that it was possible to reach the riches of India by sailing around South Africa. Did the Portuguese see any maps of America? Was America considered to be a barrier on the way to India, which should be avoided?

A map of Florida, based on a French expedition in 1564, (11:210-211) shows three names that may indicate an early Moorish settlement there. The names:
Mayarca (Majorca?)
Cadica (Cadiz?)
Marracou (Marrakesh?)
If these were in fact Moorish settlements, did the people come before or after 1492?

With the appearance of the portolanos in Western Europe, lands previously mapped came to be "rediscovered." The Dulcert portolano of 1339 shows the Azores Islands ... "long before their 'official' discovery in 1427." (8:11-12) "Bermuda's discovery seems to have been no less miraculous. Supposedly named after Juan de Bermudez, the man who first sighted it in 1515, it yet appears large as life on a map by Peter Martyr published four years before!" (1:55)

Why are there so few ancient maps? Over the centuries many maps must have been lost in shipwrecks ... especially portolanos, because those were the maps used by the seaman.

On land maps would have been lost if they had been stored in libraries. We know that the great library at Alexandria was destroyed several times. Who knows how many maps were lost when the Romans destroyed Carthage in 146 BC? Since Carthage had been a great naval power, they might have had some fine maps. "Arabic literature contains numerous tantalizing mentions of 'lost' maps." (4:31)

We should also consider the need for secrecy. The Phoenicians "never shared information regarding trade routes, markets, or winds and currents. The routes were their road to riches, and as such were shielded from prying potential competitors." (5:197) There is the story of the Phoenician captain on his way to get tin, who saw that a Roman ship was following him. The Phoenician deliberately scuttled his ship and was later "fully recompensed by the state for the cargo he had sacrificed to protect the secret of the route." (5:197-198)

The Carthaginians were also looking ahead to the future. They thought that they could escape to their secret lands "in case some total disaster should overtake Carthage." (5:222) But when the Romans did defeat Carthage, their ships had been sunk, and they could not escape as planned.

Maybe the big surprise should be that as many maps survived as did.

Misinformation was used to keep away the curious: sailors were warned of sea monsters, swamps, darkness, and so on. Piri Re'is wrote on his map that when Columbus asked the "Great of Genoa" to give him two ships, so he could sail to the West, he was told "O foolish man! In the West is only to be found the end and limit of the World! It is full of darkness." (4:24) Even the tale of Atlantis suddenly disappearing may have been invented to help discourage the competition.

The policy of misinformation and secrecy started so long ago is still very effective. School children are still taught that Columbus discovered America. We may never know who drew these maps of America.

The navigators of Phoenicia and Carthage were famous for their exploits. The ancient Egyptians had the requisite mapping skills. Stecchini had "uncovered evidence of extremely advanced techniques of measurements and map-making in ancient Egypt. He had spent a lifetime in the investigation of ancient measurements" (3:193) and wrote: "I was fortunate enough to come across a set of Egyptian documents, well known but neglected, that prove that by the time of the first dynasties the Egyptians had measured down to the minute the latitude and longitude of all the main points of the course of the Nile, from the equator to the Mediterranean Sea. Following this first result I have traced a series of texts (all earlier than the beginning of Greek science) which, starting from Egypt, provide positional data that cover most of the Old World, from the rivers Congo and Zambesi to the Norwegian coast, from the Gulf of Guinea to the peaks of Switzerland and river junctions in Central Russia. The data are so precise that they are a source of discomfort." (3:193-194)

Conclusion

In this issue a large amount of evidence is being presented that African Sea Kings went to America. It is not likely that we can ever prove that they used maps of America on their expeditions. Maps of America *may* have been in circulation in the Nile Valley area (the Middle East) at that time. Future finds may shed more light on this.

Bibliography

1. Campbell, Tony—*Early Maps* Abbeville Press, NY 1981.
2. Chandler, Wayne B.—*The Moor: Light of Europe's Dark Age*. African presence in Early Europe, Transaction Books, New Brunswick 1985.
3. Hapgood, Charles—*Maps of the Ancient Seakings* (rev. ed) Turnstone Books, London, 1979.
4. Hoye, Paul F. with Lunde, Paul—*Piri Re'is and the Hapgood Hypotheses* - Aramco World Magazine January - February 1980 pp. 18-31.
5. Irwin, Constance—*Fair Gods and Stone Faces* St. Martin's Press, NY 1963.
6. Morison, Samuel E.—*Admiral of the Ocean Sea* Little, Brown, Boston 1942.
7. Nordenskiold, A.E.—*Facsimile - Atlas the early history of cartography* Dover Publications, NY, 1973.
8. Putman, Robert—*Early Sea Charts* Abbeville Press, NY, 1983.
9. Sullivan, Walter—*Sixteenth Century Charts seen as Hinting Ancient Explorers Mapped Antarctica* New York Times, Sept. 26, 1984.

10. Tompkins, Peter—*Secrets of the Great Pyramid* with an appendix by Livio Catullo Stecchini, Harper and Row, NY, 1971.
11. Tooley, R.V.—*Landmarks of Mapmaking* Thomas Y. Crowell Co., NY, 1976.
12. Tooley, R.V.—*Maps and Map-makers* B.T. Batsford, Ltd., London, 1982.
13. Weihaupt, John G.—*Historic Cartographic Evidence for Holocene Changes in the Antarctic Ice Cover* EOS, Vol. 65, #35, August 28, 1984.
14. Wilford, John N.—*The Mapmakers* Alfred A. Knopf Publishers, NY, 1981.
15. World Book Encyclopedia Vol. E Field Enterprises Education Corp., Chicago, 1974.

PYRAMIDS—AMERICAN AND AFRICAN:
A COMPARISON

Beatrice Lumpkin

Anyone who has stood at the summit of the grand pyramids of America or crawled deep into the awesome pyramids of Africa has felt the great power of human genius. Far apart in geography but so similar in theme and structure, was there some connection between the African and American pyramid builders? Are these pyramids just similar expressions of the human trend to build bigger and reach higher, or did the earlier African civilization have a direct influence on America?

The purpose of this paper is to review some of the facts known about American and African pyramids, their similarities and their differences. A factual background is essential for any scientific evaluation, especially for a subject which has been clouded and distorted by the racist bias of Eurocentrism.

Toynbee's claim that Egyptian civilization was the product of white or Europeans was demolished by W.E.B. Du Bois:

> There can be but one adequate explanation of this vagary of nineteenth-century science: it was due to the slave trade and Negro slavery. It was due to the fact that the rise and support of capitalism called for rationalization based upon degrading and discrediting the Negroid peoples.[1]

A similar question of colonialism distorts American history. An early European "explorer" of Mayan pyramids exclaimed: "America, say historians, was peopled by savages; but savages never carved these stones."[2] Morley and Brainerd point out that, "The Old World of the 16th century was not content merely to destroy the Mexica, Inca and Maya civilizations. Typically, these great achievements were belittled." They quote this 1822 account by del Rio:

> The ancient inhabitants of these structures lived in extreme darkness, for, in their fabulous superstitions, we seem to view the ideology of the Phoenicians, the Greeks, the Romans ... that some of these nations pursued their conquests even to this country, where it is probable they only remained long enough to enable the Indian tribes to imitate their ideas and adapt, in a rude and awkward manner, such arts as their invaders thought fit to inculcate.[3]

In contrast to the imperialist approach, a scientific approach would study the great achievements of both African and Native American peoples. Accepting new ideas from another people takes nothing away from either because all peoples have learned from those who came before them. The leading proponent of an African role in the development of American pyramids clearly states, "This does not mean to suggest that Africans physically built the American pyramids . . . What we are speaking of is a stimulus, an influence."[4]

The Incas

Pyramids are found on both continents of the Americas and several locations in Africa. In Peru pyramids are found from Piura in the North to Ica in the South.[5] See Fig. 1. These include step pyramids with stairways and others with access ramps. Some were massive structures with bases 50 m by 50 m and served as centers of large urban complexes. Inca stone technology was highly developed. For example, the masonry used at Lake Titicaca fits together perfectly, with only the sides hollowed to take mortar.[6]

But the period of Inca expansion came later in history, c. 1400, compared to the Olmec civilization of Mexico, c. − 1200 to − 400. By the time of the Inca empire there had been repeated contact between Central America and Peru, with maize and other plants carried southward and the use of metals spread-

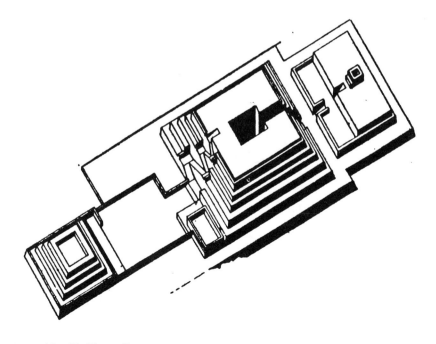

Pyramids of la Huaca Panamarca

ing North.[7] Weaver writes that "the potential of interregional diffusion of ideas should not be underestimated. Commerce provided the vehicle . . . cultural similarities between Mexico and Ecuador were so remarkable as to suggest regular communication."[8]

Since the Mesoamerican pyramids were the earliest of America, we must begin with Central America for possible African influence on American pyramid builders. Specifically, it was at La Venta, just Southeast of Vera Cruz, Mexico (-900 to -400) that the Olmec lay the foundation of Mesoamerican cultures marked by pyramid complexes and hieroglyphic writing.[9] And it is also at La Venta that we have some of the strongest evidence of a significant African presence long before Columbus.[10]

Geography

Mesoamerican pyramids are located in extremely varied geographical areas. It speaks to the strength of human cultural contact that these pyramids are so similar in different terrains. In the lowlands of the Maya South, dense rain forest now chokes off the pyramid complexes and few farmers live there today (See Figure 2). Yet these areas were densely populated in classical Mayan times. They supported a large educated class and provided sufficient surplus to feed thousands of pyramid builders.

Some Mesoamerican Pyramid Locations

The climate hasn't changed. What has changed is the political system and the method of agriculture. The ancient Maya agriculture was very efficient and well adapted to the local conditions. Raised fields (camillons) and a network of drainage canals provided fields dry enough for maize. Special seed was developed for these moist conditions, allowing two crops a year. Steep hills were terraced to prevent erosion. Building methods were also adapted to local conditions. For example, at El Tajin, Veracruz, concrete was made from available materials, seashells, sand, and wood.[11]

In North Yucatan semi-desert conditions are typical with thin soil and only a few pockets of good soil. Under the thin soil was a foundation of limestone, the basic building material of most pyramids. Large urban centers were supported by an extensive agricultural base which supplemented the maize with breadfruit, domesticated turkeys and bees as well as hunting and fishing. Wells or cenotes were an important source of water. Again, special seed was developed to produce a hardier maize for the arid conditions.[12]

Still another geographical region, the high, flat area of the basin of Mexico, was the site of later pyramid complexes. Teotihuacan with a population of 150,000 to 200,000[13] reached its height about the years 150 to 250 and declined after a fire c. 600. Tenochtitlan amazed the conquistadores by its wealth and cleanliness, surpassing the finest cities of Spain. Another pyramid center, Piedras Negras, was next to a river, in a different geographical setting. In short, cultural unity was not based on any similarity of geography.

Geography of the Nile

For the pyramids of Egypt and the Sudan the story is very different, with only minor variations in geography. The country centered about the Nile River. Everyplace, except in the delta and the Fayum, the green area of cultivation hugged the banks of the Nile. Behind the green were the desert hills and it was there that monuments and housing could be built, without danger of flooding or encroaching on valuable farm land. The need to control the river for irrigation purposes was a big incentive for the development of central government. At the same time the river connected all of Egypt. A central government in control of the river also assured access to good transportation and promoted commerce. However, despite the unity of geography, there were many changes in the Egyptian pyramid complex over the 3,000 year span of pyramid building.

Evolution of Egyptian Pyramids

Mud brick houses were built in the Nile Valley long before the beginning of history. Who were the giants who first thought of building homes with bricks? What a giant step that was, from smearing clay on a frame of reeds or tree branches to the abstract idea of forming clay into bricks and using bricks as building units!

Another giant step was to learn to fashion stone, the most durable material known to the ancients. From limestone to the harder granites and basalt, stone was a material that matched the concept of a life after death, one that would last forever. And life in ancient Egypt was so pleasant that Egyptians wanted to live forever. That was certainly true for the many Egyptians who lived off the huge agricultural surplus and could devote themselves to government, religion, science, or the arts.

In Egypt and the Sudan there is an extensive archaeological record of the development of architecture, despite claims to the contrary by the advocates of a non-African origin of Egyptian civilization. Brick construction in the Nile Valley goes back thousands of years in the prehistoric period. Even before the development of hieroglyphic writing, there were scales (balances) and standard weights[14] and no doubt some method of making commercial records.

Early Burials

Early Egyptian burials in the desert often resulted in natural mummification. Valuable personal possessions were buried with the body. As the culture developed, superstructures were often built over the burials. These superstructures evolved to a bench-like shape, now called mastabas. For better protection from robbers and the elements, stone mastabas were used by the time of the Third dynasty.

It was soon realized that bodies were better preserved by underground burial in the desert rather than above ground in the mastabas. This led to the use of underground chambers either of brick or stone.[15] Meanwhile Egyptians had mastered the technology of stone cutting and dressing as well as methods of transport from the quarries, near and distant.

The mastaba structures became very elaborate, as some at Saqqara. The underground chamber could include 5 cells and the superstructure 27 cells containing valuables. Walls were covered with lime plaster and decorated with colored geometric design. A boat cavity and a boat to carry the deceased on the journey to the afterlife were installed next to the mastaba. A wall enclosed the entire mastaba complex.[16]

The First Step Pyramid

How did the mastaba evolve into a pyramid? History credits the great Imhotep, vizier of King Zozer, for taking the next, gigantic step at the beginning of the Third Dynasty c. -2686. Imhotep did more than just make Zozer's mastaba bigger and better. See Figure 3.

Zozer's Step Pyramid and Part of Pyramid Complex

Zozer's mastaba certainly was bigger—26' high with a square base of 207 by 207 ft., each side facing one of the cardinal points (North, East, South, West). It was then that Imhotep had a stroke of genius, not only to enlarge the mastaba but to place a second smaller mastaba on top of the first. This was followed by a third, then a fourth. Finally the entire structure was enlarged and a fifth and sixth level added to make the world's first step pyramid. The final height was 204 ft. with base 411 by 358 ft., all cased in gleaming white limestone brought from the Tura quarries across the river.[17]

Zozer's successors also built step pyramids, that is until the end of the Third Dynasty. The pyramids of this period show further development toward the true pyramid shape, completing the transition between mastabas and the great pyramids of Egypt.

At Meidum the same mastaba-type base stands on a prepared platform or pavement. Layers of masonry were added to complete 8 steps, cased in smooth limestone. Then the builders filled in the steps and cased the whole structure again to make a true pyramid with an angle of 51° 53'. The pyramid now stands in a hill of rubble because the outer casing had been removed back in ancient times. However, it is the first example of a smooth pyramid.[18]

The Egyptian Pyramid Complex

We can hardly be blamed for thinking of pyramids in isolation because they dwarf the scene around them. Also little is left of the other structures which

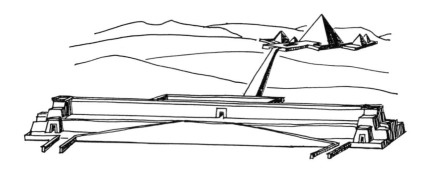

Reconstruction of the Pepi II Pyramid Complex, Saqqara

surrounded pyramids. But in their day the large pyramid was the center of a very impressive complex surrounded by a high, thick wall. See Figure 4. Zozer's pyramid, for example, was surrounded by a stone wall 33' high and over 1 mile long. The thick inner core was of masonry with the entire outer side faced in dressed Tura limestone. Many false doors were carved in the stone wall and the upper half of the wall was decorated with small rectangular inserts.[19]

The pyramid had a chapel in front of the entrance on the North side of the pyramid. In front of the Eastern face of the main pyramid stood the mortuary temple. A separate temple, now designated as the valley temple, was built at the edge of the cultivation. A long stone causeway connected the pyramid enclosure with the lower valley temple. Inside this temple stood many statues and stelae.

In addition to the main pyramid, a small pyramid with its own enclosure was built to the South, but outside the main pyramid enclosure. The small pyramid had its own chapel with two stelae in front of the Eastern face. Around the large pyramid, cut into the limestone rock, were large, boat-shaped pits.[20] At the Great Pyramid at Gizeh, these pits contained boats designed to carry the Pharaoh Khufu on his celestial journeys. One measured 43.5 m long, and 7 m deep and was covered by 41 large blocks weighing an average of 16 tons each.[21]

The Great Pyramid of Gizeh

For the purpose of comparison of Egyptian and Mesoamerican pyramid complexes, it would be useful to review some facts about Khufu's pyramid, the greatest of all. It stands on 13 acres, partly on a platform of limestone blocks and built over a rocky knoll. The causeway was of white limestone with decorated walls and sculptured reliefs. The mortuary temple had a large colonnaded court with walls of white limestone, basalt pavement and red granite pillars—a striking color combination of white, red and black.

The pyramid itself measured 146 m high and 230 m on each side of the square base,[22] using 2,000,000 stone blocks averaging 2.5 tons in weight. See Figure 5. Yet the relative error in length was only 1/14,000 in the length of the sides and only 1/27,000 in the measure of the right angles at the base.[23] Inside the pyramid, a spectacular "grand gallery" 47 m long rose 8.5 m to a corbeled vault ceiling.

Space will allow mention of only a few other interesting features of Egyptian pyramids. See Figure 6. The sanctuary of Sahure's 5th dynasty pyramid at Abusir, just North of Saqqara, had a complete drainage system. Rain ran off the roof through lion headed gargoyles and fell into channels cut in the pavement. Inside the temple, 5 large copper basins with lead plugs could also be drained. Copper pipes from the basins connected to an underground system of pipes which passed under the temple paving and ran down a long causeway to an outlet on the south side.[24]

Pyramids were also built during the Middle Kingdom but were replaced in the New Kingdom by tombs hidden in the hills for protection from robbers. Separate funerary temples were built in public locations but the burial itself was secret. Still the principle of the pyramid was retained in many tombs. A small brick pyramid, capped with a block of limestone carved with reliefs, was often placed on the roof of the tomb.[25]

The final revival of Egyptian pyramids was actually in the Nubian Sudan,

Stones of Great Pyramid (after limestone casing had been removed)

Sphinx at Great Pyramid (Facial features of King Khafre)

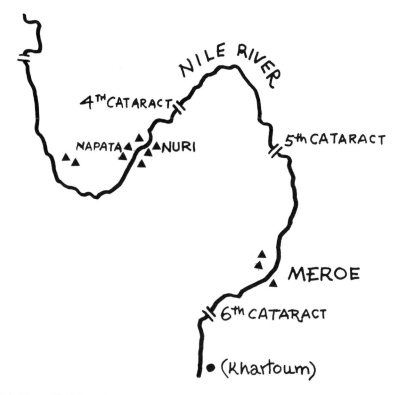

Main Pyramid Fields of Kush

that part known by the ancients as Kush which stretched as far South as the Sixth Cataract. See Figure 7. (Some authors refer to the Kushites as "Ethiopians" but that name is now used for the East African nation of the Abyssinians.) Kings of Kush rescued Egypt from foreign rule and established the XXVth dynasty which ruled all of Egypt.

The Kushite Pharaohs

When the great Piankhy responded to an urgent call from Thebes to help repel invaders, he was forced to push further North until all of Egypt was unified again. The great pyramids made a lasting impression on Piankhy. Indeed, when he returned to Kush, victorious, he ordered a pyramid built for his burial, c. 720 B.C. After his death, other members of the royal family were also buried in pyramids and this custom continued at Napata for some 400 years.

Under pressure of foreign rule of Egypt, the Kushite capital was later moved

South from Napata to Meroe near the Sixth Cataract. Pyramid building continued at Meroe and Meroe became the center of the African iron industry.
Nubian rule of Kush did not end until 350 A.D. when they were conquered by
the Abyssinians (Ethiopians).[26]

Pyramids of Sudan

Since the Kushite pyramids were contemporary with some of the Mesoamerican pyramids, they are of special interest for our study. Many authors
simply comment on their small size, compared to those of the Old Kingdom,
but miss a significant change that took place in the technology of pyramid
construction. Clarke and Engelbach give a clear description of the advanced
building methods of Kush, although their disparaging remarks about Ethiopia
reveal the bias that affected even the best of British Egyptologists.

> At or about the XXVth dynasty, a change took place in the laying of
> foundations, this period also showing a marked reaction, an effort to
> return to better forms and better sculpture. It was then discovered that it
> was well to have some regard to the foundations of a building. Advance-
> ment would not be expected from Ethiopia, yet under the princess of that
> country the buildings show a prodigality of materials in the foundations.
> Far from making a few trenches and holes to receive the walls and col-
> umns, the whole area of the temple was completely covered with carefully
> laid blocks three or four courses deep. This method continued in use until
> Roman times, and was made use of however small the building was.[27]

These pyramid superstructures were solid, built around a core of mud, sand
and small stones. The stone casing in some was smooth but in others, the
pyramid was of the step type. Unlike the Third Dynasty pyramids of 5 or 6
steps, these step pyramids were constructed of many small steps. In that
regard they looked more like the many-stepped stairways of Mesoamerican
pyramids of a later date. See Figure 8.

Piankhy's pyramid was built over a burial chamber cut out of the natural
rock. The chamber was reached by a flight of stairs cut in the rock from an
entrance outside the pyramid. A corbeled arch made of stone blocks formed
the ceiling of the burial chamber. The corbeled arch was used in many pyramids of Kush, as was the case with many of the Mesoamerican pyramids.
Piankhy's funerary chapel had high and imposing pylons sculptured with
portraits of the ruler. Considerable treasure was also supplied for the burial.[28]

Taharka, son of Pianky, was also a great warrior who defended Egypt against
the rising power of the Assyrians. His pyramid plan required more room than
available at his father's site so he built at Nuri, on the other side of the Nile.
After Taharka's death. c. − 663, more than 50 other pyramids were built at
Nuri.[29] The interior of these pyramids used blocks of well-cut sandstone, laid

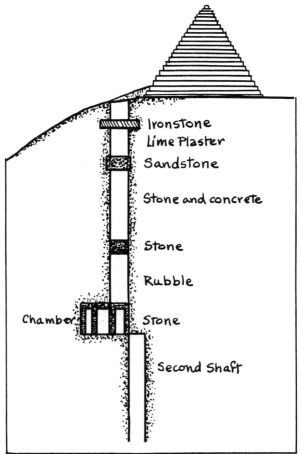

Ironstone
Lime Plaster
Sandstone
Stone and concrete
Stone
Rubble
Chamber
Stone
Second Shaft

Typical Kushite Pyramid

in regular courses like those of the Old Kingdom. The large burial chamber, carved out of the rock, had six rock-cut pillars which divided the chamber into three parts. These pyramids remained in good condition until modern times when some were dismantled by the notorious Joseph Ferlini in search of treasure.

American Pyramids

The first period of American pyramid construction actually overlapped the last stage of Egypto-Sudanese pyramid building. The American pyramid appears at La Venta in Mexico which was the center of Olmec civilization from c. − 900 to − 400. The ceremonial center at La Venta was also the site of giant stone heads carved with distinctly African features.[30] These basalt heads are believed to be actual portraits of Olmec rulers.

La Venta, itself, is a small island 30 km from the Gulf of Mexico and is totally devoid of stone. Nonetheless, the Olmecs who built the earliest American pyramid, managed to bring enormous blocks of basalt from a quarry 80 air miles to the West. The basalt was used for a system of drains as well as the colossal head sculptures.[31]

The Olmec were above all carvers of stone at La Venta, wrote Coe.[32] However, in the absence of local stone, the La Venta mounds and pyramid were made of clay, unlike later American pyramids which used local limestone. The ceremonial center was carefully planned with buildings aligned on a common North-South axis.

Throughout the Americas various peoples have built large mounds. The La Venta complex also contained a number of mounds. These were never fully explored, perhaps never will be, since the island is full of oil fields under intensive pumping activity.

A unique construction at La Venta was a massive cone with a fluted surface, 34 m high and containing 99,000 cubic meters of earth[33] At the other end of the complex are the platform remains of a step-pyramid. Bright, naturally-colored sands were used in the constructions, adding to the drama of giant heads, basalt columns, painted exteriors and numerous stelae and altars. The compound was fenced in by 2 m basalt high basalt columns set in an adobe brick wall. Just north of the main pyramid are mosaic pavements, each containing about 485 blocks of green serpentine, laid out to form jaguar masks.[34] See Figure 9.

Under Olmec influence, a vast complex was built in the Oaxaca valley at Monte Alban, some say as early as − 600. A series of 300 engravings show figures with African features, and a few that are bearded. They are called the

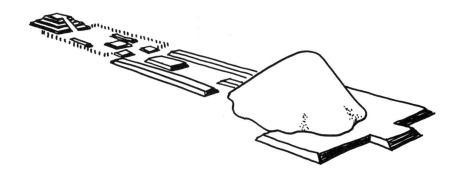

La Venta Ceremonial Complex

"Danzantes" because of their distorted positions. Already, in the Oaxaca valley, the orientation of public buildings followed the practice of La Venta. Buildings were aligned on a North-South axis, with a Northwestern deviation of 8 degrees. Many Mesoamerican centers followed this practice.

In those days the magnetic North pole was actually 8 degrees to the West of the astronomical North but there is no direct evidence to indicate that the Americans had magnetic indicators. There is, however, substantial evidence of detailed study of the stars. The 260 day ritual calendar was already in use in Oaxaca, during the Rosario phase (-700 to -500). The development of such a well organized calendar was surely preceded by many years of collective study of the sky and keeping careful astronomical records.[35] The astronomical orientation of American pyramids was similar to that of the Egyptian, except that the Egyptian alignment was to the astronomical (true) North, rather than the magnetic North pole. Also, in both the African and the American pyramids, the sides of the pyramids faced the cardinal points of North, East, South, West.

The Olmec influence is the key to a study of the pyramids of Mesoamerica. It is generally accepted that all later civilizations in Mesoamerica ultimately rest on an Olmec base. Indeed Coe goes further and says that the Olmec not only influenced the Mayans, but they *were* early Mayans. Some even see Olmec influence in the art of Peru's Chavin civilization which developed after -1000.[36]

Construction Methods

Construction techniques of the pyramid-temples varied according to the local building materials. The first stage or step of most American pyramids, according to Thompson, was built as outlined below. Succeeding levels were added and set back from the lower level, until the pyramid reached the desired height. Often a small temple was built at the top.

1. The ground was cleared of obstructions.
2. A wall enclosure was erected, made of stones set in adobe or of cut blocks of conglomerate.
3. The area enclosed by the wall was then filled with stone, conglomerate and earth in a systematic manner. Rectangular sections were filled in, one at a time, by a team of workers.
4. The outer face was made up of sloping walls, built on an inclined bank of small stones. Then 3" of concrete smoothed the surface.
5. Thin slabs of stone (andesite) were set in horizontally so the outer face projected beyond the concrete to carry the weight of decorative panels and frames. Then a wash of lime over the exterior created a smooth base for paint. Green and vermilion were used, also red, blue and black.[37]

The basic Mesoamerican pyramid complex consisted of a plaza dominated by a truncated pyramid on one side and two other buildings on facing sides of the plaza. The plaza, a clear, open space, was artificially leveled and paved with limestone cement.[38] In addition, a ball court and often ceremonial pools and buildings with astronomical applications were included in the pyramid complex. The technology for this type of construction had been developed quite early by the Olmecs. Well before the year − 600, they knew how to burn the soft limestone that was just under the soil to make cement.[39] The cement was used in building the platforms which supported many of the pole and thatch houses.

Given the thin soil of much of the Maya land, something was needed to hold house poles in place. Perhaps in answer to this need, platforms made of stones and cement were developed. In some arid areas, lined catch basins were built into the platforms to catch and store rain water.[40] Over the years the platforms became higher and bigger at the homes of the richer property owners. It would seem just a matter of time before large platforms became a status symbol.

From Platforms to Mesoamerican Pyramids

Still, a platform did not a pyramid make and it was not until smaller platforms were stacked above larger platforms that the platforms became pyramids. This required a qualitative change in architectural concepts. Such a change did take place at the Olmec center of La Venta, at the very time and place of significant African contacts.[41] Soon after, step-pyramids became the standard focus of Mesoamerican ceremonial centers.

Some Comparisons

Suppose the Africans who came to La Venta had told their hosts about the pyramids of Africa. The Africans would have found a receptive audience because Olmec civilization had developed a technology capable of large scale masonry projects. The Africans would also have found an agricultural economy rich enough to support the specialists needed to organize and plan vast building projects and to feed the thousands of workers required to build pyramid complexes.

It has been estimated that the labor required to build the major ceremonial structures at Uxmal was about 7,500,000 labor days. Construction took place at various times over 250 years.[42] This is a vast amount of labor. Still it is smaller than Herodotus's figure for Khufu's Great Pyramid at Gizeh. Herodotus estimated that 100,000 laborers worked 30 years. Multiplied out, this would come to over 1 billion labor days. Fakhry estimates that 10 years would have been needed just to construct the causeways and cut out the substructures.[43] Only highly productive economies could have supported such vast public works.

The populations of classical Mesoamerica and ancient Egypt were also of comparable size, with that of Mesoamerica estimated at .5 to 3 million.[44] Both African and American pyramid complexes often included sacred pools and systems of moats and drains. Both were highly stratified class societies with widespread use of literacy. Unfortunately we know far less about Meso-american literature than the more ancient Egyptian because of the infamous burning of the Native American books. But the little that does survive shows that the Mayans, like the Egyptians before them, were largely preoccupied with earthly matters such as agriculture and commerce.[45]

Evidently there was some class mobility, well documented in the case of Egypt. In Mesoamerica, prosperous commoners also lived very well. Their masonry houses are found clustered with those of the nobility in the Yucatan.[46] But Garza warns against extrapolating modern capitalist market relationships from the Mayan economy:

> Some authors who emphasize the similarities between the Maya markets and modern business seem to believe that the economic norms of cap-italist countries have a base in natural laws and for this reason must be universal.[47]

Often temples were placed at the summit of the pyramid, just as houses had been built on top of masonry platforms. It is believed the temples were stone copies of pole and thatch homes. For example, in the Puuc style the stone temple facades resembled the design of the tied twig walls of the Maya house.[48] The tendency of early stone architecture to imitate wood or reed construction was also seen in early Egypt. In Zozer's pyramid complex at Saqqara, stone pillars were carved in the shape of the bundles of papyrus or the palm trees that had been used as supports in the palaces of that time.

Similarities

Many of the features of the Egyptian pyramids are also found in pyramids of Mesoamerica. At Uxmal the pyramid complex was enclosed by a wall as were those of Egypt. Chichen Itza was also a walled city of 30 square km with 7 paved roads, or sacheob, several km long connecting important sites. The paved road between Uxmal and Kabah was 18 km long.[49] These roads, or sacheob, resemble the Egyptian pyramid causeways. Of course the geography was different. African use of the Nile as a river road made land connections less crucial. However, in Kush, roads were important because the cararacts interrupted river travel. Roads were needed for donkey caravans and com-munications between the towns of ancient Kush.

Astronomy and the Calendar

In both Mesoamerican and African pyramid complexes, astronomical orientation played an important role. Carter described Chichen Itza as a mile of
axial geometry anchored by huge pyramids. This tendency spanned the various periods of Mexican cultures, from La Venta to Tenochtitlan. In
Teotihuacan the huge plateau allowed an overall axial order.[50] At other sites of
more difficult terrain, the individual buildings were still laid out on a North-
South complex. Uaxactun, near Peten, gives a line of sight for the March 21
and Sept. 21 equinoxes and for the winter and summer solstices.[51] See Figure
10. For El Tigre at Mirador, about the time of the vernal equinox (March 21),
Jupiter, Mercury, Mars and Saturn all seem to rise out of the top of the Danta
pyramid.[52]

It was natural that both the Mesoamerican and Nile River civilizations, as
efficient agricultural societies, had developed scientific calendars. Common
to all agricultural societies, close attention was paid to the solar and lunar
cycles. In Mesoamerica special attention was also given to the Venus cycle
which helped shape their calendar. Unlike the classical Greeks, the Maya
knew that the Morning and Evening Stars were the same heavenly body
(Venus). The Mesoamericans calculated that an 8-year solar cycle equalled a
5-year Venus cycle, as shown in the Dresden and Grolier Codices.[53] Although

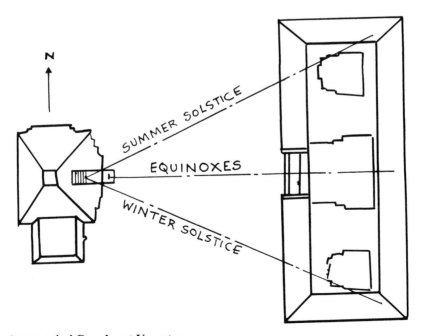

Astronomical Complex at Uaxactun

the Maya knew the solar year was a little over 365 days, they also made extensive use of a 260 day cycle[54] which had no parallel in the Egyptian calendar.

The ancient Egyptians had studied all the visible constellations in developing their star clocks. A different star was chosen every 10 days (the Egyptian week) as the new decan star to mark the last hour of night. The modern time measurement of 12 hours of day and 12 hours of night measurement had its origin in ancient Egypt. They had also developed a constant civil calendar of 365 days.[55] Of course the Egyptian calendar, with an early development date of − 4241[56] was far more ancient than that of Mesoamerica.

Mathematics was also highly developed both in Central America and Egypt of the Pharaohs. But the Egyptian number system was additive, base 10, made extensive use of fractions and did not have a symbol for zero. The Mesoamerican system used base 20, was positional, was first to invent a symbol for zero but as far as we know, did not use fractions. The scarcity of written records from Central America, a sad result of the terrible Spanish order to burn all Native American books, leaves us without detailed information about the mathematics. But Lambert, McLaughlin and McLaughlin have shown that Maya arithmetic is readily adaptable to operations of multiplication and division as well as the simpler addition and subtraction operation.[57]

Egyptian and Mesoamerican writing were each rooted in their own separate cultures and iconography. It is not known if the first use of paper in Mesoamerica received an impulse from Africans who were already familiar with papyrus writing materials. Several plant materials were used by the Maya to make "paper." The ever useful maguey cactus was used, also the amatl tree from which "amate" was made. Material from the tree was soaked, washed, pounded, cut into small pieces and pounded again, a process not too different from the making of papyri.[58]

Differences

Some of the differences between American and Egyptian pyramids have already been noted. Some other differences are more apparent than real. In this category are the differences in time and function. It is true that the famous Egyptian pyramids were built before the year − 2000 and the Classic period of Maya pyramids came after 300. But the Kushite revival of pyramids c − 700 coincides with the construction of the early Olmec pyramids at La Venta.

Egyptian pyramids were conceived as tombs, thus played a very important part in the Egyptian religion. Admittedly the American pyramids also were central to religious practice. However it is argued that they were not tombs and served some other function. The famous burial at Palenque proves that at least some pyramids also served as tombs in America. Coe goes even further to say, "The function of Maya pyramids as funerary monuments thus harks back to pre-classic times."[59]

No doubt there were differences in the precise religious function of African and American pyramids, but that is not germane to this discussion because no claims have been made as to identity of function. Also no claims have been made as to identity of composition or construction methods. In fact the Mesoamerican made extensive use of small stones, cement and stucco whereas the Egyptians used much larger stones and made only sparing use of mortar.

Conclusion

Many similarities of African and Mesoamerican pyramid complexes have been outlined above. In view of the absence of any factors which preclude African influence on the early American pyramid builders, and the evidence for an early, significant, African presence in Mesoamerica, this question must remain open for further study. This author is convinced that a definitive answer to this question still lies hidden in private collections or buried in the soil of Central America. It requires setting aside all prejudice and diverting money to research and away from weapons of destruction to free up adequate funds for this most important archaeological work.

Notes

1. W.E.B. DuBois, *The World and Africa*, N.Y.: Viking, 1946, p. 99

2. Norman F. Carver, *Silent Cities*, Tokyo: Shokokusha, 1966, p. 105

3. Sylvanus G. Morley and George W. Brainerd, revised by Robert J. Sharer, *The Ancient Maya*, Stanford: Stanford U., 1983, p. 5

4. Ivan Van Sertima, *Nile Valley Civilizations*, Rutgers: Journal of African Civilizations, 1985, p. 244

5. Emilio Harth-Terre, *Formas Espaciales Precolombinos, La piramide en la arquitectura costena del Peru*, Lima: pp. 4, 17

6. John Hemming, *Monuments of the Incas*, Boston: Little, Brown, 1982, p. 26

7. J. Eric Thompson, *Mexico Before Cortez*, N.Y.: Scribners, 1933, p. 286

8. Muriel P. Weaver, *The Aztecs, Maya and their Predecessors*, N.Y.: Academic Press, 1981, pp. 523

9. Morley, Brainerd and Sharer, op. cit., p. 53

10. Ivan Van Sertima, *They Came Before Columbus*, New York: Random House, 1976, pp. 30-31

11. Weaver, op. cit., p. 244

12. Silvia Garza Tarazona and Edward Kurjack Basco, *Atlas Arqueologico del Estado Yucatan*, Mexico: INAH, 1980, pp. 77-78

13. Weaver, op. cit., p. 204

14. Flinders Petrie, *Ancient Weights and Measurements*, London: University College, 1926, p. 42, par. 95

15. I.E.S. Edwards, *The Pyramids of Egypt*, Penguin, 1947, 1976, p. 47

16. Ibid, p. 39

17. Ibid, pp. 56-57

18. Ahmed Fakhry, *The Pyramids*, Chicago: University of Chicago, 1961, 1969, pp. 68-70

19. I.E.S. Edwards, op. cit., p. 71

20. Fakhry, op. cit., pp. 15-16

21. Ibid, pp. 106-09

22. Ibid, p. 115

23. Howard Eves, *An Introduction to the History of Mathematics*, New York: Holt, Rinehart, Winston, 1964, 1969, p. 37

24. Fakhry, op. cit., p. 171

25. I.E. Smith, op. cit., p. 246

26. Fakhry, op. cit., pp. 230-231

27. Somers Clarke and R. Engelbach, *Ancient Egyptian Masonry*, London: Oxford University Press, 1930, p. 76

28. Fakhry, op. cit., p. 241

29. A.J. Arkell, *A History of the Sudan*, London: Athlone, 1955, p. 132

30. Ivan Van Sertima, *They Came Before Columbus*, pp. 30-33

31. Richard A. Diehl, "Olmec Architecture, A Comparison of San Lorenzo and La Venta," *"The Olmec and their Neighbors*, Chicago: University of Chicago, 1981, pp. 69 ff

32. Michael D. Coe, *Mexico*, London: Thames and Hudson, 1962, p. 85

33. Jacques Soustelle, *The Olmecs*, New York: Doubleday, 1984, p. 33

34. Weaver, op. cit., p. 74

35. Ibid, p. 125

36. Michael D. Coe, *America's First Civilization*, New York: American Heritage, 1968

37. J. Eric Thompson, *Mexico Before Cortez*, New York: Scribners, 1933, p. 254

38. Andrews, op. cit., p. 11

39. Ibid, p. 72

40. Garza and Kurjack, op. cit., p. 45

41. Van Sertima, *They Came Before Columbus*, pp. 31-32

42. Andrews, op. cit., p. 73

43. Fakhry, op. cit., p. 14

44. Andrews, op. cit., p. 30

45. Garza, op. cit., p. 83

46. Ralph L. Roys, *Indian Background of Colonial Yucatan*, Washington: Carnegie Institution of Washington, 1943

47. Garza, op. cit., p. 79 [My literal translation—B.L.]

48. Carver, op. cit., p. 171

49. Garza, op. cit., p. 25

50. Carver, op. cit., p. 10

51. Andrew, op. cit., p. 71

52. Norman Hammond, "The Emergence of Maya Civilization," Scientific American, August, 1986, p. 113

53. Coe, *The Maya*, p. 160

54. Floyd G. Lounsbury, "Maya Numeration, Computation and Calendrical Astronomy," *Dictionary of Scientific Biography*, p. 760

55. Richard A. Parker, "Egyptian Astronomy, Astrology and Calendrical Reckoning," *Dictionary of Scientific Biography*, pp. 707-11

56. Carl Boyer, *A History of Mathematics*, New York: Wiley, p. 683

57. Joseph B. Lambert, Barbara Ownbey-McLaughlin, and Charles D. McLaughlin, "Maya Arithmetic," *American Scientist* Cambridge: Gallinger, May-June, 1980, p. 250

58. Hans Lenx, "La Elaboracion del Papel Indigena, *"Esplendor del Mexico Antiguo*, Mexico: Centra de Investigaciones Antropologicas de Mexico, 1959

59. Michael E. Coe, *The Maya*, London: Thames and Hudson, 1966, 1984, p. 52

LEO WIENER—A PLEA FOR RE-EXAMINATION

David J.M. Muffett

There can be no more fitting a place for this paper to be delivered than here in Boston, for its subject, who, I am convinced will come to be recognised as an Africanist—though I detest the word—of epochal stature, spent the greater part of his scholarly life working either on the faculties of Boston University or of Harvard.

Wiener's life spans the whole period of modern Western involvement with Africa. A scant thirty years before he was born, the Lander brothers had finally solved the riddle of the Niger, and in the very year itself, the search for the Nile was under way. A migration of Americans of African descent had also begun to make its mark on the Continent, with the movement of the Maroons from Nova Scotia to Freetown and with the U.S. recognition of Liberia in 1862.

But it was to be Wiener's lot to etch out the background for the examination of a migration from East to West, one which had taken place a great deal earlier, and which was a great deal more remarkable and much, much more controversial, namely that of Blacks from Africa to the Americas perhaps hundreds of years before the arrival of Columbus. His attempt was to bring him something less than the recognition to which his scholarship entitled him.

Leo Wiener was a man of Shavian ideals, endowed with an intellect (and an iconoclasm) which was Shavian as well. It is, however, not without a certain wry irony that his interest in pre-Columbian contacts between Africa and the Western Hemisphere, and the hypotheses to which this interest gave rise, seem to have run diametrically counter to the views which his wife held as to African or Black capabilities. Who can say, indeed, whether the basis of his quest for knowledge did not have its seeds in this dichotomy of domestic intellectuality.

Leo Wiener was born in Bailystock, in what is now North Eastern Poland, but which at that time was White Russia, on 26 July 1862. He was the son of a school teacher, Solomon, and his wife Freda (Rabinowicz) Wiener. He died of a stroke in Belmont Mass. on 12 December 1939 at the age of 77, having lived the last seven years as a semi-invalid subsequent to an auto accident in 1932.

Wiener's education was a good one, ranging from High School (Gymnasia) in Minsk and Warsaw, where he displayed an unusual aptitude for languages, to a brief (though unsatisfactory) medical education at the University of Warsaw (1880), followed by two years spent at the Berlin Polytechnicum which he left in 1882.

In that year he emigrated to Central America, where a somewhat idealistic endeavour to found a socialist and vegetarian commune proved abortive, and the end of the year found Wiener almost destitute in New Orleans where he worked as a floor sweeper and cotton baler in a factory. From New Orleans, he drifted West, still employed in menial occupations.

In 1883 however he obtained a teaching post in the rural school system of Odessa Mo. Then, from 1884-1892 he taught Greek, Latin and Math at Kansas City High, later moving to an appointment as an Assistant Professor of Germanic and Romance Languages at the University of Missouri at Columbia, Mo. In 1893 he married Bertha Kahn, a daughter of Henry Kahn, a department store owner from St. Joseph, Mo. by whom he had four children, one of whom, the eldest, was Norbert Wiener, an infant prodigy who obtained his Ph.D. from Harvard at the age of 18 and then went on to become famous as the mathematician and founder of the science of cybernetics.

It was at Columbia, Mo. that Wiener met and became friendly with W. Benjamin Smith, who shared the boarding house in which some of the Faculty, including the Wieners, lodged. He was "a particular crony . . . and later taught mathematics at Tulane . . ." He was also

> an unreconstructed rebel (who) . . . published a pseudo-learned book on the inferiority of the Negro, and that was too much for my Father's liberalism and for his respect for facts . . . it was on this issue that (Smith's) friendship with my father broke up many years later.[1]

This liberalism, however, did not extend to Wiener's wife, who was of Jewish extraction in all but the fact that her grandmother was not Jewish. She belonged to a family named Ellinger which had pretensions to Southern gentility.

Mrs. Wiener was an out and out bigot.

> My mother's attitude towards the Jews and all unpopular groups was different (from my Father's). Scarcely a day went by in which we did not hear some remark about the gluttony of the Jews or the bigotry of the Irish or the laziness of the Negroes.[2]

Both parents cooperated to this extent, however. They concealed from Norbert the facts of his Jewish ancentry until he was in his middle teens and even then he only found out by accident.

In 1895 Weiner left the University of Missouri consequent on a departmental reorganization and a disagreement with his employers not unconnected with political nepotism in academic appointments.

During 1895/6 he taught languages at Boston University and at the New England Conservatory of Music. At Boston he became acquainted with Prof. F.J. Child of Harvard, whom he assisted in tracing Scottish ballads through Southern Slavic languages and then, through him, later met Prof. A.C. Coolidge, to whose influence he owed his appointment in 1896 as an instructor in Slavic Languages and Literature at Harvard, where he taught Russian, Polish and Old Church Slavonic. This appointment was the first such academic post in America.

Wiener remained at Harvard until 1930, rising through successive academic promotions to full professor and Head of the Department of Slavic Languages in 1911. On his retirement in 1930, he became Professor Emeritus.

He was a small, stolidly built man, quick both in his physical movements and his intellectual pursuits. Somewhat dogmatic and unconventional, he regarded his vast knowledge of language merely as a necessary tool for a cultural historian, in which role he most clearly saw himself.

As the Dictionary of American Biography remarks:

> His broad knowledge, industrious research, and scholarly enthusiasm were, to some extent counterbalanced by too great reliance on intuitive decision and too little patience with the formalities of scholarly discipline; many of his conclusions may not, in the final analysis, be accepted by the scholarly world. Nonetheless, the great body of pertinent and provoking material assembled by Wiener, and more particularly his role as the pioneer of Slavic Studies in America, lend undoubted significance to his career.[3]

Wiener's greatest scholastic achievement must inevitably remain the monumental 24 volume translation, which he also edited, of the complete works of Tolstoy (Boston, D. Estes, 1904-5, Limited ed. of 1000 copies), but no mean accomplishments also were his other contributions to scholarship, amongst which are *A Commentary to the Germanic Laws and Medieval Documents* (Cambridge, H.U.P., 1915.). *Contributions Towards a History of Arabico-Gothic Culture* (New York, The Neale Publishing Co., 1917), *An Interpretation of the Russian People* (New York, McBride, Nast & Co., 1915.), *A History of Yiddish Literature* (New York, Scribner, 1899), *Anthology of Russian Literature* (Putnam, New York & London, 1920-3), and *A History of the Contemporary Russian Drama* (Boston, Little Brown, 1924). He also was an extensive contributor to *Webster's New International Dictionary*—and its advisor on Slavic pronunciation—as well as contributing to a wide variety of American, British, French, German, and Russian philological publications and journals.

His scholarship was thus far-ranging, his inquisitiveness pronounced and his embrace, as only a sampling of his work immediately establishes, was positively encyclopaedic in the enormous sweep of the supportive detail which he habitually applied.

It was, however the scholarship of another age, even of another culture; prolix, unstructured and undisciplined by modern American standards and lacking any identifiable frame of reference; making no pretence at all at any close or controlled analysis. Wiener was perfectly happy discussing the background, antecedents or interrelations of a hypothesis for forty-five or more pages before he even got around to stating it. In this respect of course, he not only mirrored the scholarship of his time, but also, to some extent, reflected the continuing trend of that of modern Europe in its less surgically incisive, more diffuse and less formally structured approach than that appreciated in the Western Hemisphere.

Wiener's (and Europe's) scholarship seems broader, more easy going, and less self consciously rigorous. In some respects also, it seems "happier"!

Between 1919, and 1922 Wiener published a three volume work *Africa and the Discovery of America* and in 1926 followed this up with a related volume on *Mayan and Mexican Origins*. It is to the first of these works that this paper intends primarily to apply itself, although there is an interesting similarity in respect to the appearance of all of them.

In spite of the Professor's wide ranging contacts with several major publishing houses, and in spite of his eminence as a Head of a Department at Harvard, no publisher would undertake the publication of any of these volumes. Eventually, *Africa and the Discovery of America* was printed with the aid of a private Bostonian benefactor, by Innes and Sons, Philadelphia. *Mayan and Mexican Origins* was similarly printed in Cambridge.

When volume I of *Africa and the discovery of America* was issued, it created quite a stir. *The New York Times* gave it a review of over 53 column inches exclusive of reproduced illustrations. Clearly, the reviewer was impressed:—

> That Negroes from the Northwestern coast of Africa crossed the Atlantic and landed in America an indefinite number of years before Christopher Columbus' voyage of discovery in 1492 is the arresting declaration made by Leo Wiener, Professor of Slavic Languages and Literature at Harvard University, in his most recent work, the first volume of which has just been published. ... *Africa and the Discovery of America* will be a bombshell to others than historians; it will doubtless be the father of many a debate among etymologists and archaeologists; for the acceptance of Professor Wiener's theory would be tantamount to the corollary that a great part of American archeology is builded (sic) upon the quicksand of fallacy.[4]

The reviewer added that Wiener's reputation was such that the book should be assured of "an attentive and respectful hearing."[5]

That having been said however, much of the review was then devoted to "ribbing" Wiener for the tenacity of his adherence to his convictions, though this ribbing is always circumspect and even seems to be tempered with a certain awe at the massive scholarship which the author aduces in support of his contentions.

The review of Volume II, published on 22 October 1922, was also of similar length. Again, the initial reaction was laudatory. "(The work of Professor Wiener) promises to be, when completed, a truly monumental piece of research." The review continues:

> The proof of Professor Wiener's contention (that African immigration ante-dated Columbus) . . . rests largely on philological evidence—evidence which undoubtedly must be given full weight in view of his remarkable knowledge and grasp of linguistic science.
>
> The case however relies on a great deal more than philology . . .

The reviewer, Austin Hay, then went on to observe

> When we look at the map and note the distance between the Guinea Coast of Africa, which the Mandingos inhabited, and the nearest point on the South American continent—Cape St. Roque, Brazil—is considerably less than the distance between (Europe) and North America and also less than the distance traversed by Columbus on his first voyage, there appears to be little reason why venturesome negro traders should not have crossed the Atlantic.

The review concluded with a summation which may contain within it much of the answer to why Weiner's work was so slightly regarded thereafter. It also injected a perfectly justifiable note of criticism, the substance of which has already been touched upon here.

> The importance of Professor Wiener's work will be readily appreciated, not only by historians but . . . by students of the native civilization of America. Nevertheless, the fact remains that Columbus was the discoverer of America, for it was the result of his labor that the New World was opened up by the people of old. For this reason Professor Wiener is scarcely justified in speaking of the "so called" discovery of America by Columbus. The fact that African negroes possibly did visit and trade with America in pre-Columbia days is of only minor importance from the stand point of the history of exploration. . . .

Justifiably, the reviewer then adds:

> Before Professor Wiener concludes his work it is hoped that he will gather together his results in a clear summary of the whole case. He pours forth his knowledge so copiously that he appears to be somewhat unmindful of arrangement. . . .[6]

There the matter rested. A diligent search has failed to uncover any review at all of the third volume. Was this due to the papers' disillusionment with the scope of the work and the repetitive nature of several parts of the volumes? Or was it due to outside pressure from interest groups?

Whatever was the case, nothing further happened in regard to Wiener's work apart from the appearance of a brief (and almost equally unremarked) little pamphlet relating to it, for almost fifty years.[7]

Clearly, however, enormous relevance and validity was then given to his theories by the experiments in trans-Atlantic passage which were undertaken in the late sixties by Thor Heyerdahl, and by the failure of his *Ra I* expedition and the success of *Ra II*.

Indeed, to me, *Ra I*'s failure was probably the more significant in terms of supportive theory than was the success of the second venture, and I am compelled therefore to make some reference to it.

Ra I was constructed by Buduma boat builders from Lake Chad. They are a people with whom I have had some aquaintance, and Heyerdahl perceived them as being the most readily available sucessors to the Nile Valley boat builders of Pharaonic times.

The Chad lake, however, though large is also shallow, and the Buduma boats have frequently to be pushed—from behind. Gradually, therefore, a pattern évolved in which the stern was cut square, or else gently rounded, while the prow still follows closely the toomb frescoes of the earlier age in Egypt. Heyerdahl demanded a *Ra I* with a high stern, and the Buduma builders sought to oblige him. Unfortunately, their technology was unequal to the task, and their new-pattern stern disintegrated under the stress of the crossing, which had to be abandoned some way short of Barbados. Heyerdahl then tried again.

The second attempt used the boat building skills of the Aymara Indians in Peru's Lake Titicaca. These are the people (with others) whom Heyerdahl regards as stemming from the Nilotic tradition. Moreover, their boats though relatively much smaller, match the Nilotic pattern precisely both as to prow and stern. Four Aymara boat-builders were therefore flown to Cairo, and it was their boat which crossed successfully.[8]

Wiener makes no attempt to link his theory of African emigration with any Nilotic Civilization. His thesis is concerned with the period a century, or at the most three hundred years before Columbus. Say from 1100 A.D. onwards. Yet clearly, Heyerdahl and Wiener are not incompatible. There is, in fact, an innate acceptability in placing the onset of African exploration much further back than Wiener sets it.

By doing so, also, a puzzling phenomenon which he does not touch upon at all, but which has exercised scholars for close on a century, is at once accommodated and explained.

Since the days of Joel Chandler Harris at least, and, in fact from days still earlier, scholars concerned with the Amazon Valley in general and the Tupi Indians in particular (and in fact, also with the generality of "Red-men") have noted the occurrence of animal stories of the "Bear Rabbit" pattern as being entrenched in indigenous American folklore.

In fact their existence has led to sharp and even acerbic disagreement amongst distinguished folklorists and anthropologists which has persisted to the present day.

As late as 1956, even so eminent an authority as R.M. Dorson was stating

> The first declaration to make is that this body of tales (i.e. those subsequently contained in his two volume work *American Negro Folktales*) does not come from Africa.[9]

Much earlier, however, the same view was advanced by Professor J.W. Powell of the Smithsonian Institution. Harris quotes him as being disinclined to give credence to the African theory of origin for the animal tales in that he himself had identified some of the *Uncle Remus* stories "in a number of different languages and in various modified forms" among the North American Indians and therefore was of the opinion "that they are borrowed by the negroes from the red-men."[10]

At about the same time that Harris was reporting Powell's views, however, H.H. Smith[11] who had clearly been in correspondence with him for some time, also noted, apparently in a personal letter to Harris, that

> It is interesting to find a story from Upper Egypt (that of the fox who pretended to be dead) identical with an Amazonian story and strongly resembling one found by you (Harris) among the Negroes . . .[12]

He then continues:—

> Varnhagen the Brazilian historian[13] (now Visconde de Rio Branco), tried to prove a relationship between the ancient Egyptians, or other Turanian stock, and the Tupi Indians. His theory rested on rather a slender basis, yet it must be confessed that he had one or two strong points.[14]

It can thus be reasonably argued that data arrived at from study of folklore, which neither Wiener nor Heyerdahl appear to have considered at all, may well serve to reinforce the theories which both of them have advanced. It is also not unworthy of note that Varnhagen was advancing these same theories a good 70 years before Wiener and a hundred and twenty before Heyerdahl finally put them to the test.

Thus it is that Wiener is a link with Heyerdahl in the 1970's, Harris and Smith in the 1880's and Varnhagen in the 1850's.[15] Such a link and those who came before it, more than merit a searching re-examination.

If Varnhagen is right, then the extraordinary circumstance of animal etc. folktales of an almost incredible similarity existing both on the African and

American continents prior to any substantial historical conviction of contact between them is completely explained.

So are such variations as exist between the Amazonian, Red Indian, and Plantation *corpora*. The first two would represent an injection dating from any time from about 100 years B.C., re-inforced, possibly, if Wiener is correct, by an almost continuous flow up to the 14th or even 15th century. The second would represent another injection, this time fully documented and dating broadly from the middle of the seventeenth century to the first two or three decades of the nineteenth.

Since, however, the origins of both stemmed at least in part from the same source, namely the ancient civilizations of the upper Nile Valley, it would hardly be remarkable if, whilst retaining the central features, they showed considerable divergence as to detail and emphasis. This is precisely what they do do, and the divergence is just as supportive in this case as is that of the differences in capability between Heyerdahl's boat builders, one set from Chad and the other from Titicaca.

Norbert Wiener described his father as

"a man . . . ready to defy the Almighty Jehovah himself . . ."[16] *Africa and the Discovery of America* reflects much of this attitude. His contemporaries clearly regarded some of his scholarship as spurious. Yet the enormous grasp of mind which he brought to his endeavours, his huge intellectual reach and the vast detail of the evidence on which he draws, embracing linguistics, art, artifacts, cultigens, totemism, burial customs, etc., etc., etc., almost *ad infinitum*, all merit a new examination in the light of the purely pragmatic confirmation which Heyerdahl's work now lends to his hypotheses, and the confirmation—at least in part—which the scholarship of my colleagues will add to its validity.

No one should claim that Wiener was right in all his assumptions but it is doubtful, nowadays, if any one single scholar has the competence to criticise his work in its entirety. Yet that it should be the subject of a searching re-examination on the basis of an interdisciplinary approach is the plea which this paper endeavours to advance. Too long has what Wiener wrote been buried in the archives. It is time now to bring it into the open and into the full glare of scholarly and critical re-evaluation.

An added compulsion, if such is needed, has been provided by the discoveries of the Smithsonian Institution's archeologists in 1975 and by those of other researchers in Mexico and Texas. On these, and on other evidence that Africans did succeed in making the ocean passage several hundred years before Columbus, my colleagues on this panel will address you in terms far more erudite and explicit than I myself could ever hope for.

What the *effect* of these incursions was on the societies with which they came in contact will, I suggest, be exercising scholars for years, maybe decades, to come, and in the pursuit of those answers it is my conviction that they will find themselves giving pride of place in pre-eminence and honor to the name of Leo Wiener.

Notes

1. Norbert Wiener *ExProdigy: My Childhood and Youth*: M.I.T. Press, 1953, pp. 28, 29.
2. *Op. cit.* p. 146.
3. *D.A.B.* Vol. II. Suppl. One and Two. To this same source the writer is indebted for details of Wiener's career, much of which is also drawn from Norbert Wiener *op. cit.*
4. *New York Times* Aug. 29, 1920, III, 18:1.
5. *Ibid.*
6. *The Dark Race in the Dawn*; Kathryn M. Johnson, William-Frederick Press New York, 1948. This is a small booklet of sixteen pages. I am, however deeply indebted to it and to Ms. Johnson for sparking my own interest in Wiener's work.
7. In 1971, Wiener's three volumes were reprinted by the Kraus Reprint Co., New York.
8. Several accounts of this expedition have appeared. The earliest can be found in *Nat. Geographic*, Jan. 1971. also the documentary film: *The Ra Expeditions*, nominated for an "Oscar" as the best documentary film of 1972. Heyerdahl's book, *The Ra Expeditions*, was published in 1971 by G. Allen & Unwin, London and can currently readily be found in paperback.
9. Published by Harvard University Press in 1956 (in part) and Indiana University Press (Bloomington) in 1958.
10. *Uncle Remus* (Introduction) *op. cit.* p. IX.
11. Author of *Brazil: The Amazons and the Coast*: Scribner, New York, 1879.
12. Introduction to *Uncle Remus, His Songs and his Sayings* by J.C. Harris; Appleton & Co. New York. Edition of 1899 p. XII. Note, the same introduction and this statement, can be found in earlier editions also.
13. Author of *Historia Geral Do Brazil*: Rio de Janero 1854-57. Francisco Adolfo de Varnhagen, 1816-1878.
14. *Uncle Remus op. cit.* p. XII.
15. For further discussion of this point, see Muffett D.M.J., "Uncle Remus was a Hausaman?," *Southern Folklore Quarterly*, Gainesville, Vol. 39, No. 2, June, 1975.
16. Norbert Wiener, *op. cit.*, p. 26.

FIRST REVIEW OF LEO WIENER

Africa and the Discovery of America. Volume I. By Leo Wiener, Professor of Slavic Languages and Literatures at Harvard University. Innes & Sons, Philadelphia, Pa., 1920. Pp. i-xix, 1-290. Reviewer: Phillips Barry, A.M., S.T.B.

The present volume is the first of a series in which Professor Wiener will show that Arabicised Negroes, chiefly Mandingoes, brought to America as slaves, profoundly influenced the culture of the Indians, and were an important, if not always direct factor in establishing the *modus vivendi* between the Indians and the Europeans, which made practicable the colonization of the New World.

The book is packed with valuable data, newly discovered, and brought together for the first time. It should be read slowly, and read through at least twice before judgement is passed on it. With the first reading comes a shock. One learns that the *Journal of the First Voyage*, and the *First Letter of Columbus* are literary frauds, though containing material which came from Columbus's own pen, and that tobacco, manioc, yams, sweet potatoes and peanuts are not gifts of the Indian to the European. Yet with a more intimate study of the subject matter, the conviction increases that the author has built upon the bed-rock of fact, and that his position is unassailable.

It is impossible, within the limits of a review, to do more than to emphasize the most important of his discoveries. In his studies of the *First Letter*, and of the *Journals* giving account of the first and the second voyages of Columbus, Professor Wiener seeks to determine how much testimony they give pertaining to Indian names and things, after the elimination of all that is not Indian. The non-Indian elements are of two sorts; the names of the Islands, and the words for "gold," etc. Columbus, dominated by the fixed idea, that, sailing westward, he would find a short cut to India, China and Japan, began with the first sight of land, to be engrossed with the task of identifying each newly discovered country with some island or district of the Far East, named on his maps. He was an ignorant man, though he knew Ptolemy and Marco Polo by heart, credulous, uncritical, not consciously dishonest, but unready to correct false impressions caused by his ignorance and gullibility. His notes, as may be seen from a reproduction of a page of his manuscripts (facing p. 38), were in an execrable hand. The forger of the *Journal of the First Voyage* was no puzzle expert, and made mistakes in deciphering scrawls. Thus, for example, he notes *Giaua min., i.e.,* Java minor, was read *Guanahin,* the same destined to

Reprinted from the *Journal of Negro History* (Vol. 5, Nọ. 3, July 1920).

masquerade as *Guanahani*, the Indian name of the first island sighted on October 12, 1492.

Perhaps the best specimen of such ghost-words in the *Journal* is the name *Carib*. This is nothing but Marco Polo's *Cambalu*, the capital of the Grand Khan, successively misread as Canibal, Caniba, Cariba. So also, "canoe" is a ghost-word, traced to a misreading of *scaphas* as *canoas* in the manuscript, or the Gothic text of the Latin version of the First Letter. It is interesting to learn that *maize*, in the forms *masa, maza*, utlimately from Portuguese *mararoca*, is the African name of Guinea corn. The transference of the name from Guinea corn to Indian corn, "rests on a misunderstanding of a passage in Peter Martyr's *First Decade*" (p. 123).

The question arises whether or not there had been a colony of Europeans, with African slaves in America, before the arrival of Columbus.

Fray Ramon Pane, Oviedo, and Las Casas give *conico* as the Indian word for "farm, plantation." This is clearly the Mandingo *kunke* "farm." The Indian word for "golo," according to the Journal entry for January 13, 1493, is *caona*. It is found also in the name of *Cacique Caonabo*, called in the *Journal of the Second Voyage* "master of mines,"—the name being explained in the Libretto as "lord of the house of gold." Now the words for "gold" in the Negro languages are mostly derived from Arabic *dinār*, which, through Hausa *zinaria*, and Pul *kanyera*, reaches Vei as *kani*. Evidently *canoa*, written also *guani*, is nothing but this Vei word. In "Cacique Caonabo," we have three Mande words in juxtaposition. *Cacique* is not far removed from *kuntigi*, Soso *kundi*, "chief,"—*caona*, that is *kani*, is "gold," and *boi*, Arabic *beii, bai*, is "house." The chance that three such words should be identical in the dissimilar languages of Africa and America, is *nil*. The words are African, though represented as belonging to the spoken language of the New World. Moreover, Ramon Pane, in the account he wrote for Columbus of the Indian religion, gives as Indian words, the Mande *toto*, "frog," and the Malinke *kobo*, "bug." What is more important, he imputes to the Indians, a knowledge of the terrible West African itch, or *craworaw*, which he calls by the supposed Indian name *caracaracol*. The critic faces a dilemma. Either Roman Pane lied, or he told the truth. Either he fabricated stories of Indians, which he drew from books or manuscript relations by Spanish and Portuguese traders, who were writing about Negroes in Africa, or there had been in Hispaniola, a pre-Columbian colony of European adventurers, with their African slaves, who taught the Indians the Negro words for "farm, gold, frog, bug, itch," etc., and also African folk-lore. No other hypothesis is possible.

The documentary and philological history of tobacco smoking and the cultivation of edible roots, shows additional convincing evidence of the influence of Africa on the culture of America in the colonial period. Columbus never saw the Indians smoking tobacco. According to the *Journal of the First Voyage*, on October 15, 1492, an Indian brought him a ball of earth and certain precious dried leaves. On November 16, two Spaniards reported that the Indians, carrying firebrands and leaves, used them to "take incense." In the *Journal of the Second Voyage*, Columbus (this part of the Journal is definitely ascribed to him by his son) writes of Indians spreading powder on a table, and sniffing it through a forked reed, thereby becoming intoxicated. Now the first account is suspiciously like a book-story of Oriental hashish-taking,—the second has no implication of smoking at all, while the third describes nothing but the process of taking a sternutatory. Indeed this last account is clearly based on a book account, in which there was a play on the Arabic words *tubbāq* "styptic" and *tabaq* "table." Ramon Pane, when he tells of Indians sniffing the powder, calls it *caboba*, a mere Italianisation of the Arabic *qasabah* "reed," transferring the name of the inhaler to the drug. Smoking tobacco through a forked reed of the sort described, has been proved by trial, to be impossible. As late as 1535, Oviedo is unable to tell a straightforward story of Indians smoking tobacco, but he adds the significant fact that the Negroes in the West *Indies* smoked and cultivated tobacco. Negroes, by the way were first allowed to come to America in 1501,—two years later, Ovando, the governor of Hispaniola complained that they joined with the Indians to make trouble. By 1545 "smoking had become fairly universal in America" (p. 127). It cannot be argued that half a century is too short a time for a new vice to become so widespread. Consider the case of banana culture. Oviedo says that the first bananas were introduced into America in 1516. Within twenty years, the fruit was universally cultivated, while the Spanish name *platano* has survived in a large number of derivatives in the Indian languages.

As far as the linguistic history of the tobacco-words in the Indian languages is concerned, it leads back to an eastern origin. In Arabic, *tubbāq* means "styptic." Tobacco leaves were used as a styptic by the Indians of Brazil in the sixteenth century. The Low Latin equivalent of the Arabic *tubbāq* "stypic," is *bitumen*, whence Portuguese *betume*, and French *betun, petun*. "The French traders," says Professor Wiener, "at the end of the sixteenth century, carried the word and the Brazilian brand of tobacco to Canada, and *petun* became imbedded in several Indian languages. The older Huron word for "tobacco" is derived from the Carib *yuli*, which itself is from a Mandingo word. Thus, while the Carib and Arawak influence is apparent in the direction from Florida, to the Huron country, the Brazilian influence proceeds up the St. Lawrence. The whole Atlantic triangle between these two converging lines was left uninfluenced by these two streams, and here, neither Carib nor Brazilian words for "tobacco," nor the moundbuilders' craft have been found. Here the "tobacco" words proceeded northward from Virginia, where the oldest form of the words is an abbreviated Span. *tobaco*, or Fr. *tabao* (p. 191). The Carib *yuli* "smoke," is found in Carib and Arawak, side by side with derivatives of Mande *tama, tawa*, which are also in the Algonkian languages. The fact that the Hurons, apparently the first Indians to plant tobacco, have no native word for the plant is significant. It shows that the Hurons learned to smoke from the Arawaks or Caribs, then already under Negro influence, and at a time prior to the introduction of the tobacco-plant into Canada by the French. When we consider, then, that tobacco is native to Africa, that *tubbāq* and *petun* are the ancestors of the Indian names for the weed, that by 1503, Negroes in large numbers were living in America, deserting their masters to join the Indians, that the Negroes in America smoked and raised tobacco, the conclusion is inescapable that tobacco smoking was discovered and taught by them to the Indians and the Europeans.

"The tobacco-pipe in America," says Professor Wiener, "began its career as a Mandingo amulet" (p. 184). This statement will distress the American archaeologists, but the arguments in support of it cannot be overcome. A counter-claim of pre-Columbian antiquity for pipes found in the mounds cannot be made, since it is so clearly shown that the mounds are not prehistoric, but were fortifications erected along the lines of communication from Florida to the Huron country, to protect the overland trade established in the beginning of the sixteenth century.

In the *Journal of the First Voyage*, we find mention of *ajes* and *niames*, as name of edible roots, but the account hopelessly confuses reports of yams, sweet potatoes and manioc. Neither yams nor sweet potatoes are native to America, and both bear in America, only African names. Oviedo indeed, says distinctly, that the *name* is "a foreign fruit, and not native to these Indies,"—also, that "it came with that evil lot of Negroes, . . . of whom there is a greater number than is necessary, on account of their rebellions" (pp. 203-4). Now in Africa the yam (Dioscorea), cultivated before the coming of the Europeans, is known by names derived from Arabic *arum* and *gambah, e.g.,* Ewe *adĕ, adže,* Mandingo *nyambe,* Malinke *nyeme ku,*—whence the supposed Indian names, *aje, age, niame, igname,* used indiscriminately of any edible roots. The African names of the manioc have come from Arabic *'uruq* "roots," notably in the Congo languages, *yōka, yēke, edioiko,* plural *madioka,* whence, as the plant was introduced into America, it was known there as *vuca, mandioca.* As to sweet potatoes and peanuts, the former were cultivated in Asia before the discovery of America, while the latter, mentioned by Ibn Batutah as an article of food in Africa, took to the New World, their African names *mandube, goober* and *pinder* (compare Mozambique *manduwe,* Basunde *nguba,* Nyombo *pinda*). Professor Wiener's conclusion is that manioc culture was taught to the Brazilian Indians before 1492 by Portuguese castaways, who knew of the economic importance of the plant in Africa, while the peanut, spreading north and south from the Antilles, may also have reached America a few years before Columbus.

The numerous full-page illustrations are extremely helpful in aiding the reader to a clear understanding of difficult points in the discussion.

The book is epoch-making. To all seekers of the truth, the coming of the second volume, in which Professor Wiener will deal exhaustively with the Negro element in Indian culture, will be an eagerly anticipated event.

Phillips Barry, A.M., S.T.B.
Cambridge Massachusetts

MANDINGA VOYAGES ACROSS THE ATLANTIC

Harold G. Lawrence (Kofi Wangara)

Two precise accounts of pre-Columbian West African expeditions across the Atlantic have survived. The older of these accounts appears in Al-'umari's fourteenth century *Masalik* and relates how a Mandinga emperor, after careful planning, launched two expeditions to discover the western limits of the Atlantic. These voyages which took place between 1307 and 1312 A.D. involved 2,400 ships, or *almadias*. One of the ship captains, after sailing for a lengthy period, returned to his home port to inform his emperor of the fleet's encounter with one of the Atlantic currents. After hearing this report, the emperor launched a second expedition and decided to lead it personally across the ocean. He and his companions were never heard from again. Almost 200 years later, the *Journals* of Christopher Columbus recorded the resumption of, or continuation of, these expeditions. We learn that West African merchant-marine fleets periodically left the Guinea Coast and sailed to the Middle Americas with gold and other merchandise. African merchants established trading stations in the Antilles and around the Gulf of Mexico.

From these colonies, Black people, specifically identified as Mandinga, introduced the West African gold trade and the art of alloying gold with copper and silver into the Americas. Gold, so alloyed, was named after the Mandinga province of Ghana from which the art originated. The African merchants in the Americas were Muslims and exhibited many Islamic customs; they also bore Islamic names and titles expressed in a Mandinga form. These African settlers attempted to name, or rename, areas they settled after important localities in West Africa which were under under the authority of the Mandinga emperors of Mali.

The cotton *almaizar*, or the art of making it, was also introduced into the Americas by West Africans. This and other cotton stuffs, made from the silk-cotton tree, were, as they were in Africa, sometimes used as currencies. Reports from Columbus and those who followed him specifically relate the American cotton weaving art to that of West Africa.

In a few words, we will show here that West Africans made several deliberate voyages to the Americas where they established trading colonies. The voyagers and the settlers can both be identified as Islamized Mandinga merchants who introduced the African gold and cotton trade to the Americas. Both tribal and

place names where Black populations settled in the Americas can be identified as Mandinga.

Al-'Umair's Report on Mandinga Atlantic Expeditions

When Mansa Kankan (Gonga) Musa, the most famous of the Mandinga
experors of Mali, stopped in Cairo on his way to Mecca in 1324, he reported
that his predecessors had launched two expeditions to discover the limits of
the Atlantic. Al-'umari, writing a few decades after Musa's visit, left the following notice of these voyages:

> "I asked the Sultan Musa," says Ibn Amir Hajib, "how it was that power
> came into his hands. 'We are,' he told me, 'from a house that transmits
> power by heritage. The ruler who preceded me would not believe that it
> was impossible to discover the limits of the neighboring sea; he wanted to
> find out and persisted in his plan. He had two hundred ships equipped and
> filled them with men, and others in the same number filled with gold,
> water and supplies in sufficient quantity to last for years. He told those
> who commanded them: return only when you have reached the extremity
> of the ocean, or when you have exhausted your food and water. They went
> away; their absence was long before any of them returned. Finally, a sole
> ship reappeared. We asked the captain about their adventures.'
>
> 'Prince,' he replied, 'we sailed for a long time, up to the moment when we
> encountered in mid-ocean something like a river with a violent current.
> My ship was last. The others sailed on, and gradually as each one entered
> this place, they disappeared and did not come back. We did not know
> what had happened to them. As for me, I returned to where I was and did
> not enter that current.'
>
> 'But the emperor did not want to believe him. He equipped two thousand
> vessels, a thousand for himself and the men who accompanied him, and a
> thousand for water and supplies. He conferred power on me and left with
> his companions on the ocean. This was the last time that I saw him and
> the others, and I remained absolute master of the empire.'"[1]

The monarch who preceded Mansa Musa was Abu Bakr II, known in
Mande dialects as Abubakari, Bubakari, or Bogari.[2] He either reigned from
1305 to 1307, or from 1310 to 1312, depending on whose chronology one holds
the most valid. At any rate, the expeditions reported by Al-'Umari would have
taken place in either 1307 or 1312. Although some scholars have questioned
the existence of Abubakari II by reinterpreting the basic sources from which
we determine the chronology of Mali kings, such opinions yet remain theoretical. Consequently, we will consider Abubakari II the legitimate pre-
decessor of Mansa Musa.[3]

From Al-'Umari's account of these Mandinga voyages, we can arrive at
several immediate conclusions. First, while planning the expeditions,

Abubakari could have drawn from all the geographical and scientific knowledge extant in his empire. This would include the experiences of the coastal ship builders, expert at building maritime craft, and the coastal seamen known to make extensive excursions on the high seas.[4] Secondly, the fact that this monarch launched such large expeditions and chose to accompany his men on one indicates that he was fairly certain of success. Thirdly, we note that one of the ship captains of the first attempt found no difficulty returning to his home port after an extended period on the high seas. And, finally, this same captain gave a fairly good description of one of the Atlantic currents in his report to the emperor. The "river with a violent current" encountered in "mid-ocean" could be one of these currents, all of which drive towards various landing points in the Middle Americas.

The Atlantic Currents

Ships leading due west from points along the Upper Guinea Coast after a few days sailing would inevitably pick up one of the Atlantic currents. Just which current would depend on the time of year and the distance from the African coast. The North Equatorial Current could be picked up by West African seamen "midway" between Africa and the Antilles, while one would have to be actually in the Americas before picking up the South Equatorial or the Caribbean [Antillean] Currents. Because of its geographical position the North Equatorial Current is more than likely the one described by Abubakari's ship captain.

Cortesão informs us that off Cape Verde in Senegal "the North Equatorial Current makes directly for the Antilles across the Atlantic. It attains its greatest volume and velocity during the season of the northern summer. When it enters the Caribbean Sea, driven by the force of the southeast tradewinds, it forms the Antilles [or Caribbean] Current which flows into the Gulf of Mexico."[5] The South Equatorial Current also joins the others when it enters the Caribbean Sea [see the following maps]. At any rate, they all provide natural "conveyors" for small boats on their way to landing points around the Caribbean Sea and the Gulf of Mexico. Muhammed Hamidullah, the Algerian scholar, believes that the Mali expedition had already reached the mouth of the Amazon River at the moment it encountered the current.[6] From the Al-'Umari account we note that the Mali expedition had "sailed for a long time" and that its "absence was long." This suggests that the voyage had already been at sea sufficiently long enough to make the 1,500 to 1,600 mile trip to the Americas. As Hamidullah has stated, the fleet could have reached the Caribbean by the time the captain decided to turn his ship around.

Ships leaving river ports along the Upper Guinea Coast, steering due west, would pass the Cape Verde Islands just north of latitude 10° N, and scientific tests have shown "that any floats drifting in the eastern Atlantic between

Movements of Atlantic Ocean Currents

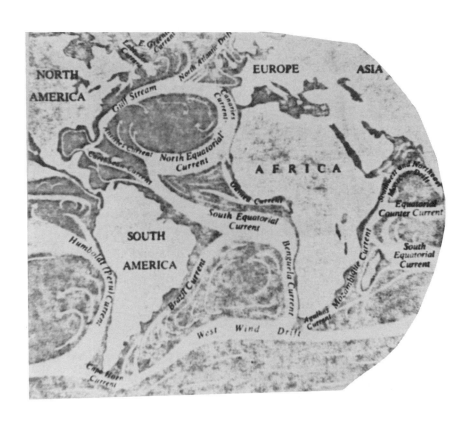

Names of Atlantic Ocean Currents

The North and South Equatorial Currents and the Caribbean and the Antillean Currents are the Atlantic surrents that would facilitate West African voyages to the Americas. The Caribbean and Antillean Currents are for the most part segments of the same oceanic stream.

latitude 10° N and the southern limits of the Sargasso Sea [20° N] are *irresistibly carried by the sea currents to the Antilles.*[7] From this, we conclude that if any of the 2,400 ships launched by Abubakari II stayed afloat they would have been swept automatically to the Antilles, or to other points bordering the Caribbean and the Gulf of Mexico.

Large Fleets of Almadias Were Not Uncommon to West Africa

An expedition of over 2,000 ships may appear an exaggeration, but the availability of such large fleets has often been reported in chronicles on West Africa. Al-Kati, the Timbuktu historian, informs us that Mansa Musa, while returning from his illustrious pilgrimage to Mecca in 1324, assembled a large number of *almadias* to transport his wives, members of the Qoreish family and their baggage from Timbuktu up the Niger to his capital.[8] The same chronicler further relates that in 1469 Sonni Ali, then emperor of Songhay, employed 400 of the same type craft which were part of his river navy to block his enemies' escape from Timbuktu when he laid seige to the city.[9] One hundred years after Ali's death, in 1591, Askia Ishaq, the last of the Songhay emperors, used close to 3,000 boats to evacuate Gao, his capital, in face of an invading Moroccan army. The *Tarikh el-Fettach* states:

> Four hundred kantas would suffice to transport the entire house of Askia, his baggage, his wives, his articles of exchange and his riches in three days. Besides these *kantas*, there are from Goima to Gadia, in regard to large *almadias*, a thousand boats belonging to Askia, without counting the *almadias* of the businessmen, those of Askia's daughters, and those of the inhabitants of the city. Finally the little *almadias*, which are found in the same strait reach, I believe, the figure of six or seven hundred.[10]

Although this impressive display of naval resources took place some 280 years after the Mali expedition, it gives a good account of the number of water craft along the Niger which would have been available to Mandinga emperors of the fourteenth century. Even as late as the eighteenth century, we hear of a "powerful shipowner in Sansanding" who controlled "the greater part of the canoes trading with Timbuktu."[11]

At any rate, the tribal-nations under Mali authority, along the Guinea Coast where it faces the Atlantic, were capable of supplying a like number of boats.[12] Two eighteenth century European observers noted the presence of large fleets along this coast. Both Barbot and Benezet reported that as many as 800 canoes left the Gold Coast [Modern Ghana] daily on fishing excursions.[13] At least one of the port towns in this area, Elmina, was to some extent controlled by the Mandinga when the Portuguese first arrived there in the fifteenth century. We conclude that 2,400 *almadias* was not an exceptionally large number for a well planned West African maritime venture, and that this number was not unusual for West African fleets.

Christopher Columbus' Account of West African Voyages

The second report of West African voyages to the Americas comes from the logs of Christopher Columbus. On his third voyage in 1498, he stopped at one of the Cape Verde Islands en route to the West Indies and while there he was informed by some of the people that West Africans were making maritime expeditions to the Americas. Las Casas, a personal friend of Columbus, who accompanied the Admiral on a later voyage, left a clear notice of these activities:

> Certain principal inhabitants of the island of Santiago came to see them and they say that to the southwest of the Island of Huego [Fogo, or Fuego] which is one of the Cape Verdes distance 12 leagues from this, may be seen an island, and that the King Don Juan [Dom Joäo II of Portugal] was greatly inclined to send to make discoveries to the southwest, and *that canoes had been found* which start from the coast of Guinea and navigate to the west with merchandise.[14]

West African seamen had either passed Brava, the most westerly of the Cape Verdes, which lies to the southwest of Fogo, approximately 500 miles off the Upper Guinea Coast, or had been *found* at some island in the Antilles, or South America, over 1,500 miles away. (See the following maps.) The fact that the African seamen carried *merchandise* indicates that their actions were certain and deliberate.

This precludes that the Portuguese must have known of some land in the Americas before Columbus' first voyage. They had either been there, or had been told about it. The king of Portugal would hardly wish to send expeditions to the tiny Island of Brava; other objectives to the southwest of Fogo are obvious. A number of researchers, including Elmer Merrill, the plant geographer, believe that the Portuguese had visisted western lands before Columbus.[15] Cartographic evidence as well as narratives and legends led Cortesäo to conclude that "the Antilles group of islands show in the 1424 Chart should be regarded as the first cartographical representation of Eastern America."[16] This would place the Portuguese presence in the Americas prior to the 1424 Chart's publication. The Andrea Biancho map of 1448 supports Cortesäo's conclusion. The map depicts what Biancho calls an "authentic island . . . distance 1500 miles from Cape Verde."[17] This island, far too large to represent any of the Cape Verdes, resembles in form and location the northeast corner of Brazil which is approximately the same distance from the Cape Verde Point in Senegal.

We recall that when Columbus took plans for his projected voyage to Por-

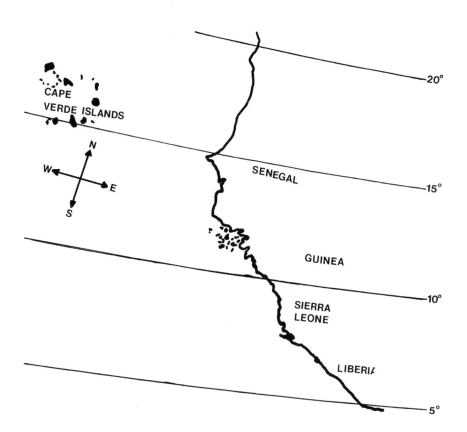

The Upper Guinea Coast and Cape Verde Islands

tugal in 1484 to gain financial support, the king told him, "I know all about that land, and it's mine."[18] King Dom Joäo II, probably the same monarch, a few years later would speak of *continental land*, not then known to Spain, to the south of the Antilles. Las Casas' report continues:

> The admiral [Columbus] says again that he wants to go south, as he believes . . . he will be able to find islands and lands; . . . and because he wants to know what was the meaning of King Dom Joäo of Portugal when he said that there was *tierra firma* [continental land] to the south; and for this reason he [Columbus] says that the King of Portugal had differences with the kings of Castille, which were settled when it was decided that the King of Portugal should have 370 leagues to the west, beyond the islands of the Azores and Cape Verdes, which belong to him . . . ; and he

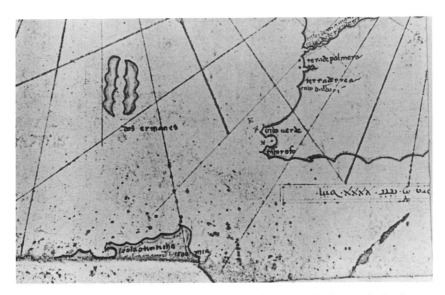

A portion of Andrea Biancho's Map of 1448 A.D. The inscription on the land mass represented in the lower left hand corner of the map reads "ixola otinticha xe longa aponente 1500 mia," which translates from the medaeval Italian into modern English as "Authentic island is distant 1500 miles to the west." This would be to the west of the Cape Verde point of the Upper Guinea coast. A tracing from an enlarged photograph of this "authentic island" gives a clearer representation of the inscription:

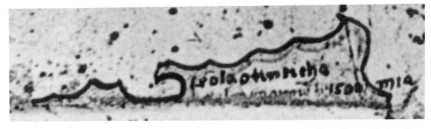

Although this land mass is drawn much closer to Cape Verde than Brazil actually is, the notation "1500 miles to the west" erases any doubts about its geographical position. The long stretch of coastline, drawn with great care, corresponds to the shape of the northeast corner of Brazil.

[Columbus] says that King Dom Joäo considered it certain that inside those limits that he was going to find many things and famous lands.[19]

The Portuguese were so certain that there were "famous lands" to the southwest of the Cape Verde Island that they were willing to make a treaty with Spain which would concede to Portugal all territory within the limits of 370 leagues [about 1,100 miles] to the west of those islands. Since Brava, the most westerly of the Cape Verdes, is some 500 miles off the West African mainland, the limits agreed upon by Portugal at the Tordesillas Treaty of 1494 adds an additional 1,100 miles to the 500 which totals some 1,600 nautical miles. This distance corresponds favorably with the "authentic island" represented on Biancho's map, which was later realized as the land of Brazil.[20] If African seamen had been sighted in the neighborhood of this "authentic island," then their presence on the northern shores of South America is documented for the fifteenth century. Again this agrees with Hamidullah's conclusion which placed the Abubakari expedition at the mouth of the Amazon River when it encountered "a river in the middle of the ocean."

In any case, Columbus, in his quest to reach continental land to the southwest, was convinced enough by what he had been told that he decided to follow the trail of the African seamen. He ordered his own course "laid to the way to the southwest, which is the route leading from those islands to the south, . . . because then he would be on a parallel with the lands of Sierra Leone and Cape Santa Ana in Guinea, . . . and after that, he would navigate . . . to the west, and from there [South America?] would go to this Española, in which way he would verify the said opinion of King Dom Joäo."[21]

The African Gold Trade in the Americas

Black seamen, who can be specifically identified as Mandinga, brought the West African gold trade to the Americas. This is established through African designations for gold, the West African method of alloying gold, its ceremonial as well as trade value and, more important, the identity of the Blacks who trafficked in it.

Upon reaching the Americas, Columbus was informed by the Indians of Hispaniola that boats carrying black men had arrived at this island. Thacher translates Las Casas:

> [Columbus] thought to investigate the report of the Indians of this Española who said that there had come to Española from the south and southeast, a black people who have the tops of their spears made of a metal they [the black men, or Indians] call 'quanin', of which he had sent samples to the Sovereigns to have them assayed, when it was found that of 32 parts, 18 were of gold, 6 of silver and 8 of copper.[22]

The *quanin* brought to Hispaniola by black men was a common West African gold alloy, know by the same name and bearing identical proportions of silver and copper. About 1275, Al-Quazwini, referring to the gold producing areas of West Africa, at that time under the authority of Mali, wrote that "[Ghana] is in the Land of Gold, the gold is named after it."[23] The *quanin*, recorded by the Spaniards, is the Arabico-Berber plural for *ghana*, which is *ghanin*. The initial phoneme *gh-* [Arabic ‏غ‎], is sometimes noted as *g-*, was generally recorded as *g-, ga-, go-, gu-*, and *gui-* by fourteenth and fifteenth century Spanish writers.[24] In some manuscripts relating to the Spanish Conquest, *guanin* also appears as *goanin, caona* and *guani*.[25] Here the initial *go-, ca-* and *gu-* sounds represent the Arabic ‏غ‎ or *gh-*.

The ancient West African words for gold, *ghana* and *ghanin*, as they were represented in Arabic, still survive in some Mande dialects. The Arabic ‏غ‎ , or *gh* is generally recorded as *k*.[26]

DIALECT	WORD	MEANING
Sarakole Soninké Gadsago	kane	gold
Vai Mende	kani	metal (gold/silver)
Kissi	kanie	gold
Kono	kanine	gold
Peul	kanne	gold

The older *g/k* sound has been replaced by *s/z* recently in some Mande language groups. As a result, the *g* and *k*, which are basically the same sounds, are interchangeable with *s* and *z*.[27] Thus we have other important Mande words for gold.[28]

DIALECT	WORD	MEANING
Mandinka, Dyula	sāni	gold, or purity
Malinké Khassonké	sano, or sanu	gold, or purity
Bambara	seni	gold, or purity

In these latter cases, the words for gold and purity have somehow become synonymous. The Modern Soso dialect may offer a clue to the origin of this phenomenon. Delafosse records:

xema, for gold

séni, for purity

[*x* is equal to *kh, gh, k*, or Spanish *jota*]

The Middle American *guanin* and its derivatives are the same as their West African counterparts which date back at least to the thirteenth century. When assayed in Spain, these *guanines* brought to Hispaniola by black men were found to have "18 parts gold, 6 of silver and 8 of copper." This method of alloying gold is typical to West Africa. Bosman, who spent fourteen years in Africa before 1705, noted that "gold is frequently mixed with a third part, and sometimes with half silver and copper." He added that this "artificial" gold was found all along the Guinea Coast.[29]

The custom of making spears and other armaments of gold and such alloys has a long tradition in West Africa. Such practices date back as far as the time of the Romans. Jobson, who visited the Gambia in 1620, relates that the Romans had a great desire "to search the south parts [West Africa], in regard they were thereunto invited by those *rich and golden armes, they found those blacke people to come against them withall, where of so many golden shields, were carried to their famous City.*"[30] This is the earliest known reference to the West African practice of making golden armaments. Later references were more explicit.

Al-Bakri's account of ancient Ghana states that when the emperor "gives audience to his people, to hear their griefs and remedy them, he is seated on a pavillion, around which are ranged ten horses comparisoned in golden quilts; behind him are *ten pages carrying shields and swords mounted in gold . . .*"[31] Although this report does not mention spears, or lances, specifically, we can assume that this weapon was treated in similar fashion. The report also does not state that silver and copper were alloyed with the gold of these weapons. Nonetheless, both silver and copper were worked throughout the empire. Al-Bakri's account continues, "The door of the pavillion is guarded by dogs of an excellent breed, who almost never leave the place where the king is found; *they wear gold and silver collars garnished with bells of the same metals.*"[32] From this passage, it appears that gold and silver were alloyed in the collars for the king's dogs. Copper, although not mentioned in this respect, was at the same time as a currency.[33]

Two fourteenth century reports describe the custom of displaying golden armaments, including spears and lances, at the emperor's court in Mali. One indicates that gold and silver were alloyed in their manufacture. Ibn Battuta, who visited Mali's capital in 1352, wrote of these ceremonial arms. "The armor-bearers," he tells us, "bring in magnificent arms-quivers of *gold and silver*, swords ornamented with gold and with golden scabbards, *gold and silver spears*, and crystal maces."[34] Al'Umari gives a similar description which reads that the Sultan *"has near him his arms which are all in gold, saber, spear, quiver, bow and arrows."*[35] These accounts were written a few decades after the two Mali expeditions of 1307/1312 whereupon large quantities of gold were carried. And since the emperor Abubakari II elected to accompany his men, it is more than likely that an impressive array of ceremonial arms would be taken along.

In Ashanti, where Mandinga contacts had existed at least as early as the fifteenth century, similar notices have been made. Dupuis, who visited Ashanti before 1824, recorded:

> Several cabaciers in waiting were decorated with massive gold breast plates, chains of the same metal, and solid lumps of rock-gold, of the weight, perhaps, of a pound or more each. The Royal messengers stood behind the sovereign, shouldering by the blades large crooked sabres, the emblems of their offices, and displaying in reversed hilts, *cased in thin gold sheathing*. In another position, at the back of the king's chair, a select few stood erect as guards, and were armed with common English *muskets in gold casing* . . .[36]

Over 500 years after the Mali expeditions, the custom of making gold, or gold-plated, armaments still prevailed in West Africa. By 1824, this tradition was nearly 2,000 years old. It is readily understandable why African nobility and African merchant seamen would introduce this custom to their colonies and clients in the Americas. The black merchant seamen who brought those spear points made of gold alloyed with silver and copper to Hispaniola were extending the African gold trade to early America.

Other Mandinga Designations for Gold Used in the Americas

Besides *guanin*, two other words were commonly used to designate fifteenth century American gold. Las Casas records *nucay*, or *nozay*, employed in San Salvador and other insular points, and *tuob* in some parts of Hispaniola.[37] All these terms have Mandinga, and possibly Arabic, affinities. The Mande *negé* [nuh-GHAY] and nexe [nuh-khuh] which means "metal" in general and "iron" in particular are also used to refer to "any kind of metal ornament, or jewelry."[38] In this respect, they are the same as the Antillean *nucay*, or *nozay*, where the *s/z* and *g/k* interchange is apparent. The -*c*-[k], in this case, is the same as -*z*-. *Tuob* can also be identified with the West African gold trade. Jeffreys records that a small, red and black bean, known in the Senegambia regions as *sabu tubab*, was used as a standard for weighing gold. He further records that *tubab* is also expressed as *tubako* and dates back to an eleventh century migration of Himyar Arabs, called Tubba, Tuab, or Teda, into the Western Sudan. In 1740, Moore noted that a powerful Mandinga alcaide who lived along the Gambia River was known as Tobauto Mansa. The Gambia, of course, was one of the chief gold trading centers in West Africa. A number of locations called Tuba yet remain in the gold-producing districts of Mandinga.[39]

The *tuob* mentioned by Las Casas was sometimes recorded as *tumbaga* in the northern regions of South America and at other points in Middle America. Morison tells us that the word *guanin* was later replaced by *tumbaga* in some areas.[40] Detailing the diffusion of this term throughout the Americas, Jenner states that *tumbaga* "was known above all in Colombia and in Chiriqui [SW Panama], but also on the Peruvian coast, in Northern South America all the way to Guiana, in the Antilles, and northwards as far as Mexico."[41] *Tumbaga* is the same as *tuob* and all their West African counterparts. The distribution of this metal indicates the trail of Mandinga gold merchants in the Americas.

These African gold-words have affinities with the Arabic language. The Arabic غِنَى [ghi-NAY] and غَنَا [gha-NA] mean "wealth, affluence and riches," while غُنم [ghunm] and غَنِيمة [gha-NI-mah] indicate "spoils, booty, loot, prey, gain, profit."[42] All of these terms are analogous with the West African *ghana* and the American *guanin*. There is also the Arabic نُقُود [nuQUD] for "gold," نُحَاس [nuHAS] for "copper" and نَقِى [na-qty] meaning "pure, clean."[43] *Tuob* could be expressed in تِبْر [tibr] which refers to "gold dust."[44] The importance of these Arabic affinities rests on the fact that the Mandinga hierarchy was strongly connected to the Islamic world through commerce, diplomacy and the Koran. Because of the commercial ties particularly, the *guanin, nucay* and *tuob* of the American gold trade initiated by the Mandinga would naturally find representations in the Arabic language.

Other Designations for Ghana Reproduced in the Americas

The word *ghana*, in West Africa, has historically been used to designate other things besides gold. All of these things though were linked in some manner with the gold trade. *Ghana* was the title of the king and the name Arab writers also gave to both his capital and his country. When used as a title for the king, *ghana* meant "war leader," or "war king," and still survives in Mande dialects as *gana* and *kana*.[45] This same phenomena is reproduced in pre-Hispanic America. L'Abbé Brasseur de Bourbourg lists the following American tribal/nations whose names relate to "war":[46]

> *Caribe* signifying "warrior."
> *Guarani* signifying "war."
> *Guarani-hara* for "warrior."

It is quite likely that these words derive from, or at least express the concept of, the African *Ghana*, or "war leader." Delafosse tells us that in Mande "the consonant *n* takes the place of the nasalized *r*; also, it often replaces an *l* or a nasalized *d* [-nd] . . ."[47] The name *Caribe* was also recorded in some documents on early America as "*Cariba, Caniba, Cannibal, Canima* and *Calibi.*"[48] The interchange of *-r-, -n-,* and *-l-* is obvious here and reflects a distinct Mande characteristic. The suffix *-ba* in Mandinga indicates augmentation, such as "great" after a name. The *-ma,* when added to a noun, suggests "intensity," or more appropriately "master of."[49] All these *Caribe* words if interpreted by Mande sounds and forms would mean either "great warrior," of "Master Warrior." In this respect they are the same as the African *Ghana. Guarini* is the same as *Guanini,* or *Ghanini,* and is an exact reproduction of the African *Ghana* and its derivatives. As we shall see, it not only relates to the gold trade, but to a number of other Mandinga designations which stem from the same root.

The earliest known dynasty of the ancient Ghana Empire was called *Kaya Magha; Kaya* means "treasury" and *Magha* is the same as *Magan* and *Ma,* which mean "master," or "master of" if they follow a noun. The author of the *Tarikh el-Fettach* translates *Kaya Magha* as "King of Gold."[50] We find kings in Hispaniola and other parts of the Americas called *Caonabo* which Refinesque translates as "gold in the house,"[51] but more logically should be "House, or Dynasty or Gold." *Caona* has already been identified as one of the American forms of the African gold-word *ghana;* the suffix *-bo* which means "house" in one of the dialects of Hispaniola is identical with the Mande *-bö* which means the same thing and can be used in the same form.[52] In the Sarakole dialect, we get *kane-bö* which like its American counterpart means "House of Gold."

Not only was the West African *ghana* reproduced in early America to mean "gold," "King of Gold" and "war leader," but, as we shall subsequently see, it was also used to designate a "black people," a "country, or nation" and a number of "cities" which were associated with gold mining and the gold trade.

The Evolution of the West African Ghana and Guinea

The modern term *guinea* derives from *ghana.*[53] The evolution of the association of these two terms can easily be traced. Although they later became synonymous, they may have had different beginnings. We first hear of Ghana through the eighth century writings of Al-Fazari who was quoted in the works of Al-Mas'udi (c. 956 A.D.). Al-Fazari states that the territory of Ghana was very vast and calls it "the Land of Gold."[54] On the other hand, Guinea, as a corrupted form of Ghana, first appears in fifteenth century Portuguese writings as *Guiné.*[55] From that point on the two terms were used in the same manner, except that Guinea never designated a king's title.

The exact origin of the word *ghana* is obscure. Besides its relationship to "gold" and "war leader," there are other possibilities. From the earliest notations on the Berber dialects, we learn that *guan* means "son," or a "person," and the plural *quanin* means "people." We further note that the Canary Island Berbers, themselves called Guanches, use *quanâc* to refer to a "state," or "republic."[56] These Berber forms could have easily derived from, or formed the bases for, the designation *ghana*, especially since the Berbers were a significant element in the Ghana Empire.

Yakūt (1179-1229), in his *Mu'djam al-Buldan*, provides a clue to the origin of the fifteenth century *Guiné*. He "mentions a land Gināwa, which according to him received its name from its inhabitants; the Gināwa are said to have been a Berber tribe who penetrated into the Sūdān and became neighbors of Ghāna."[57] The proximity of these two lands might have led to a confusion between the two terms. The Gināwa are cited in the same general area where Marty, doing an ehtnographic study of the Sudan, identifies a people called *Gouanin*, or *Gouanan*; their singular form being *Gouanini*, or *Gouanani*, which can also denote the total people. After the traditions of the Tagant in Mauritania, the Gouanin were among the first immigrants from the East [Yeman] who settled in that area. They have mixed with the local populations, and the word *Tagant* [ta-gana-t] is the Berber form of the same name.[58] The similarity between the traditions of these people and those on the origin of the first ruling dynasty of Ancient Ghana is apparent. The word *Tagant* may explain why Ghana was sometimes recorded as *Ghanata* in some ancient texts.

It has been necessary to deal with the origins of *ghana* and *guinea* in order to understand why they had a plurality of meanings, i.e., gold, a king's title, a people, an empire and its capital city, throughout much of West Africa. These same designations were duplicated in the Americas where they were connected with the gold trade of obvious Mandinga inspiration. So far, we have only dealt with the American *ghana, guana*, or its plural *guanin*, as a gold term and a title for a king, or a war leader. Now we can proceed to examine its other American meanings in a West African context.

Mandina Traders and Settlers in the Americas

The black men who brought those golden spear points to Hispaniola [Haiti] were the Mandinga/Sarakoles, known also in early times as Mandinga/Caragoles, or Caragolis.[59] The identical nature of Sarakole and Caragoli is explained through the Mande interchange of *s-* and *k-* [hard *c-* in this case].[60]

Father Roman (Ramon Pane), one of the first twelve missionaries to visit the Americas after Columbus' "discovery," states that the African gold merchants who came to Hispaniola were called the *Black Guanini*.[61] Rafinesque asserts that *Guanini* implies "the Golden Tribe," or, in other words, black merchants who trafficked in gold.[62] The significance in West Africa, as we have seen, is the same. The Guanini, if the traditional histories of America do

Gerhard Mercator *Africa ex Magna Orbus Terrae Descriptione*, Amsterdam, c. 1552/1595.

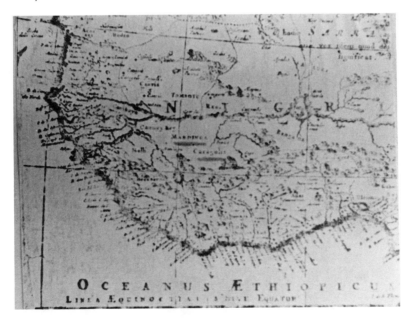

John Ogilby *Africae Accurata Tabula*, Amsterdam, 1670

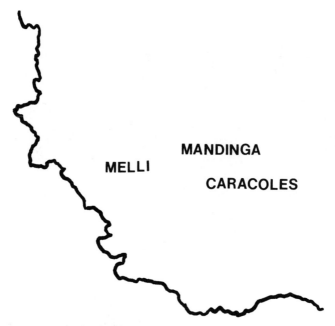

Henricus Hondius *Africae Nova Tabula*, Amsterdam, 1631

Frederick Dewit *Totius Africae Accuratissima Tabula*, Amsterdam, 1671

Nicolas Sanson d'Abbeville *L'Afrique, ou Lybie Ulteriere: ou Sont le Saara, ou Desert, le Pays des Negres*, la Guinée et les Pays Circonu Paris 1679/88

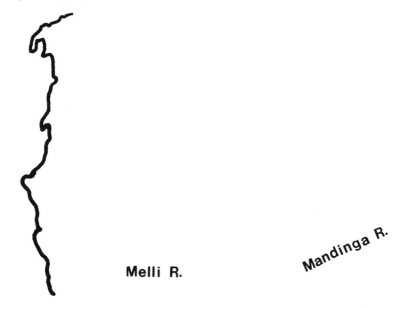

Johann Matthias Hase *Africa Legitimas Projectionis Stereographicae Regulis*, Nürnberg, 1737

not deceive us, intermarried with another black tribe called *Caracols*, or *Caracoles*, who occupied a portion of Hispaniola [Haiti]. They later diffused throughout the Lesser Antilles and the northern shores of South America up to the Isthmus of Panama [Darien]. The American Guanini and Caracoles were the same as their Mandinga counterparts in West Africa.

Leo Wiener, one of the first to single out the Mandinga as the black merchant seamen who crossed the Atlantic to pre-Columbian America, claims that they did so in less than fifty expeditions.[63] If these alleged expeditions in any way approached the size of those initiated by Abubakari II, then the West African impact on pre-Hispanic America must have been tremendous. To be sure, the Mandinga had been in Panama so long before the arrival of Europeans there that L'Abbe Brasseur de Bourbourg, an expert on Middle American traditions, classed them as indigenous to the area. He wrote that "it is thus that today we distinguish the indigenous people of Darien under two names, the *Mandingas* and the *Tulé*, whose difference perhaps yet recalls their distinct origin."[64] These Mandinga were the remnants of a colony of blacks from Upper Guinea, who might have been shipwrecked in Darien. Both Gomara and Martyr, while recording the activities of Balboa in 1513, noted their presence. Gomara tells us that when Balboa "entered the Province of Quareca, he found no gold, but some black slaves belonging to the king of the place. Having asked this king where he had obtained these black slaves, he [Balboa] received as an answer that people of that color lived quite near to there and that they were constantly at war with them." Gomara adds "that these Blacks were *entirely like the blacks of Guinea* . . ."[65] Peter Martyr's account of the same event differs, but slightly. He states, "They found there [in Quareca] black slaves, having come from a region a distance of only two days march, and which produces people of that color, fierce and above all cruel. It is believed that *such blacks came long ago from Africa* with the intention of robbing and that, having been shipwrecked, established residence in those mountains.[66] These statements, when interpreted in the light of the previously mentioned maritime ventures, explain the origin of the Mandinga in this area. The Martyr account, however, should more appropriately read "trading," instead of "robbing."

Concerning the same period, Rodrigo de Colmenares, in his *Memorial* against Vasco Nuñez de Balboa, wrote that "a captain brought news of a *black people* located east of the Gulf of San Miguel—'*i que habia alli cerca gente negra* . . .'"[67] These may have formed the core of the "moon-eyed Negroes" and "Albinos" seen around Panama by some early European arrivals, or some of the tribes of Chocó, such as the *Guanas*, or *Chuanas*, who were as black as any African.[68] *Cuana* and *Chuana* are obvious variants of the already mentioned *Guana* and *Guanini*. *Chuana* may very well be a transitional form which links *Guana* to the *Cuna*, who still reside in the Darien region.

Marquez, while correlating archaeological evidence with traditional histo-

ries, informs us that "Some tribes of Darien say that when for the first time
their ancestors arrived in that region, it was occupied by small black men who
later retired to the forests; and the PAYAS and the TAPALISAS, or the
CUNACUNAS, have their origin date back to one man and two women—one
Indian and the other Black, who lived on the shores of the Tatarcuna."[69] We
should not, therefore, be surprised to learn that the *Handbook of South American Indians* lists the MANDINGA as a "hybrid negroid group," living among
the Cuna.[70] The work also notes the following Cuna relationships:[71]

$$
\text{CUNA}\ldots
\begin{cases}
\text{Mainland Cuna}\ldots \quad \text{CUNACUNA} \\[1em]
\text{San Blas Cuna}\ldots
\begin{cases}
\text{Chucuna,} \\
\text{TULE, MANDINGA,} \\
\text{Bayano, Chepo,} \\
\text{Chucunaque, PAYA,} \\
\text{Caiman}
\end{cases}
\end{cases}
$$

It is clear, from both written and oral sources, that the Mandinga should not
be termed a "hybrid" group, but rather the Cuna who, at least in part, own
their origin to combined African and Middle American elements, which Brasseur de Bourbourg found represented in the Mandinga and the Tulé.

African elements were also found farther north in Honduras. Ferdinand
Columbus informs us that people of the Black African type were seen there by
his father. "But the people who live farther east [of Ponte Cavinas], as far as
Cape Gracios a Dios," he relates, "*are almost black in color*," and adds that
they "pierce holes in their eyes large enough to insert hen's eggs . . ."[72] Piercing
the ears in this manner still prevails among the womenfolk of many West
African regions where the Mandinga predominate. To the southwest of Cape
Gracias a Dios, at Tegucigalpa, near the Honduran-Nicaraguan border, other
Blacks were sighted who might well have been an extension of those seen by
Columbus. They were the *Jaras* and *Guabas*.[73] *Jara*, spelled *Jarra* by Gambians, and *Diâra* in Senegal and Mali, represents a very ancient clan and
territorial designation among the Mandinga-Sarakoles. When the ancient
Ghana Empire fell, this clan migrated southward and established itself along
the banks of the Niger and later on in the Gambia. At the time Abubakari
launched his Atlantic expeditions, this clan constituted an important literate
element in Mali.[74] Much the same can be said of the *Guaba*; it, likewise, is a
Mandinga clan/territorial designation. As a clan name among Mande speakers, it appears as *Kaba*, or *Kabba*, and as in the case of the *Jarras*, its members
have often been associated with the literate aspects of Islam. Kangaba, one of
the ancient capitals of Mali kings, has been frequently shortened to *Kā-ba*;
furthermore, Niani, another famous Malian capital, sometimes called "Mali"
after the empire, contained a district within its walls called *Niani Kaba*. Since
these two former Mandinga capitals have been connected with the designation
Kàba, the term takes on added importance. The roots of this designation may

well be analogous to the *Ka'ba*, the "cubical" shrine of Mecca,or *al-Ghaba*, the sacred grove of the Sarakole kings of Ancient Ghana. Both these designations were established concepts among the Mandinga centuries before Abubakari took to conquer the limits of the Atlantic.[75] At any rate, the *Jaras* and the *Guabas* of Honduras were the pre-Columbian remnants of Mandinga settlements in the Americas, and their counterparts can still be found today in West Africa under the names *Jarra*, or *Diâra*, and *Kaba*, or *Kabba*.

Mid-nineteenth-century surveys for the Darian Ship Canal disclosed that a number of Mandinga place names still existed in Panama at that time. The Africans who came there, it appears, attempted to name, or rename, certain sites after important places in their original homeland. Thus, we get the following correspondences:[76]

The above comparisons corroborate the Mandinga/Caragoli presence at the Darien/Panama Isthmus, and the pre-Columbian nature of this presence has already been established.

Black Caribs, Also Known as Black Guanini, Claifurnams and Garifs

A Black African element existed in the Antilles prior to the Hispanic invasion of these islands. When Europeans first landed on the Island of St. Vincent, they found there two distinct Carib populations, one with a reddish-yellow complexion, and the other black.[77] The latter, decidedly Africanoid, came to be known as the *Black Carib, Black Guanini*, or *Claifurnams*.[78] *Califurnam*, sometimes shortened to *Garifuna* and *Garif*, is the Mande *Ka-lifa-nami* which represents the Arabic خليفة النبي[khalīfatu-'n-nabi]; the نبي [nabi] either remains the same or changes to *nami*, or *nambi*, in Mande. From the entire phrase, we get the English translation, "Caliphate of the Prophet." *Garif* is only a segment of the total phrase and represents the Mande *kalifa, kal'fa, karifa*, or *Kar'fa*, which are the Arabic خليفة [khalīfatu], and the English "Caliph."[79]

Levy, in *The Social Structure of Islam*, explains the duties of the Caliph:

> The Caliph, like the Prophet, was always, if not actually than in theory, in supreme command of the forces of Islam. To him belonged the authority to use troops and the power to dispose as he wished of all the military equipment and supplies.[80]

In the medieval world of Islam, it was not uncommon to find titles and place names derived from some form of the word "Caliph." The title was frequently associated with troops, or the commanders of troops. *Califurnam* and *Garif* were in this light the Islamic versions of the already discussed *Cariba, Caniba*, Canima and Calibi, which relate to "war" and "war leader." *Garif* and *Carib*, therefore, are somewhat synonymous, but do *not* stem from

PANAMA	WEST AFRICA
Sierre de MALI 1)—A mountain range in Darien which corresponds to the general location where the Indians of Quareca told Balboa Blacks resided. 2)—This range lies east of the Gulf of San Miguel, approximately where one of the Colmenares' captains reported the presence of Blacks.	MALI 1)—A vast West African empire whose center lay in the mountainous area at the headwaters of the Senegal/Niger. 2)—Niani, one of the famous Mandinga capitals, was also called by this name. 3)—A synonym for Mandinga.
MANDINGA 1)—A town of anchorage located on a Bay of the same name, both facing the Gulf of San Blas. 2)—A river flowing across Panama and emptying into the MANDINGA BAY. 3)—A black people who live among the Cuna Indians near San Blas.	MANDINGA 1)—The name of an extensive geographical region in West Africa, which was the nucleus of the Mali Empire. The name was often used as a synonym for Mali. 2)—One of the most numerous ethnic confederations in West Africa. They have diffused throughout much of that area.
CANA GAUNA 1)—CANA was the name of a town where an important gold mine was worked. It was located on a river by the same name. 2)—GAUNA, also known as Chuana, was a black tribe which migrated south of Darien into the province of Chocó. They are believed to be the remnants of the Blacks seen by Balboa and Colmenares around 1513.	GHANA 1)—The name of an ancient West African empire and its capital city. It later became a province of Mali under Mandinga authority. 2)—A name for gold. 3)—The title of a king which meant "war leader" in Mandinga. 4)—The name of a people who were a significant element in the province of Ghana.
CARACOLE 1)—A pointe of land in southwest Panama.	CARAGOLE, CARAGOLI, SARAKOLE- 1)—A branch of the great Mandinga family. CARACOLE, or CARAGOLI, are the more ancient forms which were used as generic names for Mandinga.
BARBACOAS- BERBICE- 1)—BARBACOA is a town on the Chagres River. The name is also used to refer to a tribal/linguistic group scattered throughout Panama and extending southward into the southern regions of Colombia. 2)—A swampy lowland area in Panama.	BARBACUA BARBACIS BARBASINS- 1)—BARBACUA was the name of a port town at the mouth of the Senegal. 2)—BARBACIS, or BARBASIN, was the generic name for the Serers who live in the general area of BARBACUA and who were ocean-going fishermen under the authority of Mandinga.

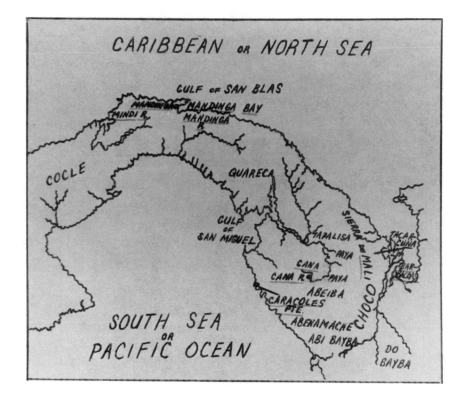

The Isthmus of Panama (Darien). Several important locations that relate to the pre-Columbian Mandinga presence in the area are noted. Most of these sites were outlined in Cullen's surveys for the Panama Canal and Railroad. (See Bibliography for this chapter).

López: Atlas de la América (París, 1758).
López' map of this area shows one of the earliest representations of Mandinga and Caracoles Pointe.

the same root, as has sometimes been assumed.[81] This implies that Islamic influences had penetrated some areas of pre-Columbian America—which is precisely the case. Additional Islamic elements among the Caribs as well as other pre-Columbian black populations will be covered in more detail later.

St. Vincent was not the only place where Black Caribs were found. They were also seen on the Island of Santa Lucia and at the mouth of the Orinoco River.[82] Those sighted on Santa Lucia may have come from St. Vincent, but the origin of those around the Orinoco is uncertain.

It is very significant that wherever we find the Caribs we often discern an element of black people. This is not to say that the Caribs were Africans, but that they were rather influenced by, or modified by, an African presence. Humboldt notes that at the source of the Essequibo River, not far from the mouth of the Orinoco, Blacks were seen living among the Caribs. He arbitrarily assigsn a "fugitive-slave" origin to these Blacks, but, as in other instances of this nature, *no evidence* is produced to support this assumption.[83] The Black Caribs of the Essequibo owe their origin to the same historical factors which produced those of the St. Vincent and Santa Lucia Islands, which are the same analogical causes that produced the Black Guanini, *gente negra* of Herrera's account,[84] who came to Hispaniola to barter gold *guanines*.

Black Muslims in Early America

The Caribs, in general, and the Black Caribs, specifically, present a number of qualities which associate them with the Islamic religion. These qualities have not only been found in the antilles, but also along the northern coast of South America and westward into Central America.

The Black Caribs possessed an Islamic name because they were, for the most part, Muslims, or at least their traditions say they were. P.V. Ramos in his "History of the Caribs," an article which appeared in *The Daily Clarion*, relates that when Columbus came to the West Indies he found a "wooly-haired" people who were "Mohammedans" and whose "language was presumably Arabic."[85] Taylor who quotes from Ramos fails to examine this tradition in context with other Islamic customs among the Carib and goes on, erringly, to label it a "distortion."

In respect to diet, Muslims have traditionally adhered to the Levitical Code, and eating the flesh of swine is one of its major taboos.[86] We should, therefore, not be surprised to learn that the Caribs did not until very recently add pork to their diet, although they were aware of its food value. Davies' translation of Rochefort's historical work on the Caribs states that "Nor is there any Swines' flesh eaten among them, which they call *coin-coin* and *bouïrokou*."[87] In other respects, the dietary evidence is not as strong. The fact that the Caribs *ate no crabs or lizards*, which were also Islamic taboos, while at sea, for fear of not being able to reach land,[88] implies religious motives. These items, it appears, were eaten on other occasions. On the other hand, geese, also an Islamic taboo, were raised for food along with other fowl.[89] Fish, however, provided the principal source of meat for the Caribs. The strongest point of similarity between Caribban and Islamic dietary habits is the taboo against eating pork. Prohibitions against eating swines' flesh have been the most strongly adhered to dietary taboo in the world if Islam. Other dietary prohibitions vary in importance from place to place. The Caribs present no exception in this respect.

The crescent, or half-moon, has been an important symbol in Islamic blazonry since the eleventh century. This same emblem had gained importance in pre-Columbian America, extending from the Antilles through parts of South and Central America as far as Mexico.[90] The *Handbook of South American Indians* states that "the most prized possession of the [Carib] men was the *CARACOLI, A CRESCENT-SHAPED ALLOY OF GOLD AND COOPER FRAMED IN WOOD*, which the warriors obtained during raids upon the continental [South American] Arawak. Some of the *CARACOLI* were small and served as ear, nose, or mouth pendants; others were large enough to be worn on the chest. They were a sign of high rank, being passed down from generation to generation, and were worn only upon ceremonial occasions and during journeys."[91] Rennard's on-the-scene observation of this phenomenon differs in several respects from the *Handbook's* report. First, he suggest that SILVER might have been an additional alloy in these CARACOLIS, which make the alloys identical to those of the gold *guanines*. Secondly, Rennard refutes the notion that the Caribs obtained their CARACOLIS by raiding the continental Arawaks. Instead, he contends that the Caribs were friendly with certain Arawaks who in turn exchanged the CARACOLIS for gifts presented by Carib warriors.[92] The word *CARACOLI* definitely links these crescent-shaped objects to the Muslim Mandinga whose early presence in the area has already been established.

The Arawaks, also known as Caribisce, possessed a number of physical characteristics which indicate African contacts. "Those who live near the coast," Prichard tells us, "are of a *very dark brown, sometimes as dark as what is termed a yellow Negro*; but the straight, strong, black hair, small features, and well-proportioned limbs are peculiarities that never allow these Indians to be taken as Africans."[93] Prichard's concern about the African characteristics among the Arawak is understandable. His assessment of Arawak hair texture, although consistent with that of most observers, is not entirely right. The *Handbook* again informs us that "among certain individuals of the Arawak tribes . . . the incidence of *wavy and frizzly hair is rather great*."[94] Although this analysis weakens Prichard's conclusion considerably, it does not infer that the Arawaks were Africans, but that they were rather, like their Carib cousins, modified by an African element. This African element was, as the CARACOLIS verify, of Mandinga derivation.

One of the main sub-groups of the Arawaken family was the Guaná, sometimes referred to as Chaná, or Chané. The name of this group betrays the Arawak's association with the Black Guanini and the African gold trade in the Americas. Like a number of West Africans, the Guaná were known to "file their incisor teeth to give them a sawlike appearance." This subgroup constituted the southernmost branch of the great and widespread Arawakan family, whose center of diffusion was north of the Amazon River, or in the neighborhood of the Carib and Black Guanini.[95]

Moving westward into the Isthmus of Darien, we find that a number of kings of that area, particularly in the neighborhood of Chocó, where black tribes and Mandinga place names are noted, possessed Islamic, or Biblical names. Brasseur de Bourbourg states, "Let us further add here the names, preserved in the time of the Spaniards, of several princes of this country [Darien]: *Do-Bayba, Abi-Beiba, Aben-Amechy, Abrayba*, etc., that to us seem to have a completely Moorish, or Biblical form."[96] Herrera devotes an entire chapter to these kings, but fails to deal with their physical appearance.[97] The fact that these kings ruled over populations which were significantly Africanoid indicates a mutal exchange of customs: either the kings were in part of African origin, or the subjects of Islamized African influences.

Groups of Muslim blacks called *Almamys* inhabited Honduras prior to the arrival of the Spaniards there. These Africans were either the same as, or related to, the Jaras [Diaras] or Guabas of Tegucigalpa, or the blacks sighted by Ferdinand Columbus along Honduras' norther coast. Cauvet, while mak-

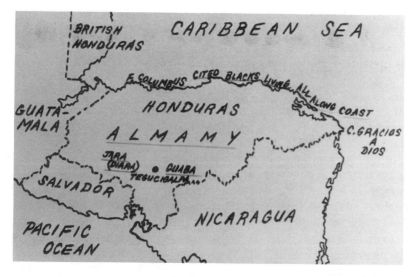

The General location of pre-Columbian African Peoples in Honduras.

ing an ethnographic comparison between Africa and the Americas, asserts that "a tribe of *Almamys* inhabited Honduras . . . having preceded by little the arrival of Columbus there." He adds that the title *Almamy* does not antedate "the twelfth century of our era," which is the earliest date that Black African Muslims would have been conveyed to the American Isthmus.[98] Cauvet further theorizes that the localization of these Africans at a central American landing point supports the possibility of their recent arrival. His conclusion compares favorably with other documented evidence dating Mandinga voyages to the Americas.

Almamy is the Mandingo form of the Arabic *Al-imāmu* ألإمام , which means "leader, chief, or chieftain."[99] This title not only applied to Islamic religious leaders, but was often, as in the case of the Mandinga, used to designate their followers and institutions. The Portuguese who visited the Upper Guinea Coast in the fifteenth and sixteenth centuries witnessed various applications of this term. Speaking of the Mandinga along the Gambia, Alvares d'Almada notes, "The majority of these religious people are called ALMAMY, which is like the dignity of Guardian or Provincial among us, and they wear a ring like a Bishop. And all three of these principal houses are on the north bank of the river." He further states that a Mandinga came to the Kind of Casamance and told him of the *three religious houses along the Gambia River called AL-MAMY*.[100] These religious houses were small kingdoms, or nations within an nation, and the word *Almamy*, like *Ghana*, pertained to a leader, a nation and its people. Significantly, this form, which was used to designate the Blacks of Honduras, was used almost exclusively by the Mandinga prior to the seventeenth century. The Fula of Guinea's Futa Jallon did not adopt this title until after that time. *Almamy*, like so much of the other evidence, specifically identifies the Blacks of Honduras with the Islamized Mandinga of Upper Guinea and also provides a general date of their arrival in the Americas, which would be somewhere between the twelfth and the fifteenth centuries.

The evidence of Islam in pre-Columbian America is not overwhelming, nor was such the case for West Africa during the same period. We recall that Islam prior to the fifteenth century was found mainly among the Mandinga hierarchy: the nobles, the military leaders and governors, the merchants and technicians, plus the *literati* and foreigners who had come from the Eastern countries. The base people, that is, the laboring classes and serfs, from which most of the seamen came, for the most part held to their traditional beliefs. The former would, therefore, have been far less numerically important as the latter in their American settlements, and the significance of Islam there would not have been so apparent.

Fugitive Slave Theories

Customarily, observers have attempted to explain the presence or black populations among the Indians by arbitrarily assigning them a *fugitive slave origin.* Often, in these cases, no evidence can be produced to support these conclusions. Yet, where there is such evidence, there are often like indications that Blacks existed in these areas before the importation of African slaves. Circumstances surrounding the origins of the Black Caribs and the blacks tribes neighboring the Isthmus of Darien afford typical examples of this latter point.

Concerning the origins of the Black Caribs, the outstanding conclusions are: 1)—that the presence of Blacks in the Antilles, or Carib Islands, before the arrival of the Spaniards, was recorded in local traditions; 2)—that black populations living among the Caribs and in neighboring areas were reported by the first Europeans who came to the West Indies and Central America; 3)—that Black Carib traditions also point to an Afro-Islamic origin; and 4)—that all evidence of this nature predates any notices of the arrival of fugitive slaves in the area.

Quatrefages, after examining the documents relating to the situation, wrote the following summary on Black Carib origins:

> When the Europeans landed on this latter island [St. Vincent], they found there two populations, or better two distinct races. One part of the islanders had the ordinary reddish-yellow complexion; the others were Blacks. In order to explain this latter peculiarity, one has generally admitted that a ship carrying slaves had been wrecked on these shores and that the Blacks set free, in this manner, mixed in with the ancient inhabitants. It is possible that this hypothesis is true, but not necessarily the reason which explains the formation of this mixed race. It would appear more probable that the color of the Black Caribs holds to the same analogical causes as those which gave rise to the complexion which characterizes the Charuas and the Yamassee. They [Black Caribs] could very well be the descendants of the Africans who were conveyed to St. Vincent by the currents and the winds, such as was in the case of those who had landed towards the mouth of the Orinoco, in Brazil, in Florida and at the Isthmus of Darien. They might even be the descendants of those *black men*, who during the time of Columbus, were from time to time making incursions to Haiti, well before slavery had brought Negroes to America. It is useless to return on the manner which might have given birth to this population that Herrera, cited by Brasseur [de Bourbourg], calls *quento negra* and which he clearly distinguished from the Caribs whom he called *Caribales.*[101]

This very lengthy summary brings the situation into sharp focus, except in one respect: it is not "useless" to attempt to identify the origin of the pre-Columbian black populations in the area. For some, their Mandinga origins have already been outlined. Other pre-Columbian black populations, those mentioned by Quatrefages, including the Charuas and the Yamasee, and those not dealt with up to this point, will be covered in a subsequent chapter.

One of the earliest documents which attempts to attribute a fugitive-slave origin to the Black Caribs comes from the British *Calendar of State Papers, 1661-1668*, which "speaks of Saint Vincent as being at that time: 'all Indians, and some Negroes from the loss of two Spanish ships in 1635.'"[102] Neither of these ships were identified, nor was their destination given, which means the number of tribal origins of these escaped slaves cannot be determined. Be that as it may, there is like evidence to indicate that Blacks were in the Lesser Antilles before the "loss" of these two ships, and certainly when the French and English began their occupation of these islands in 1625. Taylor, who has done what may be considered the most complete study to date on the Black Carib, states that ". . . It is certain, however, that Negroes were living on Saint Vincent soon after the French and English moved into the area . . ."[103] Taylor's "soon after" assessment is nebulous, but can only be interpreted to mean that as the French and English made inroads throughout the islands, they encountered Blacks already entrenched at several points.

Armand de la Paix, a French missionary, writing in 1646, tells us that Blacks and Caribs from Saint Vincent fought side-by-side against Frenchmen from Martinique on the Isle of Santa Lucia in, or before, 1635.[104] Fugitive slaves from the two wrecked, or captured, Spanish ships in question would hardly have furnished the Caribs with such formidable allies at that time.

Father Raymond, one of the earliest French missionaries to come to the Antilles, arrived in Dominica, January 17, 1641, six years after the two Spanish ships in question liberated African slaves. One of the Caribs of this island told the priest of a raid in which he and other Caribs, along with a company of Blacks, participated. This raid could well have taken place as early as 1625, the date the French first arrived in the Lesser Antilles, or certainly before 1635.[105]

A summary of the evidence shows that Blacks had occupied the Antilles before the importation of African slaves in the area, and that when Europeans first arrived in these islands they found Blacks already there. Notices of fugitive slaves in the area come much later. Consequently, the Black Caribs owe their origin to the combined pre-Columbian and post-Columbian African elements which merged with the indigenous populations of Saint Vincent, Santa Lucia and Guadeloupe.

Much of the same can be said of the black tribes which were found inhabiting the neighborhood of the Darien Isthmus. We recall that 1)—Balboa and his crew found African prisoners of war in the hands of the Indians of Quareca in 1513; 2)—that one of the captains of Comenares, a contemporary of Balboa, reported seeing a people of the black African type located near the same area; 3)—that ethnological studies of the Indians of the Darien area indicate that they attribute, in part, their origin to an aboriginal black people; 4)—that the Mandinga are considered to be among the original inhabitants of the Panamaian area; 5)—that Mandinga and other West African place names were found to exist in this area as far back as detailed maps of the area can record.

That fugitive slaves sought refuge in the Darien region at an early point in the Hispanic colonization of the area cannot be disputed. Some of these fugitives were deserters from the Spanish military and labor forces in Panama, while others had come from as far away as Jamaica. This fugitive-slave presence in the Darien region dates back at least to the early part of the eighteenth century[106] and, unfortunately, has served to obscure investigations of the pre-Hispanic Mandinga in the area. The existence of fugitive slaves has too often been tendered as the sole explanation for the presence of all early Africanoids in the Americas. Marsh's comments on the Blacks of Darien afford a typical example:

> ... The people of Yavisa were 'bush-niggers'—descendants of runaway slaves and other outlaws. They had kept up their traditions meticulously and were still a very efficient gang of cut-throats and robbers.[107]

The derogatory remarks in this statement indicate the frame of reference brought into the author's observations. Although the Blacks of Yavisa resided not too far from the regions in Panama where pre-Columbian Africans were sighted, Marsh did not think to investigate the probability of other than slave origins. He goes on instead to say that these "'bush niggers' [are] in general as primitive as their ancestors in Africa and much more primitive than the Tulé Indians."[108]

A pre-Columbian African element existed in both the Antilles and Central America before one learns of fugitive slaves there. The probability is that the Mandinga, who already occupied various sites in these regions, welcomed in their midsts fugitives who were their kith and kin. As details on other pre-Columbian Africanoids in the Americas will subsequently reveal, this may not have been a too uncommon phenomenon.

Similar conditions are present in Mexican history. Mandinga place names there have been attributed solely to the introduction of African slaves in the country. Beltran writes, "Of these Negroes, those who formed the great Mande group were, without a doubt, the ones who exercised the greatest influence in Mexico, during the entire 16th century. They entered under the general designation of Mandinga and left as a souvenir of their presence in Nueva Espaã [Mexico] a number of geographical places which bear their name and the survival of the tribal name as a popular designation of the devil."[109] These Mandinga place names in Mexico are not necessarily the result of the introduction of African slaves in the sixteenth century. Davidson questions Beltran's sweeping conclusion by provocatively asserting, "But the careful records of the Inquisition in Mexico—records that were kept as part of the process of 'safeguarding Christianity' by ensuring baptism—show that the land was fertilized by many African peoples."[110] If this is the case, then why Mandinga? Why didn't the other African groups leave like reminders of their presence? Perhaps the answer can be found in the vast number of pre-Colum-bian terra cotta and stone sculptures, precisely depicting the facial charac-teristics of Black Africans, which have been discovered on Mexican soil.[111] As yet, one cannot say that these sculptured faces belong to the Mandinga al-though Wiener has shown some corroborative features.[112] Furthermore, the same historical factors which conveyed the Mandinga to the Antilles, Colom-bia, Panama and Honduras, could very well have extended northward into Mexico before Cortés' arrival in 1519. To assign arbitrarily a slave origin to the Mandinga place names in Mexico, to the exclusion of considering the pres-ence of pre-Hispanic Africans and Africanoids in the area, is not scientific.

There is no doubt that some slaves in Mexico freed themselves by revolting against Spanish authority, and that they did establish townships on Mexican soil,[113] but these phenomena cannot specifically be connected to Mandinga place names. If this were the case, one would hope to find such designations representing other African nations which formed a part of the African slave population. There is yet the possibility that freed slaves settled in the towns that had previously been established by Mandinga traders from the Isthmus regions to the south,[114] which was the case with the Black Caribs and other Central American Black nations.

The African Almaizar and Cotton Currencies in the Americas

Gold was not the only item introduced into the Americas by West African traders. Columbus was startled to find that the Antillean Indians bartered a woven cloth, identical in style, design and purpose, to those he had seen in West Africa. His *Journal of the Third Voyages* states that the Indians "brought handkerchiefs of cotton, very symmetrically woven and worked in *colours like those brought from Guinea, from the rivers of Sierra Leone, and of no dif-ference.*" He was so struck by this phenomena that he remarked but "they [the Indians] cannot communicate with the latter [West Africans], because from where he now is to Guinea the distance is more than 800 leagues [2,400 miles]."[115] The admiral made several notices of this woven cotton and referred to it as the Moorish *almaizar*, a cloth the Moors imported from West Africa into Morocco, Spain and Portugal. The Indians seemingly wore their *al-maizars* in the same manner as the Africans. Columbus further reports, "Each one wore his cloth so woven in colours, [that he] believed it to be the 'almayzar.'"[116] Morison and Obregón explain that columbus took this to be a sure sign that the Indians "traded with Africa around the back side of the world."[117] Perhaps it did not occur to the admiral that this trade could come through transatlantic contacts although he had been continually confronted with evidence of that nature.

Ferdinand Columbus describes the Indian cotton garments as "breechcloths of the same design and cloth as the shawls worn by the Moorish women of Grenada."[118] Cortés' report on the dressing habits of the Indians of Mexico is more detailed. He remarked that "The clothing which they wear is like long veils, very curiously worked. The men wear breechcloths about their bodies, and large mantles, very thin, and painted in the style of Moorish draperies."[119] The Moorish elements described in these accounts could just as well apply to the Muslim Mandinga who at that time exhibited many of the same dress styles. The southern regions of Mauritania were under the authority of Mali from the latter part of the thirteenth through the fifteenth century.

In De Porras' manuscript on New World discoveries, he notes that the natives of Central America [Honduras?], in addition to bartering an African-type cloth and gold guanines, painted their bodies and faces like the natives of Barbary [North Africa].[120] This practice also existed among many populations along the Guinea Coast and in the interior regions of West Africa.

Wiener's studies have already instructed us that the American-made *almaizars* were manufactured from the seeds of the Silk Cotton tree, or *Bombax Ceiba*, which is the same material from which those in West Africa were made. On both sides of the Atlantic it was customary to weave cotton goods from this material.[121] The *Handbook of South American Indians* states that "The Arawakan Guaná, who were famed as skillful weavers and who still provide their neo-Brazilian neighbors with textiles, appear to have been the most likely agents for the pre-Columbian diffusion of weaving." Furthermore, "they wove textiles of such good quality that they found a market for them in neo-Brazilian cities."[122] The association of Guaná with the Mandinga has already been noted. The Guayqueri Indians, who were scattered throughout the land extending from the Guianas to Honduras, were also expert weavers of the scarves which Columbus thought were imports from Africa.[123] These Guayqueri obviously learned their craft from the Arawakan Guaná, or Guanini. Although the scarves, or *almaizars*, for the most part were not imported from Africa, the art of making them was.

Breechcloths, shawls, or *almaizars*, have long served as currencies in West Africa. As early as the eleventh century, Silla, a town on the Senegal River, under the authority of Ghana, "used millet, salt, copper rings, and *cotton breechcloths . . .* as money."[124] Cotton was such an important currency item and in such demand that "almost every house had its own cotton tree."[125] Cowry shells, euphorbium and gold were also used at that time as forms of currrency.[126] The breechcloths concern us most, and this eleventh century account provides the oldest reference to the cotton *almaizar* being used as a medium of exchange in West Africa. It was not until the fourteenth century that another of such references appears. Ibn Battuta, on his journey through that area, tells us that the food which he bought at Takedda and Tuat was "paid for with pieces of cloth." He further states that his small caravan had to pay a band of Tuaregs and "indemnity of pieces of cloth" in order to pass

through Hoggar.[127] Around the same time, Al-'Umari reports that the Kingdom of Kanem, somewhat east of Mali, placed the same value on cotton
cloth:

> . . . their currency is a cloth which they weave called *dandi*. Every piece is
> ten cubits [15 to 16 feet] long. They make purchases with it from a quarter
> of a cubit [4 to 5 inches] upwards. They also use cowries, glass beads,
> copper in round pieces, and coined silver as currency, *but all [are] valued
> in terms of that cloth*.[128]

Just as they were in much of West Africa, cotton pieces and *almaizars* were
employed as items of currency in Middle America. In the Antilles and along
the borders of the Gulf of Mexico, the Indians offered such cotton stuffs as
their chief items of barter; goods woven from this material were often worn in
the same manner as they were in Africa and bore distinct African designs. Al-
Bakri, writing about 1067, identified Terenca [Tirca, or Tirecca], a city located
on the Senegal not too far from Silla, also in the domain of Ghana, as a major
center for the manufacture or cotton breechcloths, whose length as well as
width was usually four spans.[129] Al-Bakri also noted that "the people [of
Ghana] who follow the religion of the king wear cotton, silk or brocaded
breechcloths according to their means."[130] Less than one hundred years later, a
similar notice about the same general area was made by Al-Idrisi. He observed
that the people of Silla, Takrur, Ghana and Caucau [Gao], wore the *almaizar*,
which he represents orthographically as *al-mizar*, اَلمِزَر , *al-'izar*, اَلإزَر and
izâr, إزَر .[131] Although he describes other forms of dress, Al-Idrisi fails to
speak on the manufacture of these garments.

It was not until three hundred years later that other detailed accounts
appeared on the fabrication and use of the *almaizar*. In 1455, Cadamosto,
while observing the populations around the Senegal, noted that "the chiefs
and those of standing wear a cotton garment—for cotton grows in these lands.
Their women spin it into a cloth a span in width."[132] This observation accen-
tuates the description given by Al-Bakri almost four hundred years earlier.
Leo Africanus, a half century after Cadamosto's visit to this region, wrote that
this cotton cloth was brought to North Africa "by certain merchants from the
land of the Negroes."[133] Although he does not identify these merchants, Africanus specifically locates the origin of the *almaizar* in sub-Saharan Africa, a
point of extreme importance when we attempt to trace the origin of this
cloth's presence in the Americas.

Alvares d'Almada, writing later on in the same century, lists a number of
localities in Mandinga territory where the manufacture and use of the *almaizar* prevailed. All along the Upper Guinea Coast, from Senegal to Liberia,
the *almaizar*, or more directly strips of cotton, mainly black and white, but
frequently comprising other colors, was used either as a single garment, a

piece from which larger garments were made, such as shirts and mantles, or as a medium of exchange.[134]

While visiting Sansanding on the Niger in 1795, Mungo Park recorded:

> This place is much resorted to by the Moors, who bring salt from Beero [Walata], and beads and coral from the Mediterranean, to exchange here for gold dust, and cotton cloth. This cloth they sell to great advantage in Beero, and other Moorish countries, where, on account of the want of rain, no cotton is cultivated.[135]

Park's observations synthesize the evidence. The Moorish *almaizar* was a West African product which became known in Europe by its Arabic name. West Africans cultivated the cotton, wove it into strips, breechcloths, shawls and mantles, then exported them to North Africa and the Iberian Peninsula. When the Moors occupied Spain, from the eighth to the fifteenth centuries, they familiarized the Spaniards, and consequently other Europeans, with this commodity. The probability that Moorish Spain also produced this cloth must be considered. Nonetheless, the *almaizars* which reached the Americas before the arrival of the Spaniards there came from the principal source of manufacture—West Africa. Columbua knew their source of origin; this is why he stated that the Indian *almaizar* was "*like those brought from Guinea, from the Rivers of Sierra Leone and of no difference.*"

As late as the twentieth century, the *almaizar* was still worn by many West Coast Africans. Observing the people along the Casamance River, Reeve reported that "their dress is like the negroes of Cape de Verde and the inhabitants of the River Gambia, which consists [of] a piece of cotton cloth, striped according to the custom of their country, which barely covers their privities."[136]

Leo Wiener's examination of the philological origins of American Indian trade items convinces us that the early Mexican word for *almaizar* had Mandinga origins. He shows that the Mexican *maxtli*, "waistcloth to hide the nudity," was derived from the Mande *masiti, masiri,* or *masirili,* all of which refer to an "ornament," or "adornment to tie one's toilet."[137] The Arabic *al-mai'zar* could possibly have stemmed from the same Mande roots. Unfortunately, Wiener only shows these affinities with Mexico and neglects other Middle American regions where the *almaizer* was produced and traded. Outside of the diffusion of this Mandinga term throughout other areas of the Americas, all other aspects of the Indian cloth trade are compatible with those of West Africa.

Conclusion

There are two accounts which document West African Maritime expeditions to the Americas. The older of these, Al-'Umari's *Masalik*, relates that a

Mali emperor, Abubakari II, somewhere between 1307 and 1312, made two attempts to "discover the limits" of the Atlantic; his first attempt entailed 400 ships, and his second 2,000. The only other known documentation of such voyages appears in the *Journals* of Christopher Columbus. His *Journal of the Third Voyage*, the Las Casas version, specifically states that Africans periodically left the Guinea Coast and navigated to the West with merchandise.

These two documents reveal a good deal about West African maritime activities. The Emperor Abubakari II, as the *Masalik* reports, made "careful plans" for his two expeditions; this would have enabled him to draw upon all the knowledge and skills extant in his vast empire, which were more than adequate to undertake such a venture. His persistence and the face that he elected to accompany his men on the second attempt indicate a great confidence in the successful outcome of these expeditions. One of his captains of the first expedition, after sailing for an extensive period, returned home to report how the fleet had encountered a violent current while in "mid-ocean." The current he described was either the North Equatorial, or the Antilles Current, either of whose distances from the West African Coast at that latitude would place the fleet at the doorstep of the Americas. Some of the ships of these two expeditions obviously survived the perils of the sea to reach various landing points in Middle America. Consequently, some crewmen of these ships achieved the goal of "conquering the limits of the ocean." Large fleets entailing hundreds of *almadias*, the typical West African ocean-going craft, are common to West African history. Some individual ship owners had fleets of several hundred, which would have been readily available to their emperor. The royal house, itself, may have possessed many times that number.

The Columbus report on West African maritime activities is much more general. It does not specifically identify the African group from which these commercial voyages to the Americas emanated. In 1498, on his third voyage, Columbus stopped at the Cape Verde Islands, and while there, he was informed by some of the Portuguese officials that African boats periodically left the Guinea Coast and headed towards the lands of the West with merchandise. These African merchant-mariners must have had a fairly definite destination to have carried such noteworthy merchandise. Their voyages could not have been experimental, or accidental. The Portuguese knew of these African sea routes and had, themselves, witnessed the presence of African boats in the West Indies, or in the neighborhood of Brazil. The records indicate that the Portuguese knew of these Western Hemisphere lands long before 1492. As a result, at Tordesillas in 1495, Portugal was willing to enter into an agreement with Spain which would concede the then "undiscovered" South American territories to Portuguese authority. Columbus was so concerned about this fact that he decided to follow the course of the African seamen and head for the southwest, the direction of the "new" continental lands.

The Indians told Columbus and others who arrived in the West Indies, shortly after 1492, that a black people, known subsequently as the Black Guanini, brought gold to those islands. Important Antillean names for gold had derived from earlier Mandinga forms. We have the following correspondencies:

Antillean (American)	Mandinga (W. Africa)	English
goana, caona, guani, guanin	Ghana, kane, kani, kanine, Ghanin	gold
nucay, nozay	négé, nexe [nuh-kuh]	metal: iron, or gold jewelry.
tuob, tumbaga	sabu tubab, Tobauto Mansa	gold, a gold weight, a king's title.

Besides these philological considerations, there were also other factors of association. In the West African gold trade, like in that of pre-Columbian America, gold was frequently alloyed with copper and silver. On both sides of the Atlantic these alloy proportions were the same, approximately one half gold with one quarter copper and one quarter silver added. Making ceremonial arms of these alloys, particularly spears, was likewise a common practice on both sides of the ocean. West Africans, whose traditions of making such ornaments date back to Roman times, introduced the art of alloying gold in this manner and making ceremonial arms from this alloy to the Americas.

The term *ghana*, or *ghanin*, and its Mandinga derivatives had several other traditional uses in West Africa. Besides being a synonym for gold, it was also the title of a king, which meant "war-leader," the name of a capital city and its empire, and the designation for a people in this general area. An identical phenomenon is reproduced in the Americas. We note the following American uses:

Caona	— A town in Hispaniola [Haiti] whose name when translated meant "gold." The king of the place was also known by the same name.
Cana	— A town in Panama where a very ancient gold mine was located.
Guana	— A generic name for the entire northern portion of South America in pre-Hispanic times.
Guaná	— A sub-tribe of the Arawak who inhabited the northern regions of South America.
Guanini	— A pre-Columbian Black people who trafficked in gold in the Americas.
Caribe, Caniba, Guarani	Names of Indian tribes, all of which mean "warrior," or "great — warrior."

Caonabo   — A title of a king, which is the reproduction of the Mande *kane-bö*, which means "House of Gold." It is comparable to the Ancient Ghana title *Kaya Magha*, or "Master of the Treasury." The values and intents are the same.

Besides the Black Guanini, a number of other pre-Columbian Mandinga groups can be identified at various Middle American settlements. Earlier in their history the Mandinga were sometimes called Mandinga Caragoles, or Caragolis. Caragoli is probably an older designation for Sarakollé and demonstrates the linguistic phenomenon in Mande speech where the older [k] sound evolves into the more current [s] sound. The evolution of the "gold-words" such as *kane→sani*, or the "serpent-words," *kā→sā* present typical examples. That this linguistic characteristic had found its way into the Antilles is suggested by the Indian term for "gold," *nucay*, or *nozay*, where the [k] sound as represented by [-c-] interchanges with the [s] sound, here represented by [-z-]. At any rate, we find a black tribe called Caracoles living in the Antilles before the arrival of the Spaniards. This tribe had, as their traditions attest, merged with the Guanini at some earlier point in time, and the resulting Mandinga assemblage spread throughout Middle America.

In the Panama area, we learn that the Mandinga were among the first to settle that area. Local Panamaian traditions corroborate that an early African element had mixed with some Indians to form the basis for present ethnic groups. These African settlers were still discernable when Balboa and his contemporary Colmenares arrived there around 1513. From Panama, the Mandinga migrated northward into Honduras where they were represented under the clan names Jara [Jarra, Diâra] and Guaba [Kaba, Kabba], and then southward to the province of Chocó where they appear as the Gauna, or Chuana, which are the same as Guanini and Guaná.

As late as the mid-nineteenth century, a number of Mandinga place names still survived in Panama. The name Mandinga itself appeared as a township, a river, a bay and an anchorage on the bay; Mali designated the identical area where Balboa and Colmenares reported that Africans lived in the fifteenth century; Cana was the site of the oldest known gold mine in the country; the mine was in use before the Spaniards arrived; Caracoles Pte., Barbacoas Bay and the Mindi River were other locations which show Mandinga affinities.

The Black Caribs of Saint Vincent and the islands of the Lesser Antilles also represent a pre-Columbian Mandinga element. Their proper names *Califur-nam* and *Garif* are Mandinga variants of the Arabic *Khalifatu-'n-Nabi*, which in Mande becomes *Kalifa-nami* and can be shortened to *Kalifa*, or *Karifa*, or the Black Carib *Garif*. This Muslim title can be explained by the fact that some Black Carib traditions point to Islamic origins. One of these traditions relates that when the Spaniards arrived at Saint Vincent they found there a "wooly-haired" people who were "Mohammedans," and whose language was "presumably Arabic." Carib dietary habits tend to support this tradition; it was only in recent times that the Caribs added pork, a major Islamic taboo, to their diet. Abstinence from eating lizards and crabs, also Islamic taboos, appeared to have some special religious significance among the Caribs. The crescent which has been an important symbol in Islamic blazonry since the eleventh century was highly esteemed among the Caribs and their Arawak cousins. Some of these symbols, made of gold, silver and copper alloys, were called *caracolis*, a name which betrays its connections with the Mandinga and the African gold trade. The importance of this symbol to American Indian populations seems to follow the trail of the African gold traders in the Americas.

The Black Caribs have other traditional connections with the term *caracoli*. A number of early observers concluded that the Black Carib were a faction of the Black Guanini, who, as has been confirmed, intermarried with another black American tribe known as *Caracoles*, who in turn gave their name to the crescent-shaped objects made of gold, silver and copper alloys. Here, we note the obvious link between the American gold trade and the Mandinga Caragolis who initiated it from Africa.

Returning to the Darien/Panama region, we find additional evidence of pre-Hispanic Islamic customs. When the Spaniards first arrived there, they encountered a number of kings who had Muslim names. Although these kings were not described as Blacks, it is important to note that they reigned over areas where numerous black populations, some already identified as Mandinga, resided. Further study in this direction should clarify the relationships between these two groups.

In the case of Honduras, the picture in this respect is much clearer. The Mandinga clans, the Jaras and Guabas, who had established themselves there, were Muslims. They called themselves *Almamys*, the Mande form of the Arabic *al-imamu*, meaning "leader," or "chieftain." Mandinga populations had adopted this title as early as the twelfth century A.D. to denote individuals, institutions and populations. The Portuguese found such institutions well established in the Senegambia regions when they arrived there in the mid-fifteenth century. Furthermore, the Jara [Jarra, Diâra] and the Guaba [Kaba, Kabba] clans have had a long association with Islam in West Africa.

The presence of fugitive slaves in the Middle American areas from the fifteenth century onward has obscured examination of pre-Columbian African elements. Too often, one has attempted to attribute fugitive slave origins to *all* Africanoids reported in these regions without considering pre-Columbian evidence. It appears that African slaves, escaping their European overlords, frequently sought refuge in territories where pre-Columbian Blacks had already been noted. This situation has given too many investigators a means to bypass the prospect of early African voyages to the Americas.

In addition to gold, West Africans also introduced the cotton *almaizar*, or the art of making it, into the Americas. This cloth, which originated in West Africa, was used as a currency there and in North Africa, and later throughout the Americas. The African nature of the American *almaizar* was specifically pointed out by Columbus and other Spaniards as they came upon it at various locations. The Arwakan Guaná, based in the northern regions of South America, introduced the weaving of the cloth to other American nations. The name Guaná is the same as Guanini and connects this cloth trade to the African gold trade and the Mandinga-Caragoles.

In short, we have seen that the Mandinga made several voyages to the Americas where they carried on the gold and cloth trade. A number of settlements established by them were renamed after places in their original African homeland. These settlements were bases from which this trade was extended throughout the Americas. Some of the Mandinga merchants mixed in with the local populations and passed on to them some aspects of African culture.

Notes

1. Shihab al-Din Ibn Fadl al-'Umari (al-'Omari), *Masalik el Absar fi Mamalik el Amsar*, traduit par Gaudefroy-Demombynes (Paris: Librarie Orientaliste Paul Geuthner, 1927), pp. 74-5.

2. Carter G. Woodson, *The African Background Outlined* (Washington, D.C.: Associated Publisher, Inc., 1936), p. 56; cf. Charles Monteil, *Les Empires du Mali* (Paris: G.P. Maisonneuve et Larose, 1929) pp. 83-4.

3. R. Levitzion, "The Thirteenth and Fourteenth Century Kings of Mali," Journal of African History, IV, 3, (1963), p. 341-53.

4. The *almadia* was the common type of maritime vessel used by seamen along the Upper Guinea coast. Some of the larger *almadias* had planked-up sides called *falsas*.

5. Armando Cortesäo, *The Nautical Chart of 1424* (Coimbra: University of Coimbra, 1954), p. 94.

6. Muhammad Hamidullah, "L'Afrique Découvre l'Amerique avant Christophe Colombe," *Presence Africaine*, XVIII-XIX, (Fev.-Mai 1958), pp. 177-83

7. Cortesäo, p. 94.

8. Mahmoûd Kati, *Tarikh el-Fettach*, traduit par O. Houdas et M. Delafosse (Paris: Librarie d'Amérique et d'Orient, Adrien-Maisonneuve, 1964), p. 64.

9. *Ibid.*, p. 97.

10. *Ibid.*, pp. 269-70.

11. Felix DuBois, *Timbuctoo the Mysterious*, trans. by D. White (London: William Heinemann, 1897), p. 76.

12. See Chapter VI.

13. John Barbot, *A Description of the Coasts of North and South Guinea* (London: Printed for A. Churchill, 1732), p. 156; Anthony Benezet, *Some Historical Account of Guinea, Its Situation, Produce, and the General Disposition of Its Inhabitants*, (Philadelphia, 1771), p. 26.

14. John Boyd Thacher, *Christopher Columbus* (3 Vols.; New York/London: G.P. Putnam's Sons, 1903-04), II, p. 379.

15. Elmer Dean Merrill, *The Botany of Cook's Voyages* (Waltham, Mass.: Chronica Botanica, Vol. 14, Nos. 5-6, 1954), p. 212.

16. Cortesäo, pp. 96-102.

17. H. Yule Oldham, "A Pre-Columbian Discovery of America," *The Geographical Journal*, The Royal Geographical Society, V, No. 3 (March 1895), p. 221-40; J. Batalha-Reis, "The Supposed Discovery of South America before 1448, and the Critical Methods of the Historians of Geographical

Discovery," *The Geographical Journal*, The Royal Geographical Society, IX, No. 2 (February 1897), p. 185-210.

18. Burton Kline, "American Discovered Many Times before Columbus Came," *The World's Work*, L(May-October 1925), p. 39.

19. Thacher, II, p. 379; cf. Batalha-Reis, p. 205.

20. Batalha-Reis, pp. 206, 209.

21. *Ibid.*, p. 205; Thacher, II, p. 380.

22. *Ibid.*

23. Zahariyya Ibn Muhammad Ibn Mahmud Al-Qazwini (Al-Qazwini), *Aje'ib Al-Makhlugat wa-Athar Al-Bilad*. Vol. ii: *Athar Al-Bilad*, edited by F. Wustenfeld (Gottingen: 1848), unpublished translation by Hopkins and Rajkowski, Institute of African Studies, Legon, Ghana, No. 22, p. 7 (27.6e.f.).

24. John Abercromby, "A Study of the Ancient Speech of the Canary Island," in *Harvard African Studies I: Varia Africana*, edited by Oric Bates and F.H. Sterns (Cambridge, Mass.: The African Department of the Peabody Museum of Harvard University, 1917), pp. 97, 116.

25. Thacher, I, pp. 643-44; *Ibid.*, II, p. 644.

26. Maurice Delafosse, *La Langue Mandingue et Ses Dialectes* (2 Vols.; Paris: P. Geuthner, 1929/1955), I, p. 555; II, p. 624.

27. *Ibid.*, II, pp. 312, 603.

28. *Ibid.*, I, p. 555; II, p. 624.

29. Leo Wiener, *Africa and the Discovery of America* (3 Vols.; Philadelphia: Innes & Sons, 1922) II, pp. 118-19; William Bosman, *A New and Accurate Description of the Coast of Guinea* (Liverpool: 1907), pp. 73-4.

30. Richard Jobson, *The Golden Trade, or a Discovery of the River Gambra, and the Golden Trade of the Aethiopians, 1620-21* (London: 1932), pp. 3-4.

31. Abu 'Ubayd Al-Bakri (El Bekri), *Description de l'Afrique Septentrionale*, traduit par Mac-Gucken de Slane (Algiers: A Jourdan, 1913), p. 329.

32. *Ibid.*

33. *Ibid.*, p. 325.

34. Muhammad Ibn Abdallah Ibn Battuta (Ibn Battuta), *Travels in Asia and Africa*, Trans. by H. Gibb (London: G. Routeledge, 1929), p. 328.

35. Al-'Umari, p. 65.

36. Joseph Dupuis, *Journal of a Residence in Ashantee* (London: H. Colburn, 1824), p. 74.

37. Thacher, I, pp. 556, 643-44.

38. Delafosse, II, pp. 540-41.

39. M.D.W. Jeffreys, "Maize and the Mande Myth," *Current Anthropology*, XII, No. 3 (June 1971), p. 302-03; Delafosse, II, p. 778-79.

40. Samuel Eliot Morison (ed.), *Journals and other Documents on the Life and Voyages of Christopher Columbus* (New York: Heritage Press, 1963), p. 265n;   and Mauricio Obregón, *The Caribbean as Columbus Saw It* (Boston: Little, Brown & Co., 1964), p. 162n.

41. Desmond Jenner (Ed.), *The American Aborigines* (Toronto: University of Toronto, 1933), p. 295.

42. E.A. and E.E. Elias, *Elias' Modern Dictionary: Arabic-English* (Cairo: Elias' Modern Press, 1962/63), pp. 485-486.

43. *Ibid.*, pp. 692, 727, 732; cf. English-Arabic Volume, p. 305.

44. *Ibid., English-Arabic* Volume.

45. Delafosse, II, p. 241-42; John Spencer Trimingham, *A History of Islam in West Africa* (London/Glascow/New York: Oxford University Press, 1962), p. 50.

46. L'Abbé Brasseur de Bourbourg, *Popul-Vuh: le Livre Sacré et les Mythes de l'Antiquité Americaine* (Paris: A Bertrand, 1861), p. CCIX. This book is prefaced by a long commentary entitled: "Dissertation sur les Mythes de l'Antiquité Americaine, sur la Probabilité des Communications

Existant Anciennement d'un Continent a l'Autre, et sur les Migrations des Peuples Indigènes de l'Amerique."

47. Delafosse, II, p. 528.

48. C.S. Rafinesque, *The American Nations; or Outline of a National History of the Ancient and Modern Nations of North and South America* (2 Vols.; Philadelphia: by Author, Spring 1836), I, p. 213; Brasseur de Bourbourg, p. CCXIII.

49. Delafosse, II, p. 15, 476, 479.

50. *Ibid.*, I, pp. 370, 525; Al-Kati, p. 75.

51. Rafinesque, I, pp. 202, 211; Don Fernando Colon, *Historia del Almirante de las Indias, Don Cristobal Colon,* 2 Vols. in *Colección de Libros Raros ó Curiosos que Tratan de América* (Madrid: 1892), V & VI, p. 207; Fray Ramón Pané, *Relacion de Indias 1496* (Buenos Aires: ENE), p. 60.

52. Delafosse, I, p. 525; II, p. 66.

53. Gonzalo Aguiire Beltran, "Tribal Origins of Slaves in Mexico," *Journal of Negro History,* XXXI, No. 3 (July 1946), p. 292; J.A. Rogers, *Africa's Gift to America* (New York: by author, 1959), pp. 11-14.

54. Muhammad Ibn Ibrahim Al-Fazari (C. 773 A.D.) was the author of a fragment quoted in Al-Mas'udi's *Muruj al-Dhahab wa Ma'adin al-Jawahir,* edited and trans. by Barbier de Meynard et Pavet de Courteilles as *Les Prairies d'Or* (Paris: 1861-77). Unpublished English translations by Hopkins and Rajkowski, Institute of African Studies, Legon, Ghana, p. 2.

55. *Oxford English Dictionary,* edited by J. Murray, H. Bradley, W. Craigie and C.T. Onion (13 Vols.; Oxford: Clarendon Press, 1933), IV, p. 497.

56. Abercromby, pp. 105, 111, 116.

57. *The Encyclopaedia of Islam,* edited by M.T. Houtsma and T.W. Arnold (Leydon/London: Luzac/Brill LTD., 1927), II, p. 181.

58. Paul Marty, *Études sur l'Islam et les Tribus du Sudan* (3 Vols.; Paris: Leroux, 1921), III, pp. 276-77; cf. Abercromby, p. 116.

59. See the maps and their dates of publication on the next page. It should be noted that the names Mandinga Caracoles, or Caragolis, are not orthographic errors. The fact that the map makers were of different linguistic orientations and wrote at different periods is proof of this. We have Dutch, English, French and German map makers who wrote during a period extending from 1552 to 1737.

60. Refer to Chapter III for an analysis of Mandinga.

61. Peter DeRoo, *History of America before Columbus* (2 Vols.; London/Philadelphia: J.B. Lippincott, 1900), I, p. 307; John G. Jackson, *Introduction to African Civilization* (New York: University Books, 1970), p. 233; Rafinesque, I, p. 193.

62. Rafinesque, I, pp. 121, 186-87, 194, 208-09; , "The Primitive Black Nations of America," *Atlantic Journal and Friend Knowledge* (Philadelphia: 1832/33), p. 86.

63. J.G. Jackson, p. 233.

64. Brasseur de Bourbourg, p. CCIII.

65. *Ibid.*, p. CCXXVII.

66. Pedro Martir de Angeleria, Decadas del Nuevo Mundo (2 Vols.; Mexico: Jose Porrua e Hijos, Sucs., 1964), I, p. 291.

67. Charles L.G. Anderson, *Life and Letters of Vasco Nuñez de Balboa* (New York: Fleming H. Revel Co., 1941), p. 163.

68. Rafinesque, I, p. 57; , "Primitive Black Nations ...," p. 86; Vincente Riva-Palacio, *México a Través de los Siglos* (5 vols. Mexico: Ballesca y Comp. Edits., 1887-89), I, p. 64.

69. Carlos C. Marquez, *Prehistoria y Viajes: Estudios Arquelógicos y Etnigráficos,* Segunda Edicion, Corrigida y Aumuntada (Tomo I—Editorial América; Sociedad Española de Liberia, 1920), p. 271.

70. Julian H. Steward (Ed.), *Handbook of South American Indians* (6 Vols.; Wash., D.C.: Smithsonian Institute, Bulletin 143, 1950), VI, p. 177.

71. *Ibid.*, IV, p. 64

72. Ferdinand Columbus, *The Life of the Admiral Christopher Columbus*, trans. & annotated by Benjamin Keen (New Brunswick, N.J.: Rutgers University Press, 1959), p. 234.

73. Rafinesque, "Primitive Black Nations . . . ," p. 86; Riva-Palacio, I, p. 64.

74. Sékéné-Mody Cissoko, *Histoire de l'Afrique Occidentale: Moyen-Age et Temps Modernes: VIIᵉ Siècle-1850* (Paris: Présence Africaine, 1966) pp. 29-30, 67 (map), 69, 234-46; Delafosse, *The Negroes of Africa: History and Culture*, trans. by F. Fligemen (Port Washington, N.Y.: Kennekat Press, Inc., c. 1931, reissued 1968), pp. 54, 196; Harry A. Gailey, *A History of the Gambia* (New York/ Washington: Frederick A. Praeger, Inc., 1965), pp. 1 (map), 54, 58; Trimingham, *A History of Islam* . . . ," pp. 26, 30, 45, 46, 60, 73.

75. Al-Bakri (El-Bekri), p. 328; Cissoko, p. 43 (map), 45, 54; Delafosse, *Haut-Sénégal-Niger* (3 Vols.; Paris: G.P. Maisonneuve et Larose, 1972), I, pp. 137-41; Gailey, pp. 41-59, 101, 105; Trimingham, *A History of Islam* . . ., pp. 65n., 188.

76. Edward Cullen, *Isthmus of Darien Ship Canal: A Full History of the Scotch Colony of Darien, Several Maps, Views of the Country, and Original Documents*, 2nd Ed. (London: Effingham Wilson, 1853), pp. 17, 18, 39, 40n., 52, 58, 65, 74-6, 78, 95, 159, 200;   , Papers on the Isthmus Canal *and Railroad Projects* (Society of Engineers, Transactions for 1868/69), pp. 27, 29, 31, 56-8, 63, 68-72, 88.

77. A. de Quatrefages, *Histoire Générale des Races Humaines: Introduction à L'Étude des Races Humaines* (Paris: A. Hennuyer, 1889), p. 598.

78. Rafinesque, "Primitive Black Nations . . . ," p. 86.

79. Eduard Conzemius, Ethnological Notes on the Black Carib (Garif)," *American Anthropologist*, XXX, No. 2 (April-June 1928), p. 184; Elias and Elias, *English-Arabic*, p. 112; Delafosse, II, p. 334, 345, 535.

80. Reuben Levy, *The Social Structure of Islam* (Cambridge: University Press, 1965), p. 425.

81. Conzemius, p. 184.

82. Douglass MacRae Taylor, *The Black Carib of British Honduras*, Viking Fund Publications in Anthropology, No. 17 (New York: Johnson Reprint Corporation, 1967/Wenner-Gren Foundation for Anthropological Research, 1951), pp. 17-18.

83. Alexandre de Humboldt, *L'Amérique Espagnola en 1800* (Paris: Calmann-Lévy, 1965), pp. 151-2.

84. Antonio de Herrera y Tordesillas, *Historia General de los Hechos de los Castellanos en las Islas y Tierrafirme de Mar Océano* (17 Vols.; La Academia de la Historia, 1934), II, p. 264.

85. Taylor, p. 37.

86. Lev. 11:1-47, 17:10-16; The Holy Qur'ān, ii. 168, 172-73, v. 2, 4-6, 90-91, vi. 118-19, 121, 145-46, xvi. 114-18.

87. Charles de Rochefort, *The History of the Carriby-Islands*, trans. by John Davies (2 Vols.; London: J.M. for Thos. Dring & John Starkey, 1966), II, p. 273.

88. Steward, IV, p. 554.

89. F. Columbus, p. 234.

90. Weiner, III, pp. 236-38.

91. Steward, IV, p. 553.

92. L'Abbé Joseph Rennard, *Les Caraibes, la Guadeloupe (1635-1656)* (Paris: Libraire General et Internationale—G. Ficker, 1929), p. 55.

93. James C. Prichard, *Researches into the Physical History of Mankind*, 3rd Edit. (5 Vols.; London: Sherwood, Gilbert & Piper, 1836-47), V, p. 522.

94. Steward, VI, p. 90.

95. Steward, I, pp. 238, 280, 288.

96. Brasseur de Bourbourg, p. CCIIIn.

97. Herrera, III, pp. 291-96.

98. Giles Cauvet, *Les Berbères en Amerique: la Part des Berbères dans le Peuplement de l'Amerique* (Algiers: J. Bringau, 1930), pp. 100-01, 439; cf. Hamidullah, p. 183.

99. Delafosse, II, p. 8; Elias and Elias (*Arabic-English*), p. 39.

100. André Álvares d'Almada, *Trato Breve dos Rios de Guiné do Cabo Verde, dês do Rio de Sanagá até os Baixos de Santa Ana* (*1594*), in *Monumenta Missionaria Africana: African Occidental* (*1570-1600*), edited by Padre António Brásio, Segunda Série, III (Lisboa: Agencia-geral do Ultramar, 1964), pp. 275, 291.

101. Quatrefages, p. 598.

102. Taylor, p. 18.

103. *Ibid.*

104. *Ibid.*

105. *Ibid.*, p. 17-18, 33.

106. Cullen, *Papers on the Isthmus Canal and Railroad Projects*, pp. 29, 37, 63, 66, 78.

107. Richard Oglesby Marsh, *White Indians of Darien* (New York: G.P. Putnam's Sons, 1934), p. 5.

108. *Ibid.*, p. 16.

109. Beltran, pp. 280-81.

110. Basil Davidson, *The African Slave Trade: Precolonial History 1450-1850* (Boston/Toronto: Atlantic-Little, Brown & Co., 1961), p. 103.

111. Nicolás León, *Compendio de la Historia General de México, desde los Tiempos Prehistóricos hasta el Año de 1900* (México: Herrero Hermanos, Editores, 1902), p. 14; Wiener, III, p. 322.

112. Wiener, I, p. 33n., 174n., 159-61; III, p. 365.

113. Ignacio M. Rodiles, "The Slave Trade with America: Negroes in Mexico," *Freedomways* (Fall 1961), I, No. 3, pp. 206-307; *Ibid.*, (1966), I, No. 1, pp. 39-52.

114. Wiener, III, p. 365.

115. Thacher, II, pp. 392-93.

116. *Ibid.*, II, pp. 388, 393.

117. Morison and Obregón, p. 154.

118. F. Columbus, p. 232.

119. Wiener, II, p. 37.

120. Thacher, II, p. 644.

121. Weiner, II, pp. 27-29.

122. Steward, I, pp. 239, 288.

123. Morison and Obregón, p. 161.

124. Al-Bakri, p. 325.

125. *Ibid.*, p. 326.

126. *Ibid.*, pp. 325, 331, 335.

127. Ibn Battuta, pp. 337-38.

128. Al-'Umari, *Masalik al-Absar fi Mamalik al-Amsar* in Youssouf Kamal's *Monumenta Cartographica Africae et Aegypti* (Cairo/Leiden, 1925-51), IV, 2, pp. 1236-44; also see unpublished translations by Hopkins and Rajkowski on file at the Institute of African Studies, Legon, Ghana, No. 35(2), p. 1 (23a1-23b).

129. Al-Bakri, p. 325.

130. *Ibid.*, p. 329.

131. Abu 'Abdallah Muhammad Ibn Muhammad ash-Sharif al-Idrisi (Edrisi), *Description de l'Afrique et de l'Espagne*, trad. et edit. par R.P.A. Dozy et M.J. Goeje (Amsterdam: Oriental Press, 1969), pp. 5, 8, 9, 13, 16.

132. G.R. Crone (Ed.), *The Voyages of Cadamosto and Other Documents on Western Africa in the Second Half of the Fifteenth Century*, 2nd Series, LXXX (London: The Hakluyt Society, 1937), p. 31.

133. Leo Africanus, *The History and Description of Africa*, trans. by John Pory (3 Vols.; New York: Burt Franklin, 1600), III, p. 151.

134. Alvares d'Almada, pp. 239, 245, 247, 261, 266, 279, 325, 346, 360.

135. Mungo Park, *Travels in the Interior Districts of Africa, 1795, 1796 & 1797* (2 Vols.; London: J. Murray, 1816), I, p. 303.

136. Henry F. Reeve, *The Gambia: Its History, Ancient, Medaeval and Modern* (London: Smith, Elder & Co., 1912), p. 190.

137. Wiener, III, pp. 232-33.

MEN OUT OF ASIA:
A REVIEW AND UPDATE OF THE GLADWIN THESIS

Runoko Rashidi

What we are going to try to do is build up a new theory to explain how the native American civilizations originated . . . and a first long step in this direction is to show the number, variety and location of the different peoples who were on hand when the seeds of American civilizations first began to sprout.[1]

Harold Sterling Gladwin, 1883-1983, some of whose works and ideas this essay is designed to address, comes to our attention here as a twentieth century archaeologist and historian imbued with an exceptionally keen interest in the early cultures and historical developments of the southwestern sections of the United States, including California, Arizona, New Mexico, Utah, Colorado and Texas. As for his personal history, we know that Gladwin was born in New York City and that in 1901 he attended Wellington College in Berkshire, England. From 1908 to 1922 he was employed with the New York Stock Exchange. It was not until 1924 that Gladwin, who was then an energetic forty years of age, became, in the course of a leisurely drive through the American Southwest, suddenly and incurably addicted to the archaelogical fever that possessed him for the rest of his life.

Though considered an "amateur" by some academicians because of his disdain for "formal university training," Gladwin's record in actual field research, or what might be called "dirt archaeology," was considerable.[2] Besides his position as curator at the Santa Barbara Museum, Gladwin was the cofounder and, from 1927 to 1950, Director of the Gila Pueblo Archaelogical Foundation, under whose auspices the first significant traces of North America's culture were uncovered. In addition to his extensive excavations, Gladwin either authored or co-authored 24 impressively detailed archaeological site reports and several major books, the last one of which, *Men Out Of The Past*, was completed as recently as 1975.

We are drawn to him in our current studies primarily because of his authorship of a controversial 1947 publication entitled *Men Out Of Asia*. This was the same year, by the way, that W.E.B. DuBois' *World And Africa*, and the still valuable and exciting second volume of Joel A. Rogers' *World's Great Men Of Color* were first published. Gladwin's text is of particular importance to Afrocentric analyses of American history because it is one of the few substantial studies backed by specialized field research that claims that the earliest American populations were Black. It is our firm conviction, therefore, that in an age in which a completely new vision of the Black presence in world history is being espoused uncompromisingly, the "Gladwin Thesis" and the bold, compelling and factual manner in which it is presented, cannot be ignored, overlooked or acknowledged.

In spite of the forty years that have now elapsed since *Men Out Of Asia's* initial publication, it will probably surprise few to know that the essential themes contained within it, or at least the portion of it with which we are concerned, are still unknown to all but a comparatively small number of serious students, and remain unacceptable to Western academicians as a whole. When we add to this the fact that the text is now out of print and has not been available for some time, the necessity for a critical review and reassessment of the "Gladwin Thesis" from an Afrocentric perspective becomes all the more apparent.

Diminutive Blacks: The First People on American Soil?

Although in a very remote prehistoric period small numbers of Diminutive Blacks, may have preceded them, what we are dealing with in the context of this essay as the Gladwin Thesis are the first four separate and distinct migratory waves of peoples to enter the New World. Gladwin classifies these four groups, which he calls *Australoids, Asiatic Negroids, Algonquins, and Eskimos*, as actual migrants because they came to the Americas in relatively large numbers. He further links these paleo-Americans (his *men out of Asia*) by virtue of their common use of the Bering Isthmus [Beringia] *or* (depending upon the geological period involved) the Bering Strait as their route of penetration into the Americas. Finally, Gladwin established firmly the migration of these diverse peoples through his ability to pinpoint with precision their respective Old World cultural prototypes and technologies and to trace and identify them in their subsequent New World settings. Gladwin was therefore convinced, based upon the physical evidence then available, that it had been the resulting large-scale intermingling of these various peoples that had constituted the basic ethnic composition of the Americas at the time of the European intrusions that began in the fifteenth and sixteenth centuries.

As we have previously stated (although Gladwin himself expressed doubts about their distribution in the prehistoric Americas) it appears extremely likely that small numbers of Diminutive Blacks (whose presence is suggested most strongly by the exceptionally short statures of the Yahgan and Alikuluf peoples who occupy the southernmost tip of South America on Tierra del Fuego) appeared in the New World as its first human occupants.[3]

Initially, and for the purpose of clarification, we should state that when speaking of the *Diminutive Blacks*, we are referring to the important but much romanticized subgroup of Black people (or Africoids) that are phenotypically characterized by (a) unusually short stature (b) skin-complexions that range from yellowish to dark brown (c) tightly curled hair and (d) in frequent cases, steatopygia. The Diminutive Blacks may be more familiar or better known to us by such terms (some of them pejorative) as: *Pygmies, Negritos, Negrillos, Grimaldis, Aeta, Sekai, Orang Asli, Semang, Twa, Black Dwarfs, Khoi Khoi, Hottentots, San, Bushmen, !Kung, Seed People, Little Black Men, and Little Red Men.*[4] From their initial places of origin in Mother Africa, these Blacks have scattered around the earth, and are now usually found only in isolated or heavily forested terrains. In spite of Gladwin's doubts, they were in all likelihood the first people to physically stand on American soil.

The Diminutive Blacks are of particular importance to us because they are morphologically related to the world's first Homo sapiens sapiens, and are typically found to be at the population bases of the inhabited zones of the world. In addition to a number of works by relatively early advocates of this view (Armand De Quatrefages serves as an example) we can now stand on the solid foundation of recent scientific studies. The strongest of these is the work of a team of eleven scholars, most of them based at Oxford University. After completing a meticulous analysis of nuclear DNA polymorphisms, this expert scientific body provided the following summary of its labors:

The earliest fossils of anatomically modern man (Homo sapiens sapiens) have been found in Africa at Omo in Ethiopia, Border Cave in South Africa and at Klasies River Mouth in South Africa. The data from the last site suggests that H. sapiens sapiens was present in South Africa more than 100,000 yr. ago, and an adult mandible from Border Cave has been dated to about 90,000 yr. BP. Hence, it has been argued that the evolution of modern man took place in Africa. Our data are consistent with such a scheme, in which a founder population migrated from Africa and subsequently gave rise to all non-African populations.[5] [This founder population comprised diminutive blacks].

Less than one year after the publication of this revolutionary data assessment, Oxford's Jim Wainscoat, apparently the leader and most actively involved of the scientists engaged in these studies, provided more specific evidence of their validity. In a report just published, Wainscoat elaborates on what is now being labeled "the Out of Africa hypothesis." According to him, "It seems likely that modern man emerged in Africa and ... that subsequently *a founder population left Africa and spread throughout Europe, Asia and the Americas.*"[6]

The studies of a team of scientists at the University of California at Berkeley corroborates the Oxford findings. The Berkeley study is based upon the calculation of the slow changes that have occurred in human DNA over the millennia which "indicate that everyone alive today may be a descendant of a single female ancestor who lived in Africa 140,000 to 280,000 years ago."[7]

That these early ancestors were "phenotypically Black," in addition to being native African is clear. As the brilliant, late Senegalese scholar C.A. Diop noted, "The man born in Africa was necessarily dark-skinned due to the considerable force of ultraviolet radiation in the equatorial belt."[8] Fundamental alterations of this "Africoid phenotype" (occurring after distant migrations from their original African base, with resulting adaptations to new environments) could have come about only gradually after extended passages of time.

Traces of the presence of Diminutive Blacks have been identified in the most remote periods of prehistoric Eastern Asia. Evidence has been noted of their presence, for example, near Lake Baikal in Siberia. A more recent report from Osaka, Japan states that, "The oldest Stone Age hut in Japan has been unearthed near Osaka . . . Archaeologists date the hut to about 22,000 years ago and say it resembles the dugouts of African bushmen . . ."[9] In the light of such data, it is not difficult to speculate about the probabilities of small groups of Diminutive Blacks entering the Americas in the course of their ancient wanderings.

It is generally agreed that the earliest movements of peoples into the Americas took place across the short span that is now called the Bering Strait. In other words, the first Americans wandered out of Siberia, crossed the narrow but frozen water barrier, and entered Alaska. It is entirely possible that a few of these early folk came to the New World in boats; certainly some of the later migrants from Asia to the Americas did. This very first group of migrants, however, probably entered North America without even getting their feet wet.

The first Americans are believed to have come to their new domains dry-shod because of the fact during multiple phases of the geological period known as Wisconsin Glaciation (the last North American phase of the Pleistocene Age) enormous sheets of ice covered most of the northern latitudes of the world, including both Eurasia and North America almost totally. For some reason however (probably because of the low amounts of rainfall), key zones of Siberia's eastern coastal periphery and the extreme western coast of Alaska remained practically ice-free.

The huge amounts of water that the massive northern glaciers drew from the ocean basins of the world caused the earth's sea levels to hover somewhere between 200 and 500 feet lower than today, exposing a broad, basically flat sub-continent. At certain intervals then, each of varying lengths of time (from about 70,000 to approximately 8,000 years before present), *there was no Bering Strait!* In its place was a Bering Isthmus: an approximately 3000 foot wide land bridge (sometimes referred to as Beringia) that connected eastern Siberia with western Alaska. Although controversy remains in this area, geophysicists overwhelmingly state that the existence of a land bridge connecting Asia and America is verifiable for at least three different periods of the Wisconsin Glaciation; the first of which remained unsubmerged until about 37,000 years ago.

Once having gained the assorted cultural equipment, including clothing, tools and shelter, necessary to withstand exceedingly cold climatic conditions, the existence of Beringia made it possible for early bands of men to literally walk (perhaps following the herds of mastodon, wooly mammoths, and giant bison that had gone before them) in a westerly direction over Beringia's tundra-like surface. Almost certainly without any real consciousness of the significance that modern humankind would attach to their accomplishments, these people ultimately marched directly from Asia right into North America. Eventually, after a space of time that probably consumed many generations and several millennia, they filtered all the way down to South America. These would have been the first people then, almost certainly Diminutive Blacks, to move onto American soil and wander the immense lands of the New World.

Despite the obvious implications of geophysical studies of this nature, the case for human existence in the Americas prior to 30,000 before present was basically sneered at in Gladwin's day and is still met by dogged opposition in our own. The intense debate over the earliest appearance of modern man in the Americas has now crystallized around the newly reported, but firmly documented, carbon-14 dates from the site of Boquierao do Sitio da Pedra Furada in the state of Piaui in Northeastern Brazil. This site had yielded evidence of a series of Lithic industries. It is a large, richly painted rock shelter located on the steep bank of a 100 meter high sandstone cliff, and was first reported by the joint French-Brazilian Archaelogical Mission in 1973. It has yielded carbon-14 dates from charcoal deposits at the lowest level of an impressively structured hearth. From these miniscule fragments can now be traced periodic human occupations up to 32,160 + or − 100 years before present. As far as we know this is the oldest clearly verifiable date for man's presence in the Americas.

Because human skeletal remains have yet to be excavated from the Boquierao Pedra Furada site, the identities of the shelter's first residents remains something of a mystery. Stray groups of Diminutive Blacks however (the former lords of the earth), must at least be regarded as the most serious candidates, if for no other reason than the vast antiquity of the era itself.

The First Wave: The Great Australoid Migrations

> It is extremely important to grasp the significance of these four migrations, who the people were, where they came from, when they came, the things they brought with them and the regions they occupied.[10]

> Contrary to the common belief, the earliest Americans were not Mongoloid but actually were members of the so-called Australoid family, which in the old, old days, roamed over most of the earth.[11]

The four migrations that form the basis of the Gladwin Thesis were all sporadic, probably unplanned, and occurred over long spans of time. The first migration to enter North America, Gladwin says, began about 25,000 B.C. and lasted for several millennia. Because of the regional climatic variations between Alaska and eastern Siberia during this period, the migration's approximate beginning date of 25,000 B.C. seems perfectly valid. The date coincides with the gradual reappearance of Beringia; about 26,000 B.C. to around 21,000 B.C. or beyond, when it was once again submerged under water. But even if we were to rule out Beringia's actual existence altogether we would stilll have to recognize the fact that the frigid strait separating Asia from North America could hardly have been a barrier formidable enough to prevent intercontinental movement.

Because of their close physical and cultural relationships to the people who 38,000 years ago colonized Australia and the many islands off the shores of Eastern Asia, these migrants are called Australoids (derived from "austral" or "southern"). Gladwin was not asserting, of course, that these Black pioneers to the Americas actually came from Australia, but only that they issued from the same physical type as those early folk who had moved into Asia and Australia in prehistoric times.

For a physical description of these migrants, one need go no further than their descendants—the 100,000 Blacks of modern Australia. Although known generally as "Australian Aborigines," these oppressed and much analyzed people actually call themselves Kooria ("Black people"). Similar Australoid descendant groups can be found today among the six million Mundas of East/Central India, and the easily identifiable Vedda populations of Sri Lanka.

This application of "Blackness" to the Australoid segment of humankind has been nothing less than disturbing to Eurocentric "scholars" (Gladwin was not among them). These obstinate individuals, in their apparently relentless attempts to maintain superficial divisions amongst the various members of the Black race, refuse to believe their eyes and continue to stubbornly insist (no matter how ridiculous it appears) upon the "scientific" placement of the Australoids within the Caucasoid racial family. To see the illogicality of this, one need only consider the basic question of whether there can exist groups of human beings that could be called "black-skinned white people." To us, this kind of reasoning simply does not make sense. C.A. Diop expressed it this way:

A racial classification is given to a group of individuals who share a certain number of anthropological traits, which is necessary so that they not be confused with others. There are two aspects which must be distinguished, the phenotypical and the genotypiclal. I have frequently elaborated on these two aspects.

If we speak only of the genotype, I can find a black who, at the level of his chromosomes, is closer to a Swede than Peter Botha is. But what counts in reality is the phenotype. It is the physical appearance which counts. This black, even if on the level of his cells he is closer to Swede than Peter Botha, when he is in South Africa he will live in Soweto. Throughout history, it has always been the phenotype which has been at issue; we mustn't lose sight of this fact. The phenotype is a reality, physical appearance is a reality. And this appearance corresponds to something which makes us say that Europe is peopled by white people, Africa is peopled by black people, and Asia is peopled by yellow people. It is these relationships which have played a role in history.[12]

It may help to understand the magnitude of the Australoid migrations to the New World by the fact that they filled in not only the southern section of North America, but also Central and South America. The Australoid migrations occurred during the prolonged period of high rainfall known as the Provo Pluvial, which was really just a continuation of the Wisconsin glaciation in that the rain belts which had formerly fed the massive ice sheet covering most of Canada moved into the arid regions of the North American Southwest. These southern coastal movements of the Australoids were facilitated therefore by the enormous sheets of iced then covering all but the far western extremities of North America. Again now, it should be clearly stated that all of these movements were slow and gradual processes, continuing over a span of many centuries, with numerous pauses and stops along the way.

The majority of the Australoids continued to move in a southern coastal direction but once beneath the glaciers, near the region that is now California, a few Australoid groups began an eastern trek.[13] Gladwin was able to point out numerous crania found at early sites in Southern California, Southwestern Colorado, Southern Arizona, the Texas Gulf coast, Punin and Paltacalo in Ecuador, and Lagoa Santa in Eastern Brazil, all of which demonstrated "characteristics which link these various instances together and point to their wide distribution and common ancestry with other Australoid peoples, as do also certain vestigial traces in some modern people, such as the Pericu of Lower California, the Seri on nearby Tiburon Island, and various tribes in Central and South America . . . [P]eople of Australoid type were once widely distributed, and survivals of some of their features, customs and culture are still to be found in isolated localities."[14]

Possibly the most well-documented single piece of evidence for the early presence of Australoids in the prehistoric Americas during the period of Gladwin's writing was the Punin Skull: a female crania found in 1923, embedded in a stratum of volcanic ash near the small village of Punin in the Andean region of Ecuador. In addition to the skull itself, the stratum yielded the remains of a number of long extinct mammals; including an Andean horse—an animal known to have been extinct for more than 10,000 years, The Punin Skull's recovery by the American Museum of Natural History of New York created a sensation. It was, first of all, hailed as the earliest evidence of humans in the Americas, and, secondly, it was clearly of an Australoid type. On these two issues "the leading experts" agreed. According to British anatomist Arthur Keith:

When the expedition returned to New York from Ecuador, the skull was transferred to the Anthropological side of the Museum, where it was examined and described by Drs. Louis R. Suullivan and Milo Hellman. Both anthropologists were struck by its resemblance to the skulls of the native women of Australia. I agree with them; the points of resemblance are too numerous to permit us to suppose that the skull could be of a sort produced by an American Indian parentage. We cannot suppose that an Australian native woman had been spirited across the Pacific in some migratory movement and that afterwards her skull was buried in a fossiliferous bed in the high plateau of Ecuador . . . The discovery at Punin does compel us too look in the possibility of a pleistocene invasion of America by an Australoid people.[15]

Harvard anthropologist Earnest Hooton echoed Keith, although in somewhat less detail:

The Punin skull, found in 1923 in a fossiliferous bed in the Andean highlands of Ecuador . . . is a skull that any competent craniologist would identify as Australian in type. It is easier to find Australoid-looking dolichocephals in the more ancient burials in the New World than anything in the way of a skull that resembles a Mongoloid."[16]

Gladwin's Sources

To buttress his views on the physical composition of his men out of Asia Gladwin heavily relied upon the works of three writers (two of whom, Keith and Hooton, we have just quoted) above all others. Their combined influences and interactions with him provided for Gladwin both a measure of credibility and a theoretical framework from which he could develop and grow.

The first of these writers was Sir Arthur Keith; a haughty and arrogant man who was once called the "dean of English anatomists." Keith was the former Keeper of the Hunteriana Collection at the Royal College of Surgeons and the past President of the Royal Anthropological Institute. Interestingly enough, much of Keith's academic reputation was gained as the result of his extensive studies of the famous (or infamous) fossil skull from Piltdown, England. Quite a blow it must have been for him when in his last years he learned that the prized Piltdown skull, after further studies by other scientists, was actually only a clever hoax. In 1953, through the utilization of flourine testing, the Piltdown Man's jaw was discovered to be in reality that of an orangutang and the whole fossil was declared completely fraudulent. The Keith text most utilized by Gladwin was *New Discoveries Relating To The Antiquity Of Man*, published in 1931, well before the ultimate bursting of his Piltdown Man bubble. Keith lived well into his eighties.

Earnest A. Hooton, who also contributed the Foreword of *Men Out Of*

Asia, was a constant base of reference for Gladwin. A prominent anthropologist, and the author of several major books, including *Up From The Ape*, Hooton served as Curator of Somatology of Harvard University's Peabody Museum. Hooton was trained in anthropology at Oxford University, and was at one point a professor and sympathetic advisor to the great Afrocentric scholar Willliam Leo Hansberry.

Roland B. Dixon, 1885-1934, who had a tremendous impact upon Gladwin's thought, was easily one of the most erudite scholars and scientists of his era. He was accurately described by Robert Wauchope as, "the archetypal college professor of his day, complete with pipe and tweedy clothes." Dixon was an Assistant Professor of Anthropology at Harvard University from 1906 to 1915. In 1904 he was appointed Librarian of the Peabody Museum, in 1908 Secretary of its Faculty, and in 1912 Curator of Ethnology. At the time of his death Dixon held all three offices. Like Gladwin, he was a specialist in the ancient and modern ethnologies of the North American Southwest. The author of numerous scholarly works, Dixon is probably best known for his *Racial History of Man*, published in 1923. In this comprehensive volume Dixon, through systematic and highly detailed studies of crania, was able to offer what was probably the first really scientific analysis of the racial composition of the American Indians. The book was so brutally received by fellow anthropologists, however, that Dixon was to refer to it in his later years as "my crime." Nevertheless, the fundamental conclusions presented in *Racial History Of Man* have basically been substantiated rather than disproven by the related archaeological and anthropological researches that have been conducted more recently. Dixon is also known to have spent considerable energy in attacking (some would say destroying) the diffusionist theories of Elliot Smith and W.J. Perry.

The Second Migration: The Clovis-Folsom Point Blacks

> Proto-Negroid or pseudo-Australoid. Terms such as these will be found only in technical papers on physical anthropology, but never in orthodox reconstructions of native American history. We have included them here because we think they cannot fairly be ignored, and, once you accept them as facts to be reckoned with, they turn out to be essential to an understanding of the problem.[17]

The second migration in the Gladwin Thesis began about 15,000 years ago. These migrants Gladwin calls "Asiatic Negroids." He postulates that approximately fifteen millennia ago waves of these Blacks, having entered Asia from Africa, were actively engaged in a broad, wide-ranging population movement. After firmly establishing themselves in Southern and Eastern Asia, one of their family branches dispersed towards the numerous island chains of the vast Pacific Ocean, while another, after having first penetrated its way northward up the coasts of Asia, began to gradually enter North America. Their arrival in North America differed from the earlier Australoids in that it coincided with the eastward recession of the mighty Keewatin ice sheet (which had formerly covered the mass of western Canada), creating for them a sort of corridor along the eastern foothills of the Rocky Mountains. Eventually their movements brought them onto the immense plains where roamed North America's vast bison herds.

These are the Blacks who, decades after their arrival in North America, founded the historically pivotal Clovis and Folsom fluted-point tool industries. Out of respect therefore to their unique and invaluable contribution to the techno/cultural evolution of prehistoric America, we shall henceforth disregard Gladwin's archaic "Asiatic Negroid" designation and refer to them as the "Clovis-Folsom Point Blacks." In physical appearance they closely resembled their Melanesian descendants—the proud, ancient, seafaring Black Islanders of the South Pacific.

Clovis and Folsom were the respective locations (both of them in New Mexico, U.S.A.) that provided the first evidences of the earliest projectile points associated with the Big Game Hunting Traditions of North America. Clovis points have been reliably dated to between 11,000 and 11,500 years before present. Folsom points, which are usually smaller, more refined and sophisticated than their Clovis antecedents, were actually identified before the Clovis points, and have been dated to about 10,000 B.C. Both Clovis and Folsom spearheads were several inches long and were characterized by smoothly fluted or grooved channels extending lengthwise along both faces. Their precision and firepower were revolutionary and awesome; and their rapidly widespread usage, with the increasingly greater food supplies that resulted, laid the basis for steadily larger American populations. Gladwin associated the delicacy and accuracy of the Folsom points (and the later Yuma points also) with "the better known Solutrean industry of prehistoric western Europe."[18]

It is of further interest that the first known modern discovery and revelation of the existence of these tool industries was made by an African-American; a tantalizingly and frustratingly obscure, self-taught naturalist and archaeologist named George McJunkin. The son of slaves, McJunkin, whose name may be serached for unsuccessfully in most history books, made the find in 1908 while riding out to check fence posts at a flooded creek. In 1925, three years after McJunkin's death, a dig at the Folsom site revealed a 10,000 year old spear point piercing the ribs of an extinct species of bison. It was McJunkin though, the obscure African-American, who had first documented Folsom points, which were then regarded (this was before the discovery of Ecuador's Punin Skull) as "the first unequivocal evidence of late Ice Age humans ever unearthed in the Americas."[19]

The Clovis-Folsom Point Blacks seem to have come to North America in relatively small numbers. Later migrations of essentially the same physical type populated most of the rest of North America south of Canada. Their movements into the New World were then slowed, and later halted altogether, by the Australoid populations that were already well established in the North American Southwest. The later period Basket Makers of Arizona (the pre-historic culture bearers who eventually evolved into North America's Pueblo peoples) were probably the result of a fusion of Clovis-Folsom Point Blacks with the numerically larger Australoids. Roland Dixon was such a strong advocate of this position that he is worth quoting on the subject:

> In the present area [the Southwest], the Proto-Negroid type is of relatively slight importance. In the islands off the California coast it is lacking amongst the males although present as a small minority among females; it is not found in the Pericue, and occurs only as a trace in the Ute and Pi-Ute. The Basket Maker crania, however, show a contrast to the more modern population, in that the Proto-Negroid type is present in large amounts in both sexes. This would appear to indicate that this type was at an early date quite prominent in this portion of the continent; and this belief is corroborated by the crania from the ancient burial caves of Coahuila in nothern Mexico, which exhibits this type as clearly dominant! It is interesting in this connection to find that culturally these people of Coahuila were in many respects closely allied to the Basket Makers.[20]

The Third Migration: The Coming of the Algonquin

> In dealing with the populating of the New World we are attempting to trace some of the great movements of human history, of which there is no written record and which can only be pieced together by deduction and speculation based on the disconnected and fragmentary evidence of ar-chaeology.[21]

The third migration of the Gladwin Thesis is stated to have begun about 1000 B.C. It was believed to have been made up of the people who, since their arrival in North America, have come to be best known as the Algonquin—irrespective of what they were called before they reached Alaska. The Algon-quin, whose American presence (with the aid of carbon-14 dating methods unavailable to Gladwin) have now been pushed back closer to 2,000 B.C., are specifically important to us because they are the first American arrivals who are not known to have been of a Black or Africoid phenotype. For some reason the Algonquin-speakers are the only group of migrants in the Gladwin Thesis for whom the author (much to our misfortune) provides no physical description.

What Gladwin really emphasized about the Algonquin was their pottery. He says that "once the Algonquin had settled down and made themselves at home they resumed the manufactuure of cord-marked pottery, the knowledge of which they brought with them from Asia."[22] Gladwin positively identified the Algonquin as the first American pottery makers. Their cord-marked pottery, which he defined as "a peculiar kind of prehistoric pottery which shows the imprint of twisted cords or of cord-wrapped paddles used in patting the surfaces," is now known as Jomon pottery ware; the use of which was widely employed in eastern Asia from about 11,000 to 300 B.C.

In stark contrast to the Clovis-Folsom Point Blacks, the Algonquin evidently came to North America in fairly big numbers, or so it would appear from the great quantities of pottery shards and other debris that they prominently discarded in the course of their travels. These "traveler's testimonies" have been recovered from village sites in the North American woodlands east of the Mississippi, and the northern states from the Pacific to the Atlantic coasts. These extensive areas of distribution coincide, by the way, with the domains of the known Algonquin-speaking tribes of the European phase of North American history. These tribes include: in Eastern Canada, the Micmac; in Maine, the Penobscot; in New England, the Mohican of Leatherstocking fame; in Pennsylvania, the Delaware; along the Ohio River, the Shawnee; in Illinois, the Kickapoo; near Lake Michigan, the Sauk, Fox and Menominee; and in northeastern Colorado and along the Rocky Mountains, the Blackfoot and the Cree.

Migration Four: The Arrival of the Eskimo

The Algonquin were followed, Gladwin believed, around 500 B.C. by the last of "four separate migrations, each of which was distinct from all the others in regard to both the physical appearance of the people and the culture which they brought with them."[23] The fourth migration, which had probably been in full motion well before the estimated date of 500 B.C:, was that of the Eskimo; a people that Gladwin claims showed absolutely no relationship whatsoever either in physique or culture to any of the peoples of the three earlier migratory weaves. The Eskimo entered the New World in large numbers. They came in a steady stream, and they kept on coming for a long time. It was exceedingly clear to Gladwin that *"The arrival of the Eskimo along the Arctic Coasts marked a fundamental transition in the anthropological history of North America. It was the last of a series of long-headed migrations, and the broad faces and slant eyes of the Eskimo marked the initial stage of a long period of Mongoloid domination in lands where Mongoloid people had therefore been unknown."*[24]

Mongoloid peoples, in fact, were soon coming to the Americas in such massive numbers, crossing the Bering Strait in boats rather than the Beringia land bridge, that they eventually almost totally absorbed the New World's earlier arrivals. The resulting fusion of peoples came to be *the American*

Indians. The earlier arrived Blacks (Gladwin's men out of Asia and the very first Americans) tended to fade away with increasing rapidity into the shadowy realms of fairy tales, myths and legends.[25]

Notes

1. Harold S. Gladwin, *Men Out Asia* (New York: McGraw-Hill, 1947)

2. "Harold Gladwin is not a professional archaeological in the sense of studying the subject at some university or research institute, and then making a meager living by teaching, digging, putting pots in museum exhibition cases. He is an amateur academically in that his record is not besmirched by Ph.D degree. . . . However, he had done as much dirt archaeologyy (which means real digging) in contrast to armchair archaeology (which means reading and speculating) as nearly any professional in the American field. He knows fully and utilizes skillfully the elaborate and precise techniques of the science. His excavations are models of method, his reports voluminous, orderly and overwhelmingly documented. He is not a pot hunter, not a romancer; he is an expert practitioner." E. Hooton, Foreword to *Men Out Of Asia*, x.

3. It was in 1833 that the famous British naturalist Charles Darwin, 1808-1882, the author of *Origin of Species* [1859] and *Descent of Man* [1871], found 3,000 Yahgan Indians living naked but healthy at the bleak, cold and windy tip of South America. Darwin reported that "these miserable and abject creatures" slept on the barren ground; that mothers nursed their infants while sleet fell on their naked bodies. Responding to Darwin's writings, "sympathetic Englishmen" sent clothes and blankets. Along with these new items came diseases to which the Yahgan had been previously unexposed. Dreadful and decimating epidemics among the Yahgan was the result.
Very few Yahgans now survive. It was reported in 1955 that "A shriveled old woman known only as Julia is believed to be the last pure-blooded Yahgan . . . The surveying ship Beagle picked up Jemmy Button, a Yahgan, and took him to England for education and a day at the court of King William IV. Jemmy returned two years later. Darwin, who put him ashore, regarded him as a friend and *a superior sort of aborigine.* Throwing off alien culture, Jemmy 26 years later led a massacre of missionaries." Newman Bumstead, "Atlantic Odyssey: Iceland to Antartica." *National Geographic Magazine*, December 1955, p. 765.

4.
Regions	*Designations*
Andaman Islands	Negritos
Central Africa	Negrillos, Negritos, Pygmies, Twa
China	Black Dwarfs
Ice Age Europe	Grimaldis
Malaysia	Orang Asli, Sekai, Seman
Phillipines	Aeta
Southern Africa	Bushmen, Hottentots, Khoi Khoi, !Kung, San
Taiwan	Little Black Man
Authors	*Designations*
Richard D. King, M.D.	Seed People
Albert Churchward	Little Red Men

5. J.S. Wainscoat, et al. "Evolutionary Relationships Of Human Populations From An Analysis Of Nuclear DNA Polymorphisms." *Nature*, February 6, 1986, p. 493.

6. Wainscoat. "Out of The Garden of Eden." *Nature*, January 1, 1987, p. 13.

7. "DNA Researchers Trace All Humans To Single Woman In Ancient Africa." *New York Times*, March 30, 1986.

8. Cheikh Anta Diop, "Africa: Cradle Of Humanity." *Nile Valley Civilizations.* Ivan Van Sertima, ed. (New Brunswick & Oxford, 1984), p. 27.

9. "African-Like Stone Age Hut Is Unearthed In Japan." *Associated Press*, February 15, 1986.

10. N. Guidon, and F. Delibrias. "Carbon-14 Dates Point To Man In The Americas 32,000 Years Ago," *Nature*, June 19, 1986, pp. 769-771.

11. Harold S. Gladwin, *A History Of The Ancient Southwest* (Portland, Maine: Bond Wheelwright Co., 1957), p. 16.

12. Cheikh Anta Diop, "Interview With Cheikh Anta Diop," *Great African Thinkers, Vol. 1: Cheikh Anta Diop*, ed., Ivan Van Sertima (New Brunswick & Oxford, 1986), pp. 235-236.

13. California may have been mentioned for the first time in *The Adventures of Esplandian*, a novel published in Toledo, Spain around 1516. It was noted as an island paradise wealthy in gold, silver and precious stones. A noteworthy section of the novel reads, "There is an island called California, very near to the terrestial paradise, which was peopled by black women . . ." Cortez is thought to have been inspired by the legendary riches of California.

14. Gladwin, *Men Out Of Asia*, pp. 66-67; 88-89.

15. Arthur Keith, *New Discoveries Relating To The Antiquity Of Man* (London: Williams & Norgate, 1931), p. 312.

16. Earnest A. Hooton, *Up From The Ape* (New York: Macmillian, 1931), p. 650.

17. Gladwin, p. 185.

18. P. 97.

19. Susan Katz. "Mystery: When Did Ice Age Man Discover The Americas?" *Newsweek*, November 10, 1986, p. 72.

20. Roland B. Dixon, *The Racial History Of Man* (New York: Scribner's, 1923), pp. 109-110.

21. Gladwin, p. 151.

22. P. 147.

23. P. 150.

24. P. 157.

25. "A man and his wife and their only daughter lived in a remote place. Their daughter was outside, working when she saw a big black speck moving along the ground, coming towards her. When it got closer, she realized it was a man with a sledge. The man and the sledge were all black. He came towards the house, stopped, and said to the girl, 'I have come to take you with me.' He was black all over, even his face. The girl replied, 'Very well. I'll go and tell my parents.' She entered the igloo and the man followed her. He stood outside the door and was told by the father, 'I won't have my daughter going away with a black man like you.' The stranger became angry and made a step forward with his right foot. The whole house shook. Then the father said to his daughter, 'My daughter, you'll have to go away with this man. This will go badly with us if you don't. She got ready and left the house, with the stranger behind her. Before leaving, he put his left foot down hard on the floor and the house shook again. He went out, put the girl on the sledge and shoved the sledge because it had no huskies. After a while they saw a house—the man's house. They stopped and entered. Everything inside was black, and his parents also were completely black." Edwin S. Hall, Jr., *The Eskimo Story Teller*, Knoxville, 1975, pp. 289-90.

"For the Greenlander, the color black symbolizes strength and wisdom—traditionally he was not allowed to wear black boots until he had become a skilled hunter and reached a respectable age—but black is also associated with spirits and occult forces. Jean Malaurie. Preface to *An African in Grenland*.Kpomassie, Tete-Michel. New York: Harcourt Brace Jovanich, 1983, p. x.

In the Southwest Indian story of the Emergence, a story that is as important in the region as the Book of Genesis is to Christians, *the First World is called the Black World*. John Bierhorst, *The Mythology of North America*. Quil, 1986.

Bibliography

"African-Like Stone Age Hut Is Unearthed In Japan." *Associated Press*, February 15, 1986.

Boule, Marcellin and Henri V. Vallois. *Fossil Men*. 1921; rpt. New York: Dryden Press, 1957.

Bowles, Gordon T. *The People Of Asia*. New York: Charles Scribner's Sons, 1977.

Bray, Warwick and Donald Trump. *Penguin Dictionary Of Archaeology*. Middlesex, England: Penguin Books Ltd., 1970.

Cobb, Gayleatha B. "An Interview With Roosevelt Brown: Black Nationalism In The South Pacific." *Black World*, March 1976. pp. 32-43.

Brunson, James, E. *Black Jade: African Presence In The Ancient East*. Chicago: KARA Pub., 1985.

Chang, Kwang-chih. *The Archaeology Of Ancient China*. New Haven & London: Yale University Press, 1968.

Clegg, Legrand H. II. "The Beginning Of The African Diaspora: Black Men In Ancient And Medieval America? Pt. 1." *Current Bibliography On African Affairs*, Vol. 2, No. 11, 1969. pp. 19-32.

———"Who Were The First Americans?" *Black Scholar*, Sept. 1975. pp. 33-41.

———"The First Americans." *Journal Of African Civilizations*, April 1979. pp. 98-107.

———"The Mystery Of The Arctic Twa: A Letter To The Editor." *African Presence In Early Europe*. Ed., Ivan Van Sertima. New Brunswick & Oxford: Transaction Books, 1985. pp. 245-250.

Davies, Nigel. *Voyagers To The New World*. New York: Morrow, 1979.

Diop, Cheikh Anta. "Africa: Cradle Of Humanity." *Nile Valley Civilizations*. Ed., Ivan Van Sertima. New Brunswick & Oxford: Transaction Books, 1984. pp. 23-28.

Dixon, Roland B. *The Racial History Of Man*. New York: Scribner's, 1923.

———*The Building Of Cultures*. rpt., New York: Putnam, 1974.

"DNA Researchers Trace All Humans To Single Woman In Ancient Africa." *New York Times*, March 30, 1986.

Finch, Charles S. "Race And Evolution In Prehistory." *African Presence In Early Europe*. Ed., Ivan Van Sertima. New Brunswick & Oxford: Transaction Books, 1985. pp. 288-312.

Gladwin, Harold S. *Excavations At Casa Grande*. Los Angeles: Southwest Museum Papers No. 2., 1928.

———*Method For The Designation Of Cultures And Their Variations*. 1934. In this work the development of culture was visualized as a tree with the roots forming the beginnings of a sequence, the trunk the main development, and the branches as subsidiary phases of the culture.

———"Independent Invention Versus Diffusion." *American Antiquity*, 3. 1937. pp. 156-160.

———*Men Out Of Asia*. New York: McGraw—Hill, 1947.

———*A History Of The Ancient Southwest*. Portland, Maine: Bond Wheelwright Co., 1957.

———*Men Out Of The Past*. Santa Barbara, California, 1975.

Guidon, N. and F. Delibrias. "Carbon-14 Dates Point To Man In The Americas 32,000 Years Ago." *Nature*, June 19, 1986. pp. 769-771.

Hooton, Earnest A. *Up From The Ape*. New York: Macmilllan, 1931.

Katz, Susan. "Mystery: When Did Ice Age Man Discover The Americas?" *Newsweek*, November 10, 1986. p. 72.

Keith, Arthur. *New Discovereies Relating To The Antiquity Of Man*. London: Williams & Norgate, 1931.

Kpomassie, Tet-Michel. *An African In Greenland*. New York: Harcourt Brace Jovanich, 1983.

Lemonick, Michael D. "Everyone's Genealogical Mother: Biologists Speculate That 'Eve' Lived in Sub-Saharan Africa." *Time*, January 26, 1987. p. 66.

Quatrefages, Armand De. *The Pygmies*. New York: D. Appleton & Co., 1985.

Rashidi, Runoko and Ivan Van Sertima, Eds. *African Presence In Early Asia*. New Brunswick & Oxford: Transaction Books, 1985.

Rogers, Joel A. *World's Great Men Of Color*. 2 vols. New York: Collier, 1946-47.

Rouse, Irving. *Migrations In Prehistory*. New Haven & London: Yale University Press, 1986.

Turner, Geoffrey. *Indians Of North America*. Poole & Dorset: Blandford Press, 1979.

Van Sertima, Ivan, Ed. *Great African Thinkers, Vol. 1: Cheikh Anta Diop*. New Brunswick & Oxford, 1986.

Wainscoat, J.S., et al. "Evolutionary Relationships Of Human Populations From An Analysis Of Nuclear DNA Polymorphisms." *Nature*, February 6, 1986. pp. 491-493.
Williams, Paris. "Black Beginnings In Ancient America." Oakland and Los Angeles: Unpublished, 1986.

PLATE 1
Africoid Mask—Basalt; 9″ diameter; age unknown.
Found along the North Canadian coast in 1879. National Museum of Man, Ottawa.

THE FIRST AMERICANS

Legrand H. Clegg II

Summary: *This paper lays emphasis on cranial remains in the ancient New World which establishes the pre-historic presence of "Africoid" types in the Western hemisphere. This evidence suggests, argues Clegg, that even before the great mongoloid migrations via the Bering Straits a black element, variously designated by physical anthropologists as "proto-negroid" and "pseudo-Australoid" entered both the Northern and Southern halves of the American continent.*

The history of the ancient New World will remain incomplete and will not be fully understood until the presence of the Black race, as an integral part of it, is first acknowledged by scientists and then brought to the attention of the lay public. In an effort to embark on the first step, this paper will narrowly focus on some of the cranial remains that suggest the prehistoric presence of Black folk in the Western Hemisphere.

The general history of early America is universally written in two phases: that of the pre-Columbian Indian "native" and that of the post-Columbian European colonization. Most scientists concur on the racial characteristics of the two major groups that confronted each other in the Western Hemisphere as the first phase yielded to the second.[1] The Indian or red man, it is generally agreed, was of Mongoloid stock with a broadhead, straight, black hair, broad and prominent cheekbones, and a broad and concave nose. The Caucasoid European was also broadheaded with bleached skin, a prominent nose and chin, and hair that generally ranged from straight to wavy.

Rarely considered in histories and treatises on the New World is the "Negroid" race. These long-headed, dark-skinned folk usually possess crinkled or wavy hair, a nose that ranges from broad to keen and lips that are often fleshy. Many "Negroid" people were imported by Europeans into the Americas during the early period of White colonization. Although scholars are gradually expressing a growing tolerance for historians who discuss the enslavement of Black people in the New World, any examination of the role of Blacks in the Americas prior to the slave-trade and slavery is met with bitter resistance by many of these same savants whose allegiance to outmoded tradition far outweighs their pursuit of scientific accuracy.

Before Western scientists began the *universal* suppression of the history of Black people,[2] several early scholars, primarily Latin American scholars, acknowledged and investigated evidence of an ancient Black presence in the Americas. Among those pioneers were Jose Melgar,[3] Manuel Orozco y Berra,[4] Riva Palacio[5] and Jose Villacorta.[6] In modern times, the one scholar who has synthesized the work of these and other scientists and brought a fresh approach to the history of the Western Hemisphere is Rutgers University anthropologist Ivan Van Sertima. His book, *They Came Before Columbus, The African Presence in Ancient America*, is a landmark that firmly establishes the significant role that Black folk played in the advancement of pre-Columbian, New World civilization.[7]

The contributions of the foregoing scientists are immeasurable and are slowing forcing the intransigents of the academic world to budge as the new, revolutionary school of thought gradually rises from the blight of white supremacist propaganda. One certain indication of the impact of the New School on modern science is that many archeologists, anthropologists and historians are now *listening* to the arguments of a growing number of experts on African and American history, and examining their evidence which confirms the presence of black people in the Americas between c. 800 B.C. and 1400 A.D.[8]

The New School, however, has not yet focused on the presence of Black people in *prehistoric* America, i.e., c. 40,000 B.C. to 6,000 B.C. Neither early Latin American pioneers nor their modern disciples have given this subject much attention. Yet, over the past century, a few distinguished authorities have meticulously recorded evidence in special reports and technical treatises that suggest that Africoids were the first inhabitants of the Western Hemisphere.[9] By using the term Africoid, we are speaking herein of the "Pygmoid," "Australoid" and "Negroid" peoples. Since it appears highly likely, if not absolute, that the foregoing sub-types have common ancestral roots that extend into prehistoric times and are probably traceable to the continent of Africa, we refer to these people as variants of the Black or Africoid race; and when speaking of the foregoing variants as a whole, the term Africoid is used.

The "Pygmoids" (including "Negritos" and "Negrillos") are distinguished from the heretofore defined "Negroid" subtype mainly by the fact that the former are a dwarfed people who rarely reach five feet in height. The "Australoid" subtype, on the other hand, differs somewhat from both the "Negroids" and the "Pygmoids." They are generally dark-skinned (invariably black) with a broad, flat nose and fleshy lips as are the latter two sub-types, but also possess a beetling brow ridge, a receding forehead and hair that ranges from wavy to straight.

Although the presence of Africoid people in prehistoric America is largely evidenced by cranial remains, most modern scientists ignore this and dismiss as preposterous the very possibility of such an early pre-Columbian population in the New World. Harold S. Gladwin, a distinguished pioneer in American anthropology, has summed up the present posture of the general scientific community concerning this subject:

> It has been this negative attitude of mind, for instance, which has consistently refused to recognize the definite implications of the many references by physical anthropologists to such types as Australoid or Negroid in the makeup of various Indian tribes—even though veiled by such qualifications as Proto-Negroid or pseudo-Australoid. Terms such as these will be found only in technical papers on physical anthropology, but never in orthodox reconstructions of native American history. We have included them here because we think they cannot fairly be ignored, and, once you accept them as facts to be reckoned with, they turn out to be essential to an understanding of the problem since they show that Mongoloid people could not have reached North America before the time of Christ.[10]

Prehistoric "Pygmoids"

The first of the early Africoids to reach the Americas may well have been the "Pygmoid" sub-type. Their presence, however, is mentioned here as a *possibility* rather than an established fact because the supporting evidence is extremely sparse and inconclusive.

Gladwin wonders whether the Yaghan on Tierra del Fuego are of very ancient "Pygmoid" origin. They are of surprisingly low stature, averaging about five feet with some individuals never rising above 56 inches. They are found on the southernmost islands of the archipelago lying off the tip of South America, which is refuge area and therefore typical of the present day habitats of "Pygmoids" around the world.[11]

In addition to this, Gladwin states that "there are hazy suggestions of queer faces and traits which crop out occasionally along the eastern seaboard and other out-of-the-way places, nothing that can be pinned down, but just enough to make one wonder if there may not have been a few Pygmy groups who strayed" into the Americas in prehistorictimes, "and who were pushed off to the edge and the ends when the Australoid tide flowed in."[12]

In the same vein, Latin American historian Carlos Marquez notes that "the Negroes figure frequently in the most remote tradition of some American people. Certain tribes of Darien say that when their ancestors first arrived in the region it was inhabited by *small black men* who soon afterwards retired to the forests while the Payas the Tapalisas of the Cuna-Cunas origin goes back to a man and two women, one Indian and the other Negro, who lived on the banks of the the Tatarcuna:

"The ancient skeletons which are very different from the Red American races, and have been found in various places from Bolivia to Mexico, doubtlessly belong to this race.

"It is likely, then . . . that long ago the youthful America was also a Negro continent."[13]

Were the "small black men" recalled by the ancient Indians of Central America remnants of prehistoric "Pygmoids" who were the first people to reach and settle the New World? It is impossible for us to be certain at this time, but the far flung Old World presence (e.g., Sub Saharan Africa, the Andaman Islands, the Malay Peninsula, New Guinea and the Phillipines) of the "Pygmoids" certainly suggests that they have been a migratory people over the centuries who were probably as capable of reaching the prehistoric New World as were the early "Australoids," "Negroids" and Mongoloids whose ancient presence is now confirmed. "It seems difficult to escape the theory," write J.A. Rogers, one of the most foremost authorities on the history of Black people, "that in the most ancient times a Negrito race found itself cut off in some way in the far north of both hemispheres. Northern Japan, Northern Europe, and Northern America are all inhabited by a diminutive people with hair which, though straight, is black . . . and with dark, Negroid faces with a suggestion of the Mongolian."[14]

Rogers' theory is supported by the research of the distinguished British egyptologist, Gerald Massey, who had written that "[the] one sole race that can be traced among the aborigines all over the earth or below is the dark race of a dwarf, Negrito type."[15]

Prehistoric "Australoids"

In contrast to the "Pygmoids," there is considerable evidence to suggest the prehistoric presence of the "Australoid" sub-type in the Americas. In fact, some scientists believe that these Africoids were the first inhabitants of the New World, which would mean that they reached the Americas at least 38,000 years ago (but perhaps as early as 70,000 B.C.[16]).

The eminent Harvard anthropologist, Roland Dixon, was one of the first scientists to detect "Australoid" characteristics in crania exhumed from prehistoric sites throughout the Americas. Admitting that his conclusions were "completely at variance with traditional and current theories,"[17] Dixon cautiously chose the term Proto-Australoid for the people he believed to have been the original inhabitants of the New World. This appellation served the dual purpose of saving Dixon's reputation and appeasing the scientific community which would not tolerate the suggestion that full-blown Black "Australoids" had reached prehistoric America.

"It seems on the whole probable," Dixon wrote, "that the Proto-Australoid must have been one of the earliest, if not the earliest, type to spread into the North American continent. On the Pacific coast in California and Lower California it appears to constitute the oldest stratum, characterizing as it does the crania from the lower layers of the shell-heaps from the islands of Santa

Catalina and San Clemente off the coast, and from the extinct Pericue, isolated in the southern tip of the peninsula of Lower California. It is moreover, prominent among the ancient basket-makers of northern Arizona, who represent probably one of the earliest peoples in this whole area. In the northeast the type is of importance among the Iroquois and the southern Algonkian tribes, such as the Lenape."[18]

Gladwin largely concurs with Dixon's conclusions. The former speaks of "Australoid" skulls exhumed from early sites in southern California, southwestern Colorado, southern Arizona and the Texas gulf coast; and insists that "certain vestigial traces in some modern people, such as the Pericu of Lower California [and] the Seri on nearby Tiburon Island" confirm the prehistoric presence of "Australoids" in this part of the world.[19]

Most of the scientists who have acknowledged the presence of these "Australoids" point to the evidence that has been discovered in sites south of the present-day United States—primarily in South America. Significant among these finds is a calvarium that was exhumed from a fossiliferous bed in the high plateau of Ecuador and later turned over to two distinguished anthropologists, Louis Sullivan and Milo Hellman. Struck by the resemblance of the skull to those of native women of Australia, the two scientists noted that "[either] we have, in certain parts of America, skeletal remains of a type basically related to those found also in Australia and Melanesia and fundamentally different racially from the prevailing mongoloid American Indian types, or we have a remarkable case of parallelism—parallelism sufficiently detailed to deceive physical anthropologists of very wide experience."[20] Concurring with the foregoing scientists, anthropologist Arthur Keith has stated that "[this] discovery . . . does compel us to look into the possibility of a pleistocene invasion of America by an Australoid people."[21]

This Ecuadorian or "punin calvarium" is not an isolated discovery. British anthropologist H.C. Haddon notes that "[perhaps] the oldest remains [in South America] of which we have sufficient information are those from the caves of Lagoa Santa on the eastern border of the Brazilian highlands. These skulls are small, dolichocranial, very high, with a short and wide face, medium nose and orbit and a very large palate giving marked alveolar prognathism. This is certainly an old type of skull which has affinity with various skulls from the western Pacific and elsewhere . . ."[22] In the same vein, Gladwin adds that these "Australoids" have been "found in association with extinct fauna at Punin and Pattalco in Ecuador, in the Lagoa Santa caves of eastern Brazil, and as a persisting factor in modern tribes in the southern half of the continent."[23]

Anthropologists Paul Rivet and A.H. Keene are of similar opinion. Rivet, for example, notes that from Brazil to Tierra del Fuego on the Atlantic slope, in Bolivia and Peru, and on the high plateau of the Andes are traces of this distinct folk.[24] Furthermore, Joseph Deniker, one of the first scientists to identify and define these prehistoric people, refers to them as the non-mongoloid, Paleo-American sub-race;[25] and Griffith Taylor, another distinguished anthropologist, has concluded that the foregoing evidence suggests "that the first migration into America may well have been a Botocudo or Australoid type . . ."[26]

Prehistoric "Negroids"

The "Negroid" sub-type of the Africoid race also appears to have migrated into prehistoric America. To the degree that "Negroid" remains can be distinguished from those of "Pygmoid" and "Australoid" peoples, it appears that the "Negroids" followed the latter and were the last of the prehistoric people to reach the New World prior to the great Mongoloid migrations.

Even among those scientists who recognize the prehistoric presence of "Negroid" cranial types in America, there is disagreement as to whether these early immigrants were "full-blooded Negroids" or an unnamed type evidencing a strong "Negroid" strain. The late Harvard anthropologist, Earnest Hooton, was of the latter opinion: "I do not think there is sufficient craniological or other physical evidence to support the supposition that any group of Negroes or Negritos ever reached the American continents before the coming of Europeans. But I do think that some of the earlier strata of the American population show indications of having carried with them in solution from Asia a Negroid strain of blood."[27] In sharp contrast to this, Taylor insists that existing carnial evidence "certainly indicates the presence in the far past of negroid peoples in the American continent."[28]

Evidence of the prehistoric "Negroid" people appears to be widespread in the New World. Dixon refers to crania of this type that have been exhumed from very ancient strata in Arizona, Northern Mexico, New England and from the Turner group mounds in the Ohio Valley and the grave cites of the prehistoric cist-grave people of Tennessee.[29] Gladwin believes that these ancient folk settled much of the southern and eastern regions of the United States, and mixed with many of the "Australoid" residents of the south and southwest. He also believes that these Negroids were the prehistoric Folsom people who appear to have been expert hunters and makers of fine flint spear points.[30]

Dixon and Taylor maintain that some of the prehistoric crania of South America evidence a definite "Negroid" presence on that continent.[31] Taylor and Deniker also suggest that the "wavy or frizzy" hair of living American Indians such as the Korayas of Matto Grosso, the Bakairas of the Xingu River and some Arawaks is traceable to these prehistoric "Negroid" immigrants.[32]

Conclusion

The foregoing evidence is by no means exhaustive but lays the foundation for a more detailed analysis of the arguments presented and the conclusions reached by the distinguished authorities cited. An article of this nature raises a number of questions. However, some of these are beyond our present scope. Despite this, two questions are so very compelling that a sentence or two must be devoted to a partial answer to them: From what lands did the first Americans come? And what ultimately happened to the descendants of these prehistoric settlers?

It is highly probable, though not absolute, that the prehistoric Africoids who appear to have reached and settled the New World were descendants of very ancient Black folk who migrated from Africa into Europe,[33] Western Asia,[34] India,[35] Southeast Asia and the Pacific Islands,[36] China and Japan.[37] It appears, furthermore, that, in scattered numbers, these Africoid pioneers—frist the "Australoids" and then the "Negroids"—migrated up the northeastern coast of Asia over the Bering Strait and thereafter reached the New World perhaps as early as 70,000 B.C. This theory has been very well summarized by Roland Dixon:

> "For the earliest assignable homeland or focus of dispersion of the Proto-Negroid type we may probably, although not certainly, look to northern and western Africa. As the Proto-Australoids streamed west along the southern margin of Asia, so it may be supposed the Proto-Negroids, probably at a later date, drifted eastward through India to southeastern Asia and thence through Indonesia and Melanesia to Australia, with a long arm stretched out farther through central Polynesia as far as Easter Island. Like the presumably older Proto-Australoids they followed northward up the eastern Asiatic borderlands and penetrated to the New World, drifting, or being later driven by other immigrants, southward and toward its eastern shores.[38]"

While Vasco Nunez de Balboa and other European explorers found a few Black people in the New World prior to the importation of slaves to the Americas,[39] these Blacks appear to have been recent migrants from Africa.[40] By the time of Europe's "discovery" of the New World, the overwhelming majority of American residents were Mongoloids (Indians) who, as early as 3200 B.C.,[41] appear to have begun *massive* migrations—which may have continued sporadically for several hundred years—from northeast Asia over the Bering Strait into the Americas. A number of scholars believe that for several centuries the invading Mongoloids uprooted and exterminated many of the resident Africoids.[42] In addition to this, it is highly likely that most of the Blacks who escaped extermination or expulsion from their lands probably "mixed and melted into the billion-bodied Mongoloid gene pool."[43]

We conclude, therefore, that existing cranial evidence suggest not only a prehistoric presence of Africoid or Black people in the New World, but that these people were indeed *the first Americans!* It appears, furthermore, that there is ample authority to explain the Old World origin of these early migrants, their migratory paths from the Old World to the New and their ultimate fate as well as that of their descendants who were born on New World soil.

Notes

1. We are well aware that the new anthropological party line is that "there is no such thing as 'race'," and that it is now unscientific to delimit mankind on the basis of "race." We do not accept this point of view for the following reasons: First, three major subspecies of the human family i.e., the Africoid ("Negroid"), Caucasoid and Mongoloid are readily distinguishable and can be scientifically defined without the absurd assumption that racial "purity" is widespread in either category. Secondly, it appears that the abandonment of the study of "race" by modern science is not so much an attempt to stress the unity of the human species as it is to focus away from the inevitable conclusions that such study has forced upon the academic community. Nineteenth century scientists embarked on the study of human subspecies in order to prove the superiority of the white race and it is no accident that, as their modern disciples come to the startling realization that the human family was born in Africa, that the first homo sapiens were probably Black and that Caucasians probably sprang from prehistoric Black people as a genetic mutation to albinism, these scientists are eager to suppress this information. Finally, as long as the world is dominated by White people; as long as those scientists—who now claim that there is no validity to the study of race—continue to practice racism socially and academically; and, most important, as long as the Black race bears the universal badge of inferiority forced on it by scientists who have distorted or suppressed Black history, we will not only include race as an integral part of our historical writings, but will prominently focus on it whenever and wherever the truth can be told until sincere men of science return the Black race to its former position of respect and reverence on the earth.

2. W.E.B. DuBois, *The World And Africa, An Inquiry Into The Part Which Africa Has Played In World History*, International Publishers, New York, 1961; also see Chancellor Williams, *The Destruction of Black Civilization, Great Issues of A Race From 4500 B.C. to 2000 A.D.*, Chicago, Third World Press, 1974.

3. Jose Melgar, "Notable Esculctural Antiqua, Antiquedades Mexicanos," *Boletin de Geografia y Estadistica*, Secunda Epoca, 1869, vol. 1, pp. 292-297; also see Jose Melgar, "Estudio Sobre la Antiguedad y el Origen do la Cabeze Colosal de Tipo Etiopico que Esiste en Hueyapan," *Boletin de la Sociedad Mexicana*, Secunda Epoca, 1871, vol. 3, pp. 104-109.

4. Manuel Orozco y Berra, *Historia Antigua y de la conquista de Mexico*, 1880, vol. 1.

5. Riva Palacio, *Mexico á través de los Siglos*, Mexico, Ballesca y Comp, Editores, 1889, pp. 63-67.

6. Jose A. Villacorta, *Arqueologia guatemalteca*, Guatemala, C.A., Tipografia nacional, 1930, p. 336; also see Jose Villacorta, *Prehistoria & historia antigua de guatemalteca*, Guatemala, C.A. Tipografia nacional, 1938, pp. 222-239.

7. Ivan Van Sertima, They Came Before Columbus, *The African Presence In Ancient America*, New York, Random House, 1976.

8. Ivan Van Sertima, "African-Egyptian Presences In Ancient Mexico," *Yardbird*, vol. 1, no. 2, p. 44.

9. Among the leading early anthropologists of this opinion were H. Ten Kate, "Materiaux pour servir a l Anthropologie de la île Californienne," *Bulletin Societe d' Anthropologie de Paris*, 1884, 3rd series, vol. 7; H. Ten Kate, "Sur les Cranes de de Lagoa-Santa," *Bulletin Societe d' Anthropologie de Paris*, 1885, 3rd series, vol. 8, pp. 240-244; Paul Rivet, "La Race de Lagoa Santa chez les Populations Precolombiennes de l'Equator," *Bulletin et Memoires, Society d' Anthropologie de Paris*, 1908, 5th series, vol. 9, pp. 209-274; also see 314-430 with R. Anthony; Paul Rivet, "Recherches Anthropologiques sur la Basse-Californie," *Journal de la Societe des Americanistes de Paris*, 1909, new series, vol.

6, pp. 147-253; Soren Hansen, "Lagoa Santa Racen," *Samling af Afhandlinger, Museo Lundii, 1888, vol. 1, part 5, pp. 1-37.*

10. Harold S. Gladwin, *Men Out of Asia*, New York, McGraw-Hill Book Co., Inc., 1947, pp. 184-185.

11. Gladwin, *Men Out of Asia*, op. cit., p. 61.

12. *Ibid.*, pp. 61-62.

13. Carlos C. Marquez, *Estudios arqueologicas y etnografisco*, Mexico, Bogota, D.E. Editorial Kelly, 1956, pp. 179-80, translated by Mamadou Lumumba. (Emphases added)

14. Joel A. Rogers, *Sex And Race, Negro-Caucasian Mixing In All Ages And All Lands*, New York, published by the author, 1942, p. 71.

15. Gerald Massey, *Ancient Egypt, The Light of the World*, London, 1907, vol. I, pp. 230-251.

16. Sharon S. McKern, *Exploring the Unknown, Mysteries in American Archaeology*, New York, Prager Publishers, Inc., 1973, p. 16.

While Ms. McKern, unlike the other scientists cited in this paper, does not suggest that the first settlers of America were of Africoid stock, she does hold that prehistoric peoples from northeast Asia may have reached the New World as early as 70,000 B.C.

17. Roland B. Dixon, *The Racial History of Man*, New York, Scribner's sons, 1923, p. 400.

18. *Ibid.*, pp. 401-402.

19. Gladwin, *Men Out of Asia*, op. cit., p. 67.

20. Sullivan and Hellman, *The Punin Calvarium*, op. cit., p. 323.

21. Arthur Keith, *New Discoveries Relating To The Antiquity of Man*, London, Williams & Norgate, Ltd., 1931, p. 312.

22. H.C. Haddon, *The Races of Man and Their Distribution*, Cambridge, The University Press, 1924, p. 133.

22. Gladwin, *Men Out of Asia*, op. cit., p. 59.

24. Rivet, "La Race de Lagoa Santa chez les Populations Precolombiennes de l'Equator," op. cit.; A.H. Keene, *Men Past and Present*, Cambridge, The University Press, 1920, p. 340.

25. Joseph Deniker, *The Races of Man, An Outline of Anthropology and Ethnography*, New York, Books For Libraries Press, 1971; first published in 1900, pp. 291-292 & 512.

26. Griffith Taylor, *Environment, Race and Migration*, Chicago, The University of Chicago Press, 1937, p. 247.

27. Quoted in Gladwin, *Men Out of Asia*, op. cit., p. 93.

28. Taylor, *Environment, Race and Migration*, op. cit., p. 246.

29. Dixon, *The Recall History of Man*, op. cit., pp. 403 & 409.

30. Gladwin, *Men Out of Asia*, op. cit., pp. 92-111.

31. Dixon, *The Racial History of Man*, op. cit., pp. 459-62; Taylor, *Environment, Race and Migration*, op. cit., pp. 243 & 246-247.

32. Taylor, *Environment, Race and Migration*, op. cit., p. 246; And Deniker, *The Races of Man, An Outline of Anthropology And Ethnography*, op. cit., p. 292.

33. Marcelin Boule, *Fossil Men*, New York, The Dryden Press, 1957, pp. 283-292, 294-296 & 308-329; W.E.B. DuBois, *Black Folk, Then And Now*, New York, Henry Holt and Company, 1939, p. 3; and Dixon, *The Racial History of Man*, op. cit., pp. 45-46 & 478.

34. Marcel A. Dieulafoy, *L'Acropole de Suse*, Paris, Hachette et cie, 1893, pp. 27, 44-46, 57-86, & 102-115; Diop, *The African Origin of Civilization*, op. cit., pp. 103-105 & 260-275; and Eugene Georg, *The Adventure of Mankind*, New York, E.P. Dutton & Co., 1931, p. 44.

35. Nripendra Kumar Dutt, *The Aryanisation of India*, Calcutta, published by the author, 1925, pp. 76-101; Romesh C. Dutt, *Ancient India*, New York, Longmans, Green & Co., 1893, pp. 12-19; and Guiffrida-Ruggeri, *First Outlines of a systematic Anthropology of Asia*, Calcutta, 1921, p. 53.

36. Edward G. Balfour, ed., "Negro Races," *Cyclopaedia of India*, London, Quartich, 1885, 3rd ed., vol. II, p. 1073; and Joseph P. Widney, *Race Life of the Aryan Peoples*, New York, Funk and Wagnalls, 1907, vol. II, pp. 238-239.

37. L. Carrington Goodrich, *A Short History of the Chinese People*, London, Routledge & Kegan Paul, 1950, p. 7; Kenneth Latourette, *The Chinese, Their History and Culture*, 4th edition, 1967, p. 438; J.A. Rogers, *Sex And Race*, op. cit., vol. I, pp. 62-78; Neil G. Munro, *Prehistoric Japan*, Yokohama, 1911, pp. 676-78; and Roland B. Dixon, *The Racial History of Man*, op. cit., pp. 287-292.

38. Quoted in Gladwin, *Men Out of Asia*, op. cit., p. 94.

TRAIT-INFLUENCES IN MESO-AMERICA: THE AFRICAN-ASIAN CONNECTION

Wayne B. Chandler

There are many historical problems yet to be resolved regarding the history of the landmass known today as America. One of the greatest debates being waged in this academic arena is over the possibility of trans-continental migrations and their potential influence on the ancient Meso-American civilization.

Since the mid-16th century an array of ethnologists, archaeologists, and historians have thrust themselves into an area of academic chaos, trying to put into perspective man's first attempt at civilization in ancient America.

Two major schools of thought exist on the subject; as one might expect, they are diametrically opposed. On one hand, the classic American traditionalist or isolationist camp refuses to accept the possibility of trans-oceanic cultural transmissions. This group strongly believes that ancient America evolved on its own, spiraling up and outward from a cultural abyss to attain an impressive level of achievement.

The counterpart of the traditionalist or isolationist is the diffusionist. The diffusionist believes in the spread or transmission of cultural traits from the Old World to the Americas through trans-pacific journeys by Asiatics or trans-Atlantic journeys by Africans. Both camps run the gamut from over-imaginative laymen to brilliant and serious scholars. Consequently, arguments on both sides range from far-fetched speculation to painstakingly careful analysis.

After extensive research into this subject, I have concluded that the evidence for trans-continental contacts is overwhelmingly convincing, although several problems exist. The challenge facing cultural diffusionism is the necessity to establish a valid identity and parallel between trait-complexes common to both Meso-America and those cultures from which it is claimed they have originated. The historical periods during which these traits are supposed to have been transmitted must also be established, as well as the extent of their impact upon the American cultures they may have influenced. Unanswered questions abound. The dating of these periods or phases in which the cultures made contact is a matter of very great concern.

The transmission of cultural traits from one group to another takes place in varied circumstances and the transmitter therefore affects the receiver in different ways. Sometimes a foreign trait is readily absorbed. At other times it

A. Negroid Olmec sculpture carved in jade; Mexico. 1150 B.C.

may lie submerged in comparative dormancy, only to reemerge later when socio-political or environmental circumstance favor its flowering. It may be foisted on the culture by sheer force[1] or it may be incorporated into the native system of things through the culture's own volition.

Even the most conservative of American isolationists must admit that there are startling similarities in the cultures of Asia, Meso-America, and Africa. The ambiguity surrounding the origin of America's first mother culture and civilization—the Olmec—points toward an array of transcontinental possibilities. In the words of the major isolationist scholar of Meso-America, Michael D. Coe, "We are fairly sure that the first Olmecs came to LaVenta around 1100 B.C. and we can only guess from where they came . . . On the origins of monumental sculpture at San Lorenzo, Tenochtitlan, we have little to say. There are certainly few data to support a slow and inexorable evolution of large scale quarrying, transportation and manufacture of these objects either here or at any other Olmec site."[2] Unknowingly, Coe and his colleagues have undermined their hypothesis of independent origin. In spite of this, Coe vehemently attacks the possibility of an infusion of Old World culture into America from Africa or China. His position is absurd when one considers the preponderance of evidence attesting to the many trait-complexes in Meso-America shared by these Old World cultures.

Several hypotheses have been advanced to explain these cultural similarities. Two early proponents of transpacific contact, M. de Guignes and Edward Vining, both felt that they had discovered the source of these similarities.

The French scholar de Guignes deduced from a series of Chinese documents known as Liang Shu the supposed location of a country known as Fu-Sang. The records state that in the 5th century (A.D. ?) Fu-sang was visited by five monks from Afghanistan who proceeded to indoctrinate the people of Fu-sang with Buddhist principles. Monsieur de Guignes came to the conclusion that the monks were Chinese and had gone east to reach North America. This inspired an avalanche of diffusionist speculation as to the precise location of the land known as Fu-Sang. Edward Vining meticulously dissected the Chinese codex and found in them strong evidence that this land was in fact Mexico. Although his research has some merit, readers would be well advised to be wary of his conclusions.

As to whether Fu-Sang was indeed the American continent we may never know. But recent research findings have established a definite connection between China and the New World. In the words of Jesse Jennings, editor of *Ancient Native Americans*, "There is no reasonable doubt as to the ultimate origin of the human population that finally covered this hemisphere. There is a consensus among scholars that the first American was of Asian stock. Research in biology, language, and archaeology demonstrate this; no space need

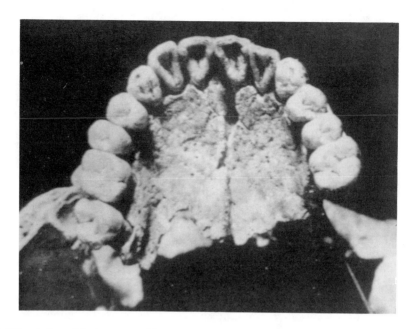

B. Shovel-shaped incisors on a Shang skull; China, Anyang period.

be wasted here in presenting the varied evidence pointing to the one conclusion. It is the timing of the entry that has not yet been determined."[3]

A joint U.S.-Soviet venture, spearheaded by Christy G. Turner II, utilized
the latest and best computer technology; this group was able to trace "the
origin of the early Americans to North China."[4] Funded by a National Geographic Society grant, Turner and his colleagues studied the teeth of more
than 6,000 early American skeletons. In 1980, Turner was then invited by the
Institute of Ethnography, Academy of Science, U.S.S.R., to conduct a large-
scale study of North Asian dental traits. "It was found that the northeast
Asian and the early inhabitants of both North and South America shared the
following dental trait complex: 1) one root upper first premolars, 2) three-root
lower first molars, 3) shovel-shaped incisors. Turner named this trait-complex
Sinodonty after the archetype from Anyang, a major royal capital of the Shang
Dynasty (1766-1122 B.C.)."[5]

Turner and his Russian colleagues further concluded that "man migrated
from North Asia to America in three waves"—the first, about 20,000 but not
earlier than 40,000 years B.P. (Before Present); the second, between 14,000 to
12,000; and the third, ca 8,700 B.P. "The roots of the first Americans lead
ultimately to Mongolia, Manchuria, and Northern China."[6]

Other studies have also been done in the area of northern China, more specifically pertaining to the Shang. The beginning of this dynasty, China's first, is as nebulous as it is mystical. "The origin of the Shang civilization is the ultimate question in the minds of many . . . Where did the Shang people come from . . . did they come from somewhere else?"[7]

Studies done on skeletal types may provide us with a few answers. Several theories have been put forward to explain the racial identity of the Shang inhabitants. The skeletal types excavated have been placed into five categories, the two largest being the Classical Mongoloid type and the Oceanic Negroid type. Of these two, the second subgroup seems to stand out as the major influence in Shang culture. Indeed, I feel it would be in order to state that it was the Shang who literally laid the cornerstone of early Chinese culture. A quotation from the Shi Jing (Book of Odes, ca. 900-500 B.C.) and Sima Qian (ca. 90 B.C.) give some historical insight into the coming of these black people to northwest China. "To the people of Shang heaven ordered the black bird to descend, and to give birth."[8]

"Jiandi, the mother of Qi [ca 2300-2200 B.C. Progenitor of the Shang Clan] . . . saw a black bird drop an egg. She swallowed it. As a result she became pregnant and gave birth to Qi."[9] These two allegorical stories suggest the coming of blacks to uplift China from its state of cultural infancy. Even the conquering Chou gave the vanquished Shang credit for their achievements: "The Chou after overthrowing the Shang Dynasty were found to be no more than barbarians with no philosophy or culture of their own. They therefore willingly adopted the Shang culture and way of life."[10]

Many references to the racial make-up of the Shang are given in the Chinese histories. When the Chou overthrew the Shang Dynasty, they described the inhabitants as having "black and oily skin."[11] In the Shang's last capital, Anyang, many "Negroid" images in stone, metal, and jade have been found. Archaeologist Kwang Chin Chang states in regards to Shang figurines, "Another miniature jade figurine from Hsiao-T'un, and Hou-Chai-Chuang suggest "Negroid" features: "flattened" nose, prominent chins and foreheads, and a lack of the epicanthus fold that Mongoloids possess."[12]

The amount of data amassed as to the racial composition of the Shang is extensive. It is not my intention to elaborate upon it here; since lack of time and space forbids such an undertaking. The rest of this paper will continue based on the assumption that the reader accepts this basic premise.

Though most diffusionists will acknowledge transpacific voyages to the New World, the subject of transatlantic journyes is rarely discussed, let alone seriously considered. This poses a problem which may endanger much of what has already been accomplished in terms of understanding ancient America's cultural milieu. Denial of transatlantic travel will forever consign archeologists, ethnologists, and historians to the impossible task of trying to fit

C. Those who doubt the amalgamation of Asian and African types should note this classic example.

D. Present day inhabitant of Inner Mongolia with children. Notice the very dark skin pigmentation.

square pegs into round holes. Why the denial? The answer is simple. Such voyages involve Africa.

The most remarkable of ancient nation-states—Egypt—arose on African soil and several great African empires succeeded it. Africa is not only the mother of mankind but the mother and midwife of many a civilization. But since the advent of colonialism the keepers of the historical record have been insistent on belittling the role Africa has played in history. It is only recently that black historians the worldover have taken pen in hand to correct this distorted historical view and restore Africa to her rightful place.

Dr. Alexander Von Wuthenau tells an interesting story which illustrates this reluctance to give Africa and Africans their proper due. After discussing with a friend, Dr. Erwin Palm, his theories on transatlantic voyages by Negroes to the New World, Palm advised: "Wuthenau, never say Negro, always say Negroid because then it would mean that the black specimens in the pre-Columbian art are derived from Melanesian Negritos and not from African Negroes."[13] Wuthenau goes on to explain that he knew Dr. Palm meant well "and probably intended to help me maintain my respectability in academic circles, because orthodox scientists are beginning to admit the possibility of Melanesian migrations to America but are deadly opposed to that of contacts from Africa across the Atlantic."[14]

This school of thought, though still in the majority, is facing a strong and growing challenge from pioneering scholars who, I feel, will eventually undermine their foundation of falsehoods. Such a pioneer is Ivan Van Sertima, whose incisive scholarship slashes through this archaic historical data like a keen new blade through ancient cobwebs. His work has done much to establish the African influence in New World culture. His evidence is so persuasive that it is impossible to sweep it all aside. As a result of these revelations, a new drama of man begins to unfold on the Meso-American stage.

Recalibrated radiocarbon dates place the beginning of the Olmec civilization around 1450 B.C. The date established for the founding of the Olmec site at La Venta, (their spiritual fountainhead in the New World), is 1100 B.C., approximately simultaneous with the collapse of China's first dynasty, the Shang.

Rafique Jairazbhoy notes that a mass exodus originated from northern China in 1121 B.C. He feels that this emigration accounts for the numerous Shang trait elements compounded with those of the Olmec. "In 1121 B.C., the Chou leader Wu-Wang attacked Chao, the ruler of Shang. But before he did so he accused him of being debauched and thinking only "of palaces, buildings, terraces, groves, dikes, pools and extravagant clothes to the neglect and ruin of the people," and he accused him further of "spreading pain and poison over the four seas." He exhorted his men to attack like tigers and panthers . . . on conquering the Shang he respected their intelligent men . . . He distinguished the families of the clever men among the enemy who had gone away."[15] In view of the preponderance of Shang trait complexes found in pre-Columbian Meso America, Jairazbhoy concludes that the final destination of the Shang exiles was Meso-America. Jairazbhoy goes on to draw striking parallels between the Shang elite who fled and reestablished their dynasty in a new land and other deposed rulers in times past who also reestablished empires in foreign lands. One such example is the Omayyad Dynasty. "The Omayyad Dynasty of Syria were all but exterminated in the 8th century A.D. and its remaining members migrated and set up a new kingdom . . . in Spain, a few years later."[16] One must admit that Jairazbhoy's theory is ripe with possibility. Key phrases in the original text appear quite significant. The phrase, "spreading pain and poison over the four seas" implies that the Shang had an idea of the oceans surrounding their continent; the phrase "he distinguished the families of the clever men among the enemy who had gone away" appears consistent with the idea of Shang nobles in exile.

Jairazbhoy goes on to further establish what he sees as profound similarities in the Shang and Olmec cultural patterns in the very heartland of Olmec territory. "We will see evidence of the Shang setting up a state system on the Gulf of Mexico . . . within a few years of living at San Lorenzo, the Shang must have decided to found their own ceremonial capital at La Venta, for it is here that Shang influences are rampant."[17] Endeavoring to draw correlations between the layout of Shang cities and those of San Lorenzo and La Venta, Jairazbhoy cites example after example, establishing his case for a Shang power structure at La Venta.

Though Jairazbhoy outlines what seems to be a fine case for the diffusion of Shang culture within the Olmec, the examples he gives to support his choice for the primary site of this influence are debatable. While the city-planning strategies used by the Olmec are in his opinion typical of the Shang, to me they seem to be an Egypto-Nubian influence.

Jairazbhoy himself acknowledges the similarities between the Olmec use of water, the Egyptian irrigation methods in the Fields of Peace (pictured as being full of a number of small pools and lakes) and the "dikes and pools to which the last Shang emperor was addicted."[18] Jairazbhoy, however, concludes that the Shang were the progenitors of La Venta and San Lorenzo.

But the Shang's transoceanic voyage would have brought them *not* to the Gulf of Mexico adjacent to these two sites, rather instead to the western coastline. Theirs was a transpacific voyage. Naturally, their journey would conclude on the western side of Mexico and not in the east. This alone leads me to a different conclusion than Jairazbhoy's. Although I believe in a powerful Shang cultural influence in Meso-America, I find evidence of their presence strongest along the west coast, and envision the influence of the Egypto-Nubians most prevalent along the eastern portion.

Olmec culture was pervasive. It reached far into the southeast, rooting itself firmly in Guatemala and Honduras, which were later to be occupied by the

Maya. Olmec culture also extended to the west, leaving its legacy at Monte Alban, and eventually spread across central Mexico, and to a much lesser degree made its way into Costa Rica and Panama. Because of the location of their entry, on the western coast, the Shang would have found it difficult to avoid making contact with Olmec culture. Thus it is on the west coast that we find the merging of Shang and Olmec trait complexes. This Shang-influenced Olmec culture approached the southern frontier and extended toward the Nicoya Peninsula; then it moved further south, showing an extensive cultural presence in Costa Rica, and finally embraced the west coast of South America, through Peru and Columbia. Along the Meso-American coast as far south as Panama, hundreds of artifacts Non-Olmec in style have been found, yet these images display distinctive Africoid features. These pre-classic artifacts give evidence to a vast Negroid constituency which I believe to be related to the Shang.

But although the Shang were a highly developed culture, their influence alone cannot account for all of the imported trait complexes found in Meso-America. The Shang, progenitors of Chinese civilization, developed a script, used on oracle bones, which was the precursor of Chinese characters. They ushered in China's Bronze Age with some of the most artistic displays of bronze-casting the world has ever seen. They also developed a martial fighting system which is still practiced not only in China but in many countries around the world. But pyramid builders they were not. True pyramids, ancient or modern, cannot be found in China. But at LaVenta we find the first true pyramid in the New World. This is an achievement which cannot be attributed to Shang inspiration. Further, since pyramid building is a very highly specialized form of construction, it is unlikely that the Olmec spontaneously developed it. There are no antecedents for this structure in the Olmec world. In Egypt, the progression in expertise can be traced from early pyramids like the stepped pyramid of Djoser, to the polished achievement at Giza. Yet in Meso-America, the art of pyramid building appears suddenly and fully developed.

The search for an explanation for the sudden appearance of these sophisticated structures in the New World takes us back to the work of Van Sertima, who credits the Egypto-Nubian element in Meso-America with inspiring and influencing the first New World pyramids. Van Sertima points out that the pyramid at LaVenta is placed "on a north-south axis, as all Egyptian and Nubian pyramids are placed ... [The] pyramid combines the same double function, tomb and temple, and their own great pyramid ... [in Teotihuacan] has a pyramidal base almost identical in proportion to that of the base of the Great Pyramid in Egypt."[19] The base of the Teotihuacan pyramid measures 225 meters square; the pyramid at Giza measures 226.5 meters square. Van Sertima goes on to mention similarities in the use of moveable capstones and also notes that the Meso-American builders used the "same standards of measurements [which had been] developed by the mathematicians and astronomers of the Nile Valley."[20]

Yet another factor points to Egypto-Nubian presence in Meso-America. Writing can be used to identify a culture. In the words of T. S. Ferguson, "The script of an ancient people, being the most complex part of their civilization, is the surest and best means of identifying that people. Script is to a people what fingerprints are to a person—the most complex and surest means of identification. An archeologist is generally happier with the discovery of ancient script than with any other thing he finds. It tells him more, and it is the most reliable source of knowledge for identification purposes."[21]

As of this date, no trace of the Shang language or written script has been found anywhere in Meso-America. Thus, Nigel Davies concludes: "The Shang Dynasty . . . admittedly possessed a form of recording found on the famous oracle bones, but it has nothing in common with Olmec glyphs . . ."[22] But although we find no evidence of Shang script in Meso-America, such is not the case with Egyptian script.

The following letter was sent to one Dr. William F. Albright, a reputable expert in the field of Old World languages and archaeology:

> Dear Dr. Albright:
> Enclosed is a copy of an impression of a cylinder seal recently excavated by this organization at Chiapa de Corzo in the State of Chiapas, Mexico. Our carbon-14 dates at this site are ranging all the way from 1,050 B.C. to 400 A.D. I am wondering if this seal resembles anything in the Near East. I would appreciate your comments on this question.
> Sincerely,
> Thomas Stuart Ferguson[23]

The seal in question was discovered by Edwards Martinez, a member of the New World Archaeological Foundation, in October of 1957. Ferguson reports on Dr. Albright's response to his inquiry.

On May 1958, Dr. Albright examined a photograph of the cylinder seal impression and made an interesting observation. This seal contains "several clearly recognizable Egyptian hieroglyphs," wrote Dr. Albright in his reply. In my personal opinion, this will ultimately prove to have been one of the most important announcements ever made. Five seals . . . (The stratum dating 300 B.C.-600 B.C.) now have been found . . . at Chiapa de Corzo.[24]

Needless to say, the announcement went unheeded by the conservative academic establishment. What is of significant importance is that the find is within the Olmec sphere of influence and that the carbon-14 dating of strata associated with these seals are consistent with the datings of the giant Africoid stone heads, which were found at La Venta and other Olmec capitals.

These and other important factors prove that, while there is evidence of Shang influence, this influence may have entered the Gulf Coast capitals of

E. Cylindrical seal found in Mexico, dated 600 B.C. Pay close attention to the Egyptian script on the seal and the identical symbol next to it on your left.

the Olmec at a later date, moving in from the opposite coast of Meso-America. Also, important cultural traits cited at La Venta and other Olmec locations are of Egypto-Nubian origin and indicate a trans-Atlantic crossing which would account for this influence.

The task of isolating specific traits and trait transmissions is a very complex one, especially when a single culture displays plural or culturally diverse trait elements. Determining the chronology involved is an additional challenge. Questions also arise over whether certain traits were transmitted and adapted, whether they lay in dormancy for a while and later resurfaced, or whether they originated in the local culture in the first place. Because of these problems, guidelines have been suggested by Paul Shao to assist us in the analysis of possible trait transmissions.

1. The simpler a cultural trait, the easier for it to be independently invented or evolved.
2. The more functionally and structurally oriented a trait, the greater the probability of independent invention.
3. Conversely, the more complex, arbitrary, and stylized a correlated trait, the higher likelihood of its being borrowed from a more advanced culture, particularly if these highly complex traits appear suddenly

without traceable developmental precedence (like some of the Olmec, Mayan and [Chavin] motifs).

4. The probability of cultural contact increases if resemblance occurs not only between individual traits of the two cultures, but also between trait-complexes—a trait-complex is composed of several traits arranged in a particular juxtaposition.

5. The significance of the similarities between arbitrary trait-complexes of the cultures multiplies if the resemblance can be correlated not only in motif-substance but also in time sequence.

6. The case for diffusion becomes more convincing if the correlated arbitrary trait complexes are unique to the two cultures being investigated.

The startling identity of unusual traits or trait-complexes has been used to show the diffusion of Old World culture to Meso-America. Massive change and innovation, occurring almost simultaneously seem to place the first phase of Old World influence at around 1450 B.C.

In the words of Stephen C. Jett, "Beginning about 1450 B.C., quantum changes, including hierarchical social organization, construction of large-scale religious monuments and ceremonial centers, extraordinary lapidary work (Middle America) and metal working (Peru), and water control appeared suddenly at San Lorenzo, Veracruz, and at Chavin de Huantar, Peru . . . Possible outside sources for [this] stimuli include Shang China . . . [and] Egypt . . ."[25]

Anthrophotojournalism, which can be defined as the use of human images in art to trace cultural influence, can also be used to support the theory of transoceanic diffusion. Van Sertima and Von Wuthenau have used the giant stone heads and the numerous Terracotta sculptures in this way. Concrete examples of trait complexes or cultural pecularities—photographs of highly specialized rituals, for example—provide some of the best evidence.

Such are the photographs we are about to examine. Through them I will show similarities in the Egypto-Nubian, Shang and Olmec cultures.

To compare the various traits and trait-complexes, I have identified several categories of subjects. The categories are as follows:

1. *Comparative traits of Shang tripod bronzes and south-west coast tripod ceramics.*
   "Chinese influences are seen in the cylindrical tripod vessles [and] in both China and Teotihuacan lids were sometimes surmounted with birds."[26] The New World vessels pictured display strong similarities to Shang vessels and the time sequence is in order.

2. *Comparative trait complexes of Serpent and Dragon; Tiger and Lion; plus the Jaguar of Middle America.*
   A saying from an ancient Chinese codex (400-100 B.C.) states: "The people of Xian Yuan [distant ancestor of Xia Yu, founder of the black Xia Dynasty, ca 2205-1766 B.C.], have human faces and snakes bodies . . ."[27]

First Category: Tripod Vessels

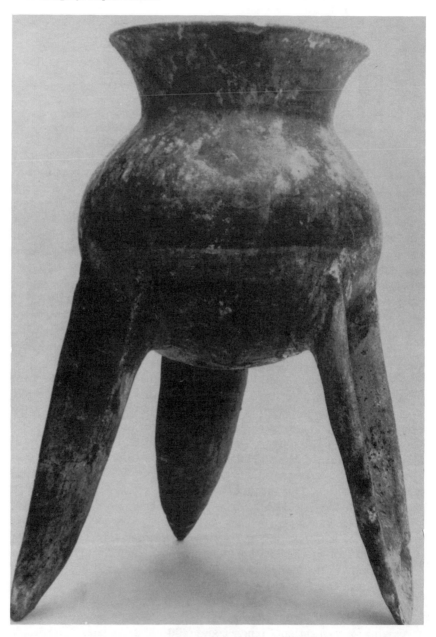

1a. One of the oldest tripod vases found in Ancient America. Ecuador, dated in the early formative period, circa 900 B.C.

1b. Shang bronze vessel; China, 11th century B.C.

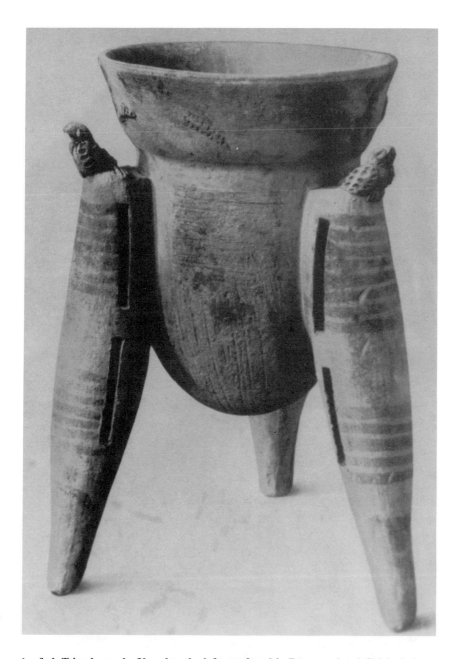

1c. & d. Tripod vessels. Vessel to the left was found in Panama, dated Chiriqui phase. Vessel on the right is Shang Dynasty, dated 12th century B.C. Note the similarities between the two, especially in the birds which ornament both vessels. The use of birds as ornamentation was very common in Shang bronze casting.

1e. The first documentation of tripod pottery in Meso-America was located on the south-west coast where Shang influence was most powerful. This fine example of well-crafted pottery is adorned with two powerful symbols, the serpent and the feline. Both symbols were intergrated into the artwork of the Egpto-Nubian, Shang and Olmec cultures. These vessels were found in Costa Rica, dated pre-Classic.

1f. Shang bronze. China, dated 12th century B.C.

Another Chinese document (Huai Nan Zi) states, "The God of Enlightenment has a human face and a snake's body . . ."[28]
The snake which took the form of the dragon in later Chinese and Indian
mysticism had long been heralded in black civilization as an all seeing
spiritual power. Thus it was worn on the helmets of Pharoahs and Gods
over the forehead to symbolize the third eye or enlightenment.
The same holds true of the black race's reverence for cats which gave birth
to the varied feline cults of Egypt, Shang China, and the Olmec of the New
World. Ennobled as a symbol of power and strength, the great cats—*Tiger*
in China, *Jaguar* in Mexico, and *Lion* in Africa are also classified as earth
gods in all regions. Motif imagery and time sequence are also in order for
this category.

3. *Comparative traits of Guizuo sitting postures.*
   This posture symbolizes man's unition between earth and heaven. Drawing
   energy from the macrocosm, man becomes a channel to the microcosm
   and sits in humble reverence of the supreme spiritual manifestation. Origins of this posture may once again be traced to the Old Kingdom in Egypt.
   Historian and archaeologist Li Chi in his investigation of this posture
   found it to be an ancient Chinese posture called Cheng-Tso meaning "correct sitting." By the end of the Han Dynasty circa 220 B.C. this posture had
   disappeared. In Japan, it is known as the Seiza posture and has its origins
   there circa 14th century A.D. Motif imagery and time sequence for Shang
   and Olmec are in order.

4. *Comparative Traits of Traditional African Sitting Posture.*
   The origin of this extremely unusual sitting posture may also be traced to
   Egypt. Two slight variation on this posture are depicted here.

5. *Comparative traits of the Bird Man.*
   "To the people of Shang, heaven ordered the black bird to descend, and
   give birth. (Shi Jing) ca 900-500 B.C. Jiandi, the mother of Qi [ca
   2300-2200 B.C. progenitor of the Shang Clan] . . . saw a black bird drop an
   egg. She swallowed it. As a result she became pregnant and give birth to
   Qi."[29]
   These phrases tell of the coming of the black race to China which became
   immortalized in the symbol of a bird man which was carried into middle
   America. Motif iconography and time sequence are in order, with regard to
   Shang and Olmec.

6. *Comparative traits in the broad ridge hair style.*
   This particular hair cut is extremely interesting. First evidenced in early
   China, worn by its black inhabitants, its influence spread through the
   Shang upon entering the New World. It was worn by blacks in ancient
   America.

Second Category: Serpent and Dragon, Tiger and Lion

2a. & b. These two exquisite artifacts exemplify the old Chinese legend that the first inhabitants of China, the legendary Xia, had human faces and snakes' bodies. The Shang vessels to the left has a snake's body extending from the back of its head. China, circa 1200 B.C. The figure on the right exhibits a strong Shang/Olmec influence; it also has a snake's body descending from the head. El Salvador, circa 200 B.C.-150 A.D.

2c. & d. Back of figures showing the snakes' bodies descending from the heads on the Shang vessel; on "c", the body wraps around the base of the vessel.

2e. Male Shang figure sitting atop dragon's head. Late Shang Dynasty, 1300-1100 B.C.

2f. Olmec figure on stela surrounded by snake/dragon image. One of very few such artifacts surviving from the formative period. La Venta, Mexico; circa 1100 B.C.

2g. Anthropomorphic jaguar; Olmec, 1150 B.C.-300 A.D.

2h. Anthropomorphic lion; Egyptian

Third category: Guizuo Sitting Posture

3a. Shang jade guizuo figure; Anyang, China, 1300-1100 B.C.

3b. Olmec jade quizuo sitting figure. La Lima Ulua Valley, Honduras, circa 1150 B.C.

3c. Shang quizuo sitting posture. China, Chou period, circa 600 B.C.

3d. Olmec quizuo sitting posture. La Venta, Mexico, circa 1150 B.C.—300 A.D.

3e. Egyptian quizuo sitting posture; Middle Kingdom.

3f. Monolithic limestone statues fashioned in quizuo sitting posture. Peru, yet to be properly dated but believed to be late pre-Classic.

3g. Olmec anthropomorphic feline in quizuo sitting posture. Puebla, Mexico, circa 1150 B.C.

3h. Anthropomorphic feline in quizuo sitting posture. Note the identical symbol used for ears of both Olmec and Shang felines. China, Shang Dynasty, late period, circa 1300 B.C.

Fourth Category: Traditional African Sitting Posture

4a. Egyptian sitting in traditional African sitting posture. Old Kingdom.

4b. Olmec jade figurine sitting in traditional African posture. Formative period.

4c. Egyptian sitting in traditional posture. Middle Kingdom.

4d. Negroid figure sitting in traditional African posture. Jalisco, west coast of Mexico, dated late pre-Classic to early Classic.

Fifth Category: Bird Men Images

5a. Olmec jade bird man. Costa Rica,
circa 1150 B.C.

5b. Shang Dynasty jade bird man. China,
1200 B.C.

5c. Mexican jade bird man. Costa Rica, 900-1500 A.D.

5d. Chinese jade bird man. Han Dynasty, 206 B.C.—220 A.D.

Sixth Category: Broad Ridge Hair Style

6a. The presence of this hair style in the Shang culture and then the Olmec denotes a
strong and definite transmission of a trait characteristic. This style of cut was originally
unique to the Shang and Olmec, but was later adopted by the Shang-influenced San
Augustin culture of Columbia. This fact is evidenced in virtually all of their stone
sculpture. This example, though Chou in time period, reflects the artistic style of the
Shang. China, 600 B.C.

6b. The evidence indicates that this hair style was originally worn only by the shamen or magicians of the Shang and Olmec cultures, much in the way that dreadlocks were originally worn only by the high-priests or Sadhu's of India. This example is Olmec, from La Venta, Mexico, 1150 B.C.

6c. Totonacan stone head with broad ridge hair style. Mexico, late pre-Classic period.

6d. Fine marblehead with broad ridge. Veracruz, Mexico, classic period.

6e. & f. Front and side views of beautifully carved marble head. Veracruz, Mexico, Classic period.

7. *Comparative traits of Anthropomorphic Tiger and Jaguars Protecting Children.*
Once again, the reverence for the feline mystique is exemplified in these unusual works of art. From Shang, to Olmec, and the Chavin-influenced cultures in San Augustin, Colombia this symbol exhibits strong cultural parallels. Time sequence in order.

8. *Comparative trait complexes of the Shaman Holding objects of ritual significance.*
A saying from an ancient Chinese text (Lu Shi Chun Qiu, circa 239 B.C.) states that the daodi images on the ceremonial vessels of the Chou people (1100-256 B.C.) were portrayed with heads but without bodies. This art style, though Shang in origin, made its way into the Chou culture, Olmec, and the contemporary South American cultures which were influenced by the Shang. Termed the man and animal interface, they consist of a lone head with hands on the side holding some sort of ritualistic symbol. Time sequence in order.

9. *Comparative trait of Nose Plugs and Rings Worn in the Nose.*
Worn extensively by the blacks in Shang China, this trait caught on first by the Priest caste of Olmec civilization. In Stela art it is symbolized by a circular ball at the very tip of the nose. Time sequence in order.

What follows is a listing of the cultures being compared:

Shang: First historical dynasty in China, culturally influenced by the black race. The black race at that time was also a sizeable component of the population. It is necessary to note, that, despite a change of dynasty occasioned by the Chou conquest of the Shang, the basic Shang styles and ways of life *persisted for centuries* almost up until the end of the second century B.C.

Olmec: A civilization in Meso-America believed to be originally Asiatic which became culturally influenced by elements from two major civilizations from abroad. The first presence was Egypto-Nubian. The second was the Shang.

Chavin:Many believe the Chavin to be a Shang-influenced culture. There are very strong similarities in many respects which have been noted by Heine-Geldern. At the same time, Signorini also drew convincing parallels between Chavin and Olmec. Apart from research which indicates trade connections between early Mexico and Peru, a separate imact of the Shang on the Chavin de Huantar culture makes sense in terms of the Pacific landfall on the west coast border of Peru. To summarize, I will quote a leading American archaeologist, Gordon Willey, who has pondered deeply on transpacific contacts and who till recently remained skeptical; he now confesses to an "uncanny feeling" when looking at some Shang Dynasty items that display "disturbing similarities" to Chavin, relating not only to content but to style."[30] Chavin and Olmec were contemporaneous with one another in time sequence.

San Augustin: "Although not adequately dated, San Augustin in Columbia certainly has some relationship to Chavin as well. Chavin and its coastal variant Cupisnique together exhibit monumental stone construction . . . large stone sculptures, tinioned stone heads in walls . . ."[31]

Egypt: Due to the cultural pervasiveness of the Egyptian civilization, many traits may be directly traced to her, especially in the Formative phases of Olmec civilization. This is dealt with extensively in the work of Van Sertima and Jairazbhoy.

Although many diffusionists have brought fresh and illuminating data and insight to the study of ancient American history, their efforts remain unacknowledged by the entrenched isolationists. Richard MacNeish, who broke new ground in his investigation of the Tehuacan Valley preceramic-ceramic sequence, but whose findings were met with an oppressive lack of acceptance, made this comment: "At the outset, let me say that it often seems that some archaeologists working in Meso-America never change their minds, no matter what the new data, or, if they do, they never admit it. Further, there is a great deal of provincialism in respect to both time and space among Meso-American archaeologists, so that sometimes they may change their minds about one aspect, usually an aspect that concerns their narrow problems, and not change their minds about other conceptions.[32] Unfortunately, MacNeish's observation appears to be quite apt. I have had some personal experience with the narrow-minded attitude of which MacNeish speaks. In July of this year, while talking to one of the country's leading archaeo-astronomers, I was informed of the existence of a small group of traditionalists who "police" history. This professor summarized the raison d'etre of this group by saying, "We keep out what we do not want."[33]

Several problems, other than the tunnel vision of the isolationist, beset the revisionist trying to establish a firm basis for cultural diffusion. One of them is particularly serious.

It is the sheer absence of original sources which would have documented the cultural dynamics of Meso-America. History has recorded many examples of the early burning of libraries by over-zealous and bigoted Christians. From Alexandria in Egypt to Cordova's Moorish Spain, thousands of valuable books and other documents were turned to ashes in the name of Christ. The very same Christians that burnt the Moorish libraries in Spain carried the torch to the New World. Diego deLanda, Bishop of the Yucatan, committed many atrocities on its native people; among them was the destruction of ancient Yucatan texts. He wrote, "These people also made use of certain characters or letters, with which they wrote in their books, their ancient matters and their sciences . . . We found a large number of books in these characters and, as they

Seventh Category: Felines with children

7a. A remarkably well-preserved figure in the form of a jaguar protecting a child. The posture and style is almost identical to that of the Shang vessel to the right. Found in Paracas Cavermas, South America, circa 400 B.C.

7b. Tiger protecting child. China, late Shang Dynasty, 1300-1100 B.C.

7c. Jaguar figure holding child in gesture of protection. Found on the west coast of South America in the Shang/Chavin influenced culture of San Augustin, 500 B.C.-200 A.D.

7d. Jaguar influenced Olmec figure holding child in protective gesture. Circa 1150-700 B.C.

Eighth Category: Shaman Holding Ritualistic Objects

8a. Shang shaman holding ritualistic objects. China, late Shang Dynasty period, circa 1200 B.C.

8b. Drawing of figure 8a on opposite page

8c. Olmec shaman holding ritualistic objects. The Olmec and Shang figures exhibit strong similarities. Pre-Classic period, circa 1150 B.C.

8d. Shaman figure in the form of a feline alter-ego, the jaguar. He too is holding what appear to be objects of ritual significance, virtually identical to objects held by figure c. San Augustin culture, circa 300-500 B.C.

contained nothing . . . [but] superstition and lies of the devil, we burned them all, which they regretted to an amazing degree, and which caused them much affliction."[34]

Spanish historian Antonio deCuidad Real recorded in 1588 "but because in these books were mixed many things of idolatry, they burned almost of them, and thus was lost the knowledge of many ancient matters of that land which by them [the Spanish] could have been known."[35] For the next several decades books were burned by the thousand. Major book burnings were recorded in 1590, 1633, and 1688. The recorded burning of 1633 is of particular interest, for the documents destroyed pertained to the origin of the Maya. "Thus he collected the books and the ancient writing and he commanded them burned and tied up. They burned many historical books of the ancient Yucatan which told of its beginning and history."[36]

The list of atrocities committed against the native people continued until it finally culminated in the extermination of a culture, its people, and history. Surviving records show that this path of destruction is littered not only with the ashes of books but also with the shattered fragments of thousands of clay and stone statues.

All those obstacles—the narrow-mindedness of the traditional isolationist, the over-active imaginations of earlier diffusionists, and the gaps in the historical record—make the task of proving trans-oceanic cultural diffusion more difficult. Ironically, even under these circumstances, a strong case for diffusionism can nevertheless be made. Even with sizable pieces of the puzzle missing, the surviving evidence is still conclusive.

The variety of races and ethnic types which culturally influenced the New World is of immeasurable historical importance. With what has recently been brought to light in terms of the varied racial types present within Meso-America between 1400 B.C. and 900 A.D., there should be no doubt that the traditional version of the New World's history will need drastic revision. That these revisions must be forced upon the reigning major-domos of Pre-Columbian academics is a sad state of affairs. Their refusal, in spite of all evidence, to acknowledge the African presence in ancient America raises the issue of racial prejudice.

The isolationist will in time come to accept what seems to me to be incontrovertible—that transcontinental crossings produced one of the outstanding civilizations of the ancient world. Tatiana Proskouriakoff reminds us that "no civilization has arisen from a single focus. If we must have a metaphor, we would do better to compare the progress of civilization to the propogation of waves on a rising ride. Its genesis is the interaction of cultures, and no isolated and homogenous culture has ever arisen much beyond its original level."[37] Thus, waves of Egypto-Nubian, and Shang, culture, converging on the ancient shores of Meso-America, all added to the rising tide of the civilization we know as the Olmec.

Ninth category: Nose Plugs and Rings

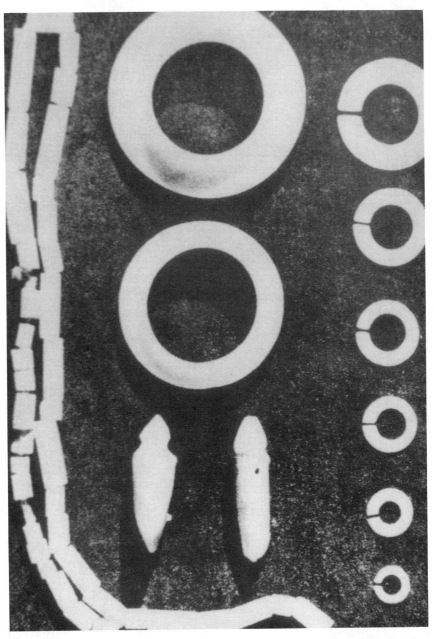

9a. Jade nose plugs, nose rings with necklace. Chinese, dated late Shang Dynasty, circa 1400-1100 B.C.

9b. Negroid Olmec priest exhibiting ball at the end of nose symbolizing nose ring or plug. LaVenta, circa 1100 B.C.-300 A.D.

9c. Olmec figure on dragon stela also exhibiting ball at the end of nose. La Venta, 1100 B.C.-300 A.D.

9d. Proper usage of jade plugs. An ancient Chinese saying states that "with jade and gold in the nine orifices, even a dead body will be everlasting." These particular plugs are adorned by a head sculptured by the Chavin de Huantar culture of Peru. This culture is said to exhibit strong Shang trait characteristics indicative of deep Shang influence. Peru, circa 900-200 B.C.

9e. Stela depicting priest with nose ball. Guatemala, circa 850 A.D.

9f. Alterpiece depicting figure with nose plugs. Mexico, late Classic period.

9g. Very fine head sculptured in marble. Note both the nose ring and the elaborate hair cut. Vera Cruz, Mexico. Classic period.

10. Shang bronze vessel cover. China, Anyang period.

Notes

For Chandler's chapter we would like to thank the Freer Gallery of Art (established by the Smithsonian Institution) and the Dumbarton Oaks Museum, department of Pre-Columbian Art for the lending of several photographs extremely pertinent to his essay. Those photographs obtained from the Freer Gallery are listed as 1-b, 1-d, 1-f, 2-a, 2-c and number 10. Those photographs which were contributed by Dumbarton Oaks are listed as 2-g, 3-g, 6-d, 6-e, 6-f and 9-g. All photographs were researched by Mr. Wayne Chandler and Mr. Gaynell Catherine as well as being photographed by them with the exception of those previously listed. Both Dumbarton Oaks and the Freer Gallery of Art are located in Washington, D.C.

1. The history of Moorish influence in Europe constitutes an excellent example of the phenomenon of trait hibernation or dormancy. The Moors, rulers of Spain for eight hundred years, excelled in many of the arts and sciences. The Renaissance, which finally illuminated Europe in the 14th-16th centuries, had actually been lit centuries earlier by the Moor's accomplishments in medicine, philosophy, agriculture, architecture, and literature. At the time of the banishment of the Moors in the 14th century, Europe's dark age must have seemed permanent. But cultural traits left by the Moors eventually brought about the great new beginning we call the Renaissance. Isolated resurgences of certain trait transmissions of Moorish culture can be traced even into the 19th century.

The transmission of Egyptian culture includes both types of exchange. Through the many military campaigns launched by Egypt's armies, subjugated countries were forced to absorb Egyptian culture. But, on the other hand, many nations eagerly visited Egypt to seek out a source of education and enlightenment. Cultural elements were then taken back to their respective countries and amalgamated with their own culture. Examples of the former include Syria and examples of the latter include Greece and Rome.

2. M.D. Coe, "San Lorenzo and the Olmec Civilization," *Dumbarton Oaks Conference on the Olmec*, Ed. E. Benson, 1968, p. 61.

3. Jesse D. Jennings, *Ancient Native Americans*, W.H. Freeman and Company, 1978, p. 1.

4. Franklin and Mary Folson, "Sinodonty and Sundadonty," *Early Man*, Vol. 4, No. 2, 1982, p. 16-21.

5. Ibid.

6. Ibid.

7. K.C. Chang, *Shang Civilization*, Yale University Press, 1980, p. 336.

8. Shi Jing (Book of Odes).

9. Sima Zian

10. H. Hardclett, *China—A History in Art*, Brown and Brown Publishers, 1968, p. 12.

11. J.A. Rogers, *Sex and Race*, Vol. 1, Helga Rogers, New York, 1967, p. 67.

12. K.C. Chang, *The Archaeology of Ancient China*, Yale University Press, London, 1968, p. 286.

13. Alexander Von Wuthenau, *Unexpected Faces in Ancient America*, Crown Publishers, Inc., New York, 1974, p. 19.

14. Ibid.

15. R.A. Jairazbhoy, *Ancient Egyptians and Chinese in America*, Rowman and Littlefield, Totowa, New Jersey, 1974, p. 102.

16. Ibid, p. 102.

17. Ibid, p. 103.

18. Ibid, p. 103.

19. Ivan Van Sertima (ed.), *Nile Valley Civilization*, Journal of African Civilizations, Ltd., Inc., 1985, p. 242.

20. Ibid, p. 242.

21. Thomas Stuart Ferguson, *One Fold and One Shepherd*, Books of California, Book of Mormon, 1958, p. 22.

22. Nigel Davies, *Voyagers to the New World*, University of New Mexico Press, 1986.

23. T.S. Ferguson, p. 22.

24. T.S. Ferguson, p. 23.

25. Steven C. Jett, *Ancient Native Americans*, Edited by Jesse D. Jennings, W.H. Freeman and Company, 1978, p. 607.

26. Nigel Davies, *Voyagers to the New World*, University of New Mexico Press, 1986, p. 111.

27. Shanha Jing (Classics of Mountain and Sea).

28. Liu An Huai Nan Zi (Book of Prince Huai Nan).

29. See #8.

30. Nigel Davies, p. 100.

31. Stephen C. Jett, p. 630.

32. Richard MacNeish, "Tehuacan's Accomplishment," *Archaeology*, 1981.

33. Statements by University of Maryland Archaeoastronomer.

34. Diego de Landa, *Relacion de las Cosas de Yucatan*. Papers of Peabody Museum of American Archeology and Ethnology, Harvard University, Cambridge, Massachusetts, 1966, Reprint, Vol. XVIII, p. 109.

35. *Antonio de Ciudao Real*, Fray Alonso Ponce in Yucatan, translated by Ernest Noyes, Middle American Research Series, Tulane University Press, New Orleans, 1932, Vol. 4, p. 314.

36. Bernardo de Lizana, *Historia De Yucatan*, Mexico, 1893, Book 1, Chapter VI.

37. Tatiana Proskouriakoff, *Olmec and Mayan Art*, Ibid, p. 119.

BIOGRAPHICAL NOTES ON CONTRIBUTORS

CHANDLER, Wayne B.

Wayne B. Chandler is an Anthrophotojournalist and Co-Chairman of What's A Face Inc. He has done extensive research into the origins of race and ancient civilizations and is co-producer and writer of A People's History To Date — 4000 B.C. to 1985 and 365 Days of Black History, parts I and II. Through the photo archives of What's A Face Inc. Mr. Chandler and his associate Mr. Gaynell Catherine have been instrumental in unearthing key photographs relating to the African presence in the Olmec civilization, as well as the civilizations of ancient India, Southeast Asia, Egypt, and China. He is a committee member of the Historian Roundtable and has lectured in various locations in the U.S. He was visiting lecturer at the University of D.C. from 1978-1983 and instructor at the prestigious Ananda Institute from 1982-1986. In 1984 he helped implement the program Genius Transformation which proved that when under-privileged children are exposed to proper historical information, along with diet and exercise, their psychological perspectives undergo a radical change for the better. From 1987 through 1989, he was working with archaeologist Dr. Edward Otter on various excavations of pre-historic Indian sites in the southeast and midwest. He has been involved with the Journal of African Civilizations since 1985 and his contributions include "Jewel in the Lotus: The Ethiopian Presence in the Indus Valley Civilization" (1985); "The Moors: Light of Europe's Dark Age" (1986); "Trait-Influences in Meso-America: the African-Asian connection" (1987); "Hannibal: Nemesis of Rome" (1988); and "Of Gods and Men: Egypt's Old Kingdom" (1989). Current project is a collaboration with Creative Fox Associates in the production of "Strangers in Their Own Land", a five part documentary involving Drs. Van Sertima, Runoko Rashidi, Asa Hillard III, and Alexander Von Wuthenau. Any comments regarding chapters published or unpublished are gladly welcome. He may be reached at P.O. Box 928, Adelphi, Maryland 20783.

CLEGG, II, Legrand

Legrand Clegg II is an instructor at Compton Community College in Compton, California. He is also Deputy City Attorney for the City of Compton. He has engaged in research on black history and culture since 1963 and his work has appeared on college and university campuses across the U.S. He has co-produced a filmstrip entitled "The Black Roots of Civilization."

COVEY, Joan

Student of diffusionist literature with special interest in voyages from the Old World to the New. Reviewed *Asians in Pre-Columbian Mexico* by R.A. Jairazbhoy for the *New Diffusionist* and *Atlantis* by Henriette Mertz for the *Anthropological Journal of Canada.*

JAIRAZBHOY, R.A.

R.A. Jairazbhoy is an independent researcher who has devoted over 30 years to tracing the rise and spread of civilizations. He has written more on the interconnections between the primary world civilizations than anyone living. His familiarity with the Old World heritage enabled him to make discoveries of their impact on the development of Pre-Columbian America. Jairazbhoy's available works are: *Ancient Egyptians and Chinese in America,* 1974; *Ancient Egyptians in Middle and South America,* 1981; *The Spread of Ancient Civilisations,* 1982. (Order from Ra Publications, 37 Hillside Road, Northwood, Middlesex HA6 1PY, England. First two $20 the set; third $15 [semibound])

JORDAN, Keith

Keith Jordan is a student of clinical psychology at Rutgers University. His work in archaeological research includes several book reviews published in the *Journal of New England Antiquities Research Association.*

LAWRENCE, Harold G. (Kofi Wangara)

Harold G. Lawrence developed an interest in African migrations to America while selling the books of J.A. Rogers during his studies at Wayne State University, Detroit, Michigan.

After receiving his B.A. in Linguistics and a Master's degree in Education, he left for Ghana in 1964. Lawrence received the African name of Kofi Wangara from the students of the Institute of African Studies in Legon, Ghana. He received a Master's degree from the Institute and left Ghana for Nigeria. He returned to the U.S. in 1965. From 1969-1983 he made several extended study and research trips to Senegal, Gambia, Sierra Leone, Liberia, Mali, Ivory Coast, Dahomey and Togo. He was forced to return to the U.S. due to failing health. He currently resides with his brother in Detroit.

The chapter published in this volume is an excerpt from a larger work *Mandinga Voyages to America,* awaiting publication.

LUMPKIN, Beatrice

An associate professor of mathematics at Malcolm X College in Chicago, Professor Lumpkin has written on the Afro-Asian foundations of mathematics for *Freedomways,* the *Mathematics Teacher, Science and Society* and *Historia Mathematica.* She has also written two major articles for Vol. 2, Nos. 1 & 2 of the *Journal of African Civilizations*—"The Pyramids—Ancient Showcase of Science and Technology" and "Africa in the Mainstream of Mathematics History." She is author of a children's book, *Young Genius in Old Egypt.*

MUFFETT, D.J.M. (O.B.E.)

Dr. Muffett was a former British administrator in Nigeria. He was a professor in African studies at Duquesne University. He chaired a panel on Pre-Columbian African Contacts at the 19th Annual Meeting of the African Studies Association held in Boston in November, 1976, at which meeting he read the paper on Leo Wiener published in this volume. He is also the author of studies in African folklore and linguistics.

RASHIDI, Runoko

Runoko Rashidi is an African-Centric historian, writer and lecturer with a pronounced interest in the African foundations of world civilizations. He has appeared on numerous television and radio programs, and has lectured extensively in India, England and throughout the United States. From 1981 to 1984 he was African History Research Specialist at Compton College in Compton, California. Among the major programs he developed and coordinated during this period were: The African People's Conference, An Evening for the *Journal of African Civilizations,* The African Presence in Early America, The African Presence in Early Europe, and The Significance of the Pyramid in African History. From 1985 to 1987 Rashidi was the History Editor for the National Black Computer Network. Since 1983, he has been an active member of the Board of Directors and the Board of Editors of the *Journal of African Civilizations.* In 1990 Rashidi was listed in the Smithsonian Institution's *Directory of African American Folkorists.*

Since 1982, Runoko Rashidi has been a major contributor to the *Journal of African Civilizations.* Rashidi's *J.A.C.* essays include: "The African Presence in Sumer and Elam" in 1982, "African Goddesses: Mothers of Civilization" in 1983, "The Nile Valley Presence in Asian Antiquity" in 1984, "The African Presence in Early Asian Civilizations" in 1985, "Ancient and Modern

Britons" in 1985, "Dr. Diop on Asia" Highlights and Insights" in 1986 (noted and reviewed in *Presence Africaine*, 2nd Qtr. 1987), "Men Out of Asia: The Black Presence in Prehistoric America" in 1987, "More Light on Sumer, Elam and India" in 1988, "Ramses the Great: The Life and Times of a Bold, Black Egyptian King" in 1988, "A Working Chronology of the Royal Kemetic Dynasties" and "The Middle Kingdom of Kemet: A Photo Essay" in 1989.

In 1988 Rashidi edited with Ivan Van Sertima *The African Presence in Early Asia* (New Brunswick: Journal of African Civilizations). One of Rashidi's most recent and comprehensive works, *A Guide to the Study of African Classical Civilization*, is scheduled for publication in March 1991 by Karnak House of London, England.

On October 8, 1987 Rashidi formally inaugurated the "First All India Dalit Writers Conference" in Hyderabad, India, and delivered a major address on "The Global Unity of African People." In 1989 he was appointed United States Representative of *Dalit Voice: The Voice of the Persecuted Nationalities Denied Human Rights,* issuing from New Delhi, India, and published in English, Tamil, Urdu, Telugu, Malayalam and Hindi. For further information write to: Rashidi, 4140 Buckingham Road, Suite D, Los Angeles, CA 90008; or call (213) 293-5807.

VAN SERTIMA, Ivan

Ivan Van Sertima was born in Guyana, South America. He was educated at the School of Oriental and African Studies, London University and the Rutgers Graduate School and holds degrees in African Studies, Linguistics and Anthropology.

He is a literary critic, a linguist, and an anthropologist and has made a name in all three fields. As a literary critic, he is the author of *Caribbean Writers,* a collection of critical essays on the Caribbean Novel. He is also the author of several major literary reviews published in Denmark, India, Britain and the United States. He was honored for his work in this field by being asked by the Nobel Committee of the Swedish Academy to nominate candidates for the Nobel Prize in Literature, from 1976-1980. As a linguist, he has published essays on the dialect of the Sea Islands off the Georgia Coast. He is also the compiler of the *Swahili Dictionary of Legal Terms,* based on his fieldwork in Tanzania, East Africa, in 1967. He is the author of *They Came Before Columbus: The African Presence in Ancient America,* which was published by Random House in 1977 and is now in its tenth printing. It was published in French in 1981 and in the same year was awarded the Clarence L. Holte Prize, a prize awarded every two years "for a work of excellence in literature and the humanities relating to the cultural heritage of Africa and the African diaspora."

He was invited by UNESCO to join the *International Commission for a new History of the Scientific and Cultural Development of Mankind.*

Professor Van Sertima is an associate professor of African Studies at Rutgers University in New Jersey and editor of the *Journal of African Civilizations*. He was also visiting professor at Princeton University from 1981 to 1983. He is editorial advisor on African Science for a projected British Encyclopedia on the Non-Western Sciences.

PATTEN-VAN SERTIMA, Jacqueline

Jacqueline Patten-Van Sertima is photographic consultant, art director and cover designer for the *Journal of African Civilizations*. Mrs. Van Sertima also established the Journal's audio arm, Legacies, Inc. As director, she produces companion audio cassettes to each volume of the *Journal of African Civilizations* as well as of various presentations made by Dr. Van Sertima and colleagues.

As a photographer, Mrs. Van Sertima has won international distinction for her hand-painted photography and its significant contribution to social awareness. Listed in the Cambridge *World Who's Who of Women* for "distinguished achievement," their *International Register of Profiles* and their *International Who's Who in America* and *Personalities of America* for "outstanding artistic achievement and contributions to society." Mrs. Van Sertima received her B.S. degree in Psychology/Sociology and M.S. in Education from Hunter College, New York.

VON WUTHENAU, Alexander

Son of Count Charles Adam von Wuthenau and Countess Marie Antoinette Chotek (sister of the wife of the Archduke Franz Ferdinand, assassinated at Sarajevo) Baron von Wuthenau was educated at the Royal Bavarian Gymnasium in Ettal and later in the universities of Freiburg, Munich and Kiel. He secured his doctorate at Kiel in International Law and became Secretary for cultural and legal affairs to the German legation in Buenos Aires, Argentina. He was also Secretary of the German Embassy in Washington, D.C. before the outbreak of the Second World War but renounced diplomatic service in protest at the racist policies of the Nazis. From 1934-1979 he did art history studies in Mexico and Latin America, finally specializing in pre-Columbian art. From 1939-1965 he was Professor of Art History in Mexico City College and the University of the Americas. His first book was published in German, French and English. The English edition of *Art of Terracotta Pottery in Pre-Columbian South and Central America* appeared in 1970 (Crown Publishers) and his second book, *Unexpected Faces in Ancient America: The Historical Testimony of the Pre-Columbian Artist* (Crown, New York) in 1975. He is the Director of the Central Archives of Human Representations in the Americas, located in San Angel, Mexico City.

ORDER FORM FOR BOOKS
Journal of African Civilizations

Books Now Available:

❑ African Presence in Early America $15.00
❑ African Presence in Early Asia $15.00
❑ African Presence in Early Europe $15.00
❑ Blacks in Science: Ancient and Modern $15.00
❑ Black Women in Antiquity $15.00
❑ Egypt Revisited $20.00
❑ Golden Age of the Moor $20.00
❑ Great Black Leaders: Ancient and Modern $20.00

Books Scheduled for Reprint:

❑ Great African Thinkers (September, 1992).............................. $15.00
❑ Nile Valley Civilizations (October, 1992)............................... $15.00

Name_____

Address_____

_____

City/State Zip_____

Checks and Money Orders should be made payable to
Journal of African Civilizations and sent to:

Ivan Van Sertima (Editor)
Journal of African Civilizations
African Studies Department
Beck Hall
Rutgers University
New Brunswick, New Jersey 08903

ANCIENT EGYPT
MEXICO
and the
UNITED STATES

R.A. Jairazbhoy

This book shows a large number of traits in early North America, which could only have been received from Ancient Egypt to which they were unique. It places them in context, so that a picture emerges of how this came about, and who were involved. The approach is largely pictorial which makes it easy even for the uninitiated to follow the argument. At the same time it also makes it impossible for the sceptics to refute the unique and identical parallels which cannot be explained in any other way than as a result of contact.

Published by **KARNAK HOUSE**

$11.95/£16.95 and available in the U.S. from Frontline Distribution, 1951 West Birchwood, Suite 1, Chicago, Illinois 60626.

Phone: (312) 743-7635

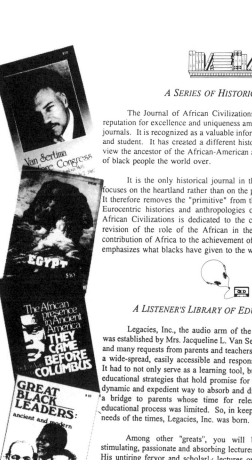

A Series of Historical Classics

The Journal of African Civilizations, founded in 1979, has gained a reputation for excellence and uniqueness among historical and anthropological journals. It is recognized as a valuable information source for both the layman and student. It has created a different historical perspective within which to view the ancestor of the African-American and the achievement and potential of black people the world over.

It is the only historical journal in the English-speaking world which focuses on the heartland rather than on the periphery of African civilizations. It therefore removes the "primitive" from the center stage it has occupied in Eurocentric histories and anthropologies of the African. The Journal of African Civilizations is dedicated to the celebration of black genius, to a revision of the role of the African in the world's great civilizations, the contribution of Africa to the achievement of man in the arts and sciences. It emphasizes what blacks have given to the world, not what they have lost.

A Listener's Library of Educational Classics

Legacies, Inc., the audio arm of the Journal of African Civilizations, was established by Mrs. Jacqueline L. Van Sertima in answer to a genuine need and many requests from parents and teachers across the country. They needed a wide-spread, easily accessible and responsible medium of communication. It had to not only serve as a learning tool, but as an informational vehicle for educational strategies that hold promise for our youths. They also needed a dynamic and expedient way to absorb and disseminate information as well as a bridge to parents whose time for relearning and participation in the educational process was limited. So, in keeping with the highly controversial needs of the times, Legacies, Inc. was born.

Among other "greats", you will be hearing the most brilliant, stimulating, passionate and absorbing lectures given by Dr. Ivan Van Sertima. His untiring fervor and scholarly lectures on history have made learning an exciting adventure through time. It is the drama of forgotten peoples and civilizations, brought to you through an unusually fresh and liberating vision of the human legacy.

BOOKS

African Presence in Early America — $15.00
African Presence in Early Asia — $15.00
African Presence in Early Europe — $15.00
Black Women in Antiquity (new essay & index) — $15.00
Blacks in Science: ancient and modern — $15.00
Egypt Revisited — $20.00
Great African Thinkers - C. A. Diop (Sept. 1992) — $15.00
Great Black Leaders: ancient and modern — $20.00
Golden Age of the Moor — $20.00
Nile Valley Civilizations (Oct. 1992) — $15.00
They Came Before Columbus — $24.00
(For this particular book, please make check payable to "Ivan Van Sertima".)

Date _____

Name _____
Address _____
City/State _____
Zip _____
Tel. No ( ) _____

Check and money orders should be made payable to: **"Journal of African Civilizations"**

and sent to:

Ivan Van Sertima (Editor)
Journal of African Civilizations
African Studies Department
Beck Hall
Rutgers University
New Brunswick, NJ 08903

Add $7.50 per book overseas airmail.

AUDIO TAPES

All audio tapes are $10 each

African Presence in Early America
African Presence in Early Asia
African Presence in Early Europe
African Presence in World Cultures
The Black Family - J.H. Clarke & Van Sertima
Black Women in Antiquity
Blacks in Science: ancient and modern
Egypt Revisited
Golden Age of the Moor
Great African Thinkers - C. A. Diop
Great Black Leaders: ancient and modern
Re-Educating Our Children
Socialization of the African-American Child - Asa G. Hilliard
They Came Before Columbus
Van Sertima Before Congress
Van Sertima's Address to the Smithsonian

Date _____

Name _____
Address _____
City/State _____
Zip _____
Tel. No ( ) _____

Check and money orders should be made payable to: **"Legacies"**

and sent to:

Jacqueline L. Van Sertima
347 Felton Ave.
Highland Park, New Jersey 08904

Please include postage:

1 tape .... .75
2 tapes 1.44
3 tapes 1.90
4-10 tapes 2.90
11-15 tapes 4.10

Please Note: *Tapes cannot be purchased through bookstores or other vendors.*

They Came Before Columbus
by IVAN VAN SERTIMA
Winner of The 1981 Clarence L. Holte International Prize

"Comprehensive and convincing evidence of links between Africa and America in the Pre-Columbian Period. Ivan Van Sertima takes the subject out of the "Lost Worlds" category and brings together all the known facts established by various disciplines... He makes an impressive case for contact... A big boost to Black Cultural History."
—*Publishers Weekly*

"The theory has been argued for years. Usually supported by enthusiasts claiming far too much on very little information. Professor Van Sertima is no such romantic... He has pursued it with good judgement and persuasive evidence drawn from a wide variety of sources. A fascinating case worth the attention it demands...."
—*The Atlantic Monthly*

"The majority of Afro-Americans and White Americans accept the slave version as the definitive story of Black presence in this land... This book will place Afro-American History in a much more important dimension than *Roots*... A remarkable work...."
—*Los Angeles Sentinel*

"This is a pioneering work that will help to bring about a reassessment of the place of African people in world history... A scholarly achievement... Calls attention to Africa's ages of grandeur and the great adventurous spirit of the Africans that brought them to the worlds beyond their shores... After the excitement over Alex Haley's *Roots*, I hope a popular and scholarly reading public will turn to this book where the roots are much deeper...."
—John Henrik Clarke, *Africa*

The great stone heads of Mexico are by far the most spectacular evidence that, as civilization was dawning in the New World more than 2,000 years before Columbus, black people from Africa had already reached these shores... The leading proponent of an African presence in the New World is Ivan Van Sertima... Van Sertima marshals many other kinds of evidence.
—*Science Digest* (September 1981)

As one who has been immersed in Mexican archeology for some forty years, and who participated in the excavation of the first of the giant heads, I must confess that I for one am thoroughly convinced of the soundness of Van Sertima's conclusions ...
—Dr. Clarence W. Weiant (Professor of Archeology)
The New York Times Book Review (Letters)

"The French translation of *They Came Before Columbus* has been very well received by the French-speaking intellectual and academic community. Already it is highly regarded as a fundamental contribution by a young Afro-American scholar to universal historical knowledge ..."
—Dr. Cheikh Anta Diop
Director, Radio Carbon Laboratory, IFAN University, Dakar, Senegal.

To order a copy, please send $21.95 plus $2.05 postage to: Ivan Van Sertima, 347 Felton Avenue, Highland Park, New Jersey 08904. Checks or money orders should be made out to "Ivan Van Sertima."

NOTES

NOTES